The Spectacle of Japanese American Trauma

The Spectacle of

Japanese American Trauma

Racial Performativity and World War II

Emily Roxworthy

University of Hawai'i Press
Honolulu

Library of Congress Cataloging-in-Publication Data
Roxworthy, Emily.
    The spectacle of Japanese American trauma : racial performativity and
World War II / Emily Roxworthy.
        p. cm.
    Includes bibliographical references and index.
    ISBN 978-0-8248-3220-9 (hbk. : alk. paper)
    1. Japanese Americans—Evacuation and relocation, 1942–1945.
2. World War, 1939–1945—Mass media and the war. 3. World War,
1939–1945—Psychological aspects. 4. World War, 1939–1945—United States.
5. Concentration camps—United States—Psychological aspects. 6. United States—
Ethnic relations—History—20th century. I. Title.
    D769.8.A6R68 2008
    940.53'1773—dc22
                                                    2008009098

Designed by University of Hawai'i Press production staff

Printed by The Maple-Vail Book Manufacturing Group

Contents

Acknowledgments   vii

Introduction   1
Staging the Trauma of Japanese American Internment

1   "A Race of Ingenious Marionettes"   19
Theatricalizing the Japanese, 1853–1946

2   Spectacularizing Japanese American Suspects   57
The Genealogy of the FBI's Post–Pearl Harbor Raids

3   Performative Citizenship and Anti-Japanese Melodrama   100
The Mass Media Construction of Home Front Nationalism

4   "Manzanar, the Eyes of the World Are upon You"   120
Internee Performance and Archival Ambivalence

5   Transnational Theatre at the Tule Lake Segregation Center   148

Notes   179
Bibliography   215
Index   225

Acknowledgments

One day over a "working lunch" at one of our usual sushi joints, my longtime adviser, Dwight Conquergood, leaned across the table with a glimmer in his eyes and mischievously remarked, "Emily, I had no idea you had become so *political*." He meant it as a compliment, and I took it as such. Dwight saw me through the most formative decade of my life, from a rather self-absorbed, apolitical undergraduate majoring in Performance Studies—en route to an acting career, no doubt—to an over-serious doctoral student bent on critique and revolution. Perhaps the transformation was not quite so dramatic, but being Dwight's advisee made one feel on the constant verge of greatness. I now realize, since his passing, that the feeling had a good deal to do with basking in his afterglow. Dwight died long before his time and certainly before this project represented anything but unrealized potential, but I dedicate the book to him nonetheless. I am one of a small army of scholars indebted to his legacy and homesick for his friendship.

I would also like to thank many other scholars who have advised me over the years, from my earliest graduate schooling at Cornell University to my doctoral studies at Northwestern University and my very welcoming first job at the University of California, San Diego (UCSD). Thank you to Jim Carmody, Tracy Davis, Paul Edwards, Brian Edwards, Takashi Fujitani, J. Ellen Gainor, Nadine-George Graves, Jorge Huerta, Dominick LaCapra, Lisa Lowe, Marianne McDonald, Lisa Sun-Hee Park, John Rouse, Rebecca Schneider, Janet Smarr, Dorothy Wang, and Mina Yang. I have also benefited greatly from my colleagues in the UCSD California Cultures in Comparative Perspective research initiative, especially from the selfless leadership of David Pellow. My graduate students in the Theatre and Drama Joint Ph.D. Program at UCSD and UC Irvine have constantly challenged the ideas with which I wrestle in this book, offering far more interesting interpretations than I ever could have mustered at that stage in my career.

I am grateful to the professional friendships I share with many, particularly Suk-Young Kim, Lon Kurashige, Sheila Moeschen, Magdalena Romanska,

Karen Shimakawa, Melinda Wilson, Harvey Young, Patrick Anderson, Shannon Steen, and the now far-flung members of the Northwestern Performance Studies ABD writing group, including Amy Partridge, Rebecca Rossen, Ioana Szeman, and Jason Winslade.

This book has profited from the research assistance of Tomoyuki Sasaki and Zachary Gill and from funding by the Northwestern University Graduate School and the Academic Senate of the University of California, San Diego. Parts of chapters 2 and 4 previously appeared in slightly different forms in *TDR* and *Theatre Journal* respectively, where the editorships of Richard Schechner, Jean Graham-Jones, and David Saltz catalyzed immense growth in my thinking on this material. For its present form, the input of Masako Ikeda at the University of Hawai'i Press—as well as the two anonymous readers she selected— proved invaluable to shaping this book's narrative arc.

Finally, thank you to my partner in all endeavors, Philip Roxworthy, and the astonishing little people we have made together. And I am forever grateful to the assiduous Margaret Colborn, who instilled the joy of research and writing in me from the very youngest age.

Introduction

Staging the Trauma of Japanese American Internment

> VICTOR: When I was in 'Nam? You know when I was hit by some
> Viet Cong mortar fire? They wouldn't pick me up, the medics. I was
> lying there, bleeding all over, they were picking everyone else up. I
> kept screaming, "I'm an American, I'm a Japanese American, I'm not
> VC." But they wouldn't pick me up. They walked right past me.
> —Philip Kan Gotanda, *Fish Head Soup and Other Plays*[1]

> The traumatic reexperiencing of the event thus *carries with it* what
> Dori Laub calls the "collapse of witnessing," the impossibility of
> knowing that first constituted it.
> —Cathy Caruth, *Trauma: Explorations in Memory*[2]

After the closure of the World War II internment camps and the "relocation" of former internees to new postwar homes, many observed the remarkable silence and stoic rebounding with which most first- and second-generation Japanese Americans (Issei and Nisei) closed that chapter of their lives. It was this silence and stoicism that contributed in large part to their designation, along with other Asian Americans, as the "model minority."[3] Conservative critics claimed this apparent lack of bitterness as proof that the internment camps were not unjust after all, that even their former inmates tacitly approved the "military necessity" that stripped them of civil liberties and segregated them from their fellow Americans after the Japanese Empire attacked Pearl Harbor. Liberal scholars have mostly chalked up this stoic silence to a diasporic retention of the Japanese cultural logic of *shikata ga nai*, or "it can't be helped"—a fatalistic philosophy that negates the efficacy of resistance or other political action. Although silence has been used to justify and minimize the impact of the internment, outside this context the concept of silence circulates widely as a telltale symptom of trauma. Shoshana Felman resurrects Walter Benjamin's term "expressionless" (*das Ausdruckslose*) in order to describe "the silence of the persecuted, the unspeakability of the trauma of oppression" experienced by "those whom violence has deprived of expression; those who, on the one hand, have been historically reduced to silence, and who, on the other hand, have been historically made faceless, deprived of their *human* face." [4] This seems an apt judgment of how historical events left Japanese Americans silent and then the historiography of these events rendered this silence expressionless and inhuman, as epitomized in the stereotype of the automaton-like "model minority." Americans have allowed the symptoms of wartime injustice to stand as apology for the injuries themselves. So what if—instead—we reinterpret former internees' silence not as a culturally conditioned response to adversity but rather as the structural outgrowth of the particular trauma of this particular internment?

I emphasize the *structure* of the internees' silence because the recent wave of trauma scholarship makes clear that traumatized responses cannot be wholly explained by the catalyzing event or by "a distortion of the event, achieving its haunting power as a result of distorting personal significances attached to it." Rather than some inherent atrociousness adhering to the event or some inherent psychosocial predisposition causing an individual or group to react in a certain way, trauma should be understood in structural terms. The pathology of trauma, Cathy Caruth insists, consists "solely in the *structure of the experience* or reception: the event is not assimilated or experienced fully at the time, but only belatedly, in its repeated *possession* of the one who experiences it. To be traumatized is precisely to be possessed by an image or event." [5] I emphasize the *particularity* of the Japanese American internment because those who have written on the trauma of this experience have, by and large, bypassed these structural aspects, instead comparing the internment *event* with other more widely recognized atrocities such as the Nazi genocide of Jews and other minorities, the experiences of U.S. soldiers during and after the Vietnam War, and generalized sexual abuse against women. By accessing Japanese American trauma through these other atrocities—none of which directly implicates the racist domestic policies of the U.S. government as the internment does—these "American concentration camps" inevitably find themselves subordinated once again in hierarchies of suffering that always privilege the point of comparison. [6] Such strategies of comparative analysis end up posing the internment as a debased mimicry of unquestioned traumatic events.

No genocide occurred against the Japanese American "evacuees" imprisoned in the "assembly centers" and "relocation centers," euphemistically named and controlled by the U.S. military's Wartime Civilian Control Agency (WCCA) and the U.S. government's War Relocation Authority (WRA), so when former internee Raymond Okamura wrote that "the linguistic deception fostered by the United States government" in regard to the internment "bears a striking resemblance to the propaganda techniques of the Third Reich," the comparison might have been instructive, but Japanese American trauma inevitably paled in comparison to the Holocaust.[7] The material losses of $200 million in Japanese American property, homes, and businesses become profane concerns when juxtaposed with the Nazi genocide.[8] Likewise, Chalsa Loo recognized the post-traumatic stress disorder (PTSD) that plagued many former internees but only did so by discussing "parallels" with the symptoms of trauma widely associated with Vietnam War veterans who had witnessed, perpetrated, and suffered horrifying violence in Vietnam and returned home to find an American public that considered them "baby killers" and did not honor their military service.[9] Although violent events did occur in many of the Japanese American camps and several internees were murdered both by U.S. soldiers guarding the camps and by fellow internees—and despite the fact that internees also experienced virulent prejudice and even violence when they returned to their prewar communities—the scale of this emotional and physical violence cannot compete (nor should it have to) with the PTSD of Vietnam veterans. Another common trope is the metaphoric equation of the violation inflicted upon internees by their own government with the experience of rape; this analogizing to the suffering of rape victims is most often voiced by male scholars of the internment and by male former internees, but the comparison also emanates from Amy Uno Ishii's oft-quoted statement: "Women, if they've been raped, don't go around talking about it. . . . This is exactly the kind of feeling that we as evacuees, victims of circumstances, had at the time of evacuation."[10] Since sexual abuse was not a systemic part of the camps, comparing the trauma of Japanese Americans to that of rape victims belittles the wartime internment and renders invisible the more subtle but no less insidious violations that made up the everyday lives of internees, such as the total lack of privacy that plagued every aspect of camp life, including toilet facilities, and the utter degradation resulting from assigning inmates numbers and lining them up in dehumanized masses for every conceivable purpose.

In this book I posit the importance of understanding the structural trauma of the internment as located in the spectacularization imposed upon Japanese Americans by the U.S. government and mass media. Unlike the Holocaust, the evacuation and internment of Japanese Americans was perpetrated in full view of the public by capitalization upon the propaganda possibilities of the U.S. "free press." Unlike the abject treatment of Vietnam veterans, who were mostly drafted into war, the Federal Bureau of Investigation (FBI) and WRA coerced Japanese Americans into "voluntary" participation with their abjection from the rest of society, demanding that they cooperate with authorities and put on a happy face for reporters and other visitors to the barbed-wire-encircled camps.[11] And unlike the sexist contract of victim-shaming that protects rapists, American politicians and pundits broadcast far and wide the violations enacted during the mass evacuation and internment, leveraging—for an audience at home as well as in the European and Pacific theatres of war—the supposedly benign captivity of ethnic Japanese as absurd proof of U.S. racial tolerance and, at the same time, melodramatically posing these "suspect" Americans as antagonists against the many heroes and heroines of the American home front. By thus spectacularizing the disenfranchisement and imprisonment of nearly 120,000 Japanese Americans, the U.S. government and mass media denied the gravity of what was taking place and disavowed the psychological suffering and material violence perpetrated against a persecuted ethnic minority. Thankfully, much has been written about the fictitiousness of the "military necessity" placed around the evacuation and used to justify the internment of all West Coast Japanese Americans, regardless of citizenship status, for the duration of U.S. hostilities with Japan.[12] But in this book I argue that an equally seductive framing device justified the camps for the wartime American public and continues to be uncritically deployed by conservative analysts like Michelle Malkin in her recent book, *In Defense of Internment*.[13] By framing the evacuation and internment as *spectacles,* the United States positioned the American public as passive spectators to the unconstitutional treatment of their ethnic Japanese neighbors and, simultaneously, cast the public as heroic "patriots" opposite Japanese Americans, who were cast in one of two thankless roles: expressionless automata or melodramatic villains.

So in the case of the internment, theories of *trauma* and theories of *spectacle* intersect and converge. Both trauma and spectacle are haunted by visuality, a visual scene/seen that inscribes its image deeply within one's psyche precisely to the extent that it alienates the subject from any comprehension of the material underpinnings of the transpired event.[14] On the side of trauma, Shoshana Felman finds that "the unexpectedness of the original traumatizing scene" is replayed in the compulsive repetitions that characterize traumatic symptoms.[15] On the side of spectacle, Guy Debord finds that the images offered up by commodity culture violently foreground the presence of the visual realm in order to absent spectators' awareness of their own exploitation and disenfranchisement under advanced capitalism. In his classic book, *The Society of the Spectacle,* Debord claims that "The spectacle's function in society is the concrete manufacture of alienation," and he describes the means of this alienation as precisely visual: "Understood on its own terms, the spectacle proclaims the predominance of appearances and asserts that all human life, which is to say all social life, is mere appearance." For Debord, "spectacle's essential character" consists in "a negation of life that has *invented a visual form for itself*."[16] The refuge taken in the visual as a means to negate life leads performance theorist Diana

Taylor to warn of spectacle's potential as an arrangement of events that rewards passive spectatorship and denies the need for active witnessing. Writing of the terrifying political spectacles staged by the Argentine government during the Dirty War (1976–1983), Taylor claims that "The onlookers, like obedient spectators in a theatre, were encouraged to suspend their disbelief. Terror draws on the theatrical propensity simultaneously to bind the audience and to paralyze it. Theatrical convention allows for splitting of mind from body, enabling the audience to respond either emotionally or intellectually to the action it sees on stage without responding physically."[17] Likewise, the failure to respond physically—on the part of both the onlooker and the victim—causes psychoanalyst Dori Laub to characterize trauma as a "collapse of witnessing." He defines the corrective to this visual refuge as an active listening; as Taylor points out, Laub defines the witness as a *listener* rather than a *see-er,* if only in the post-traumatic setting of psychoanalytic therapy or testimony-taking.[18] In addition to listening, the engaged witness refuses the visual refuge of spectacle by resisting the objectification of the other that characterizes spectacular images. As Caruth (as well as Felman) emphasizes, the mute isolation of trauma can be redressed only by engaging the other as a subject of address in order to witness how "history, like trauma, is never simply one's own, that history is precisely the way we are implicated in each other's traumas."[19]

My theoretical intervention comes at this convergence of trauma and spectacle: the spectacular structure of the Japanese American internment removed the public-as-spectator from any participation, empathy, implication, or complicity in the dramatic disenfranchisement of racialized citizens that was taking place in full view. The political spectacles staged by the U.S. government and broadcast by the American media *framed* the internment event in visual terms that objectified the Japanese American other within an economy of Debordian "mere appearance" that was based on a racialized understanding of Japan as a culture of artifice and surfaces.[20] But the most important sense in which the spectacle *became* the trauma of Japanese Americans consisted in the demand placed on internees to comply with this spectacularization so as to provide "proof" of their loyalty to the United States—a command performance that actually prevented internees from fully processing the material violence enacted against them by the internment policy. Whether called upon to "voluntarily" relocate to internment camps under intense media scrutiny or, later, asked to offer their interned bodies (and those of their sons and brothers) up to military service on behalf of a nation that impugned their loyalty, many Japanese Americans found that the only way to prove the internment policy's baselessness was to comply with the terms of its spectacularization. Caruth's insights into trauma as a "missed" event (missed insofar as "the event is not assimilated or experienced fully at the time, but only belatedly") thus illuminate the experience of internees.[21] Japanese Americans "missed" the impact of their forced evacuation and imprisonment after Pearl Harbor because their persecution was staged—over and over again for the more than three years of the Pacific War—as a series of political spectacles that denied the psychological violence and material underpinnings of what was taking place.

Every aspect of the U.S. government's (and its "fourth branch," the mass media's) framing of these events prevented those involved from fully grasping the injustice of what was taking place and from preparing to deal with a cataclysmic change. Caruth calls this aspect of trauma "the inability to fully witness the event as it occurs," so that the traumatic event carries within it "an inherent forgetting."[22] The compulsion to forget was built into the government's overhasty institution of the internment policy from its first moments, as the U.S. military posted euphemistically devastating evacuation notices throughout West Coast communities. On these notices, "aliens and non-aliens" of Japanese descent were told to report to assembly stations, taking only what they could personally carry to the camps, sometimes with as little as forty-eight hours' notice. Not only were Japanese Americans rushed through the material and psychological processing of their forced evacuation as they quickly packed up their lives and boarded a bus or train to unknown destinations for an indeterminate duration, but the harsh glare of media attention and political rhetoric spectacularized the process in a way that encouraged fellow Americans to sit back and watch in passive awe and silence. Although trauma has been most easily associated with bodily injury, Caruth reminds us that in Freud's foundational *Moses and Monotheism,* the trauma "is first of all a trauma of leaving, the trauma of *verlassen.*"[23] In their own forced leaving, Japanese American "evacuees," it should be clear, have a distinct claim on trauma.

Nearly a century before Japanese Americans were forced to leave their communities on the West Coast, the U.S. government perpetrated the opposite but complementary deception against the internees' Japanese ancestors. In 1853, the United States came to them: with the government's blessing, Commodore Matthew C. Perry led an expedition of four battleships to forcefully but peacefully open Tokyo Bay, ending Japan's two-century policy of national isolation. For a Japan that had never laid eyes on such imposingly industrialized steamships, these uninvited vessels of American modernity immediately became known as "the Black Ships." Their forced opening of Japan—what one American historian recently called *Breaking Open Japan*—resulted in the proverbial equal and opposite reaction, in the form of a stream of Japanese immigration to the Americas that would culminate in the World War II persecution.[24] But Perry's arrival also inspired a spiritual and cultural "leaving," even for those who stayed, as Japanese people at large became sudden exiles from their long-standing traditions. In addition, with Commodore Perry, spectacle became established as the mode for obscuring the psychological violence and material underpinnings of Japanese disenfranchisement. In a self-conscious national image constructed against the imperial histories of its fellow Western powers, the U.S. State Department communicated to Perry that he was to be extremely concerned to avoid any "real" violence in his mission to end Japanese isolation—he was instructed, instead, "to show an imposing *display* of power"—and, through his study-at-a-distance of Japanese culture he devised in advance a strategy for manufacturing the other's consent that centered upon the staging of spectacle.[25] Upon the mission's victorious return to America, Perry's official chronicler described the commodore's strategy for deploying spectacle to conquer "these people of forms and ceremonies":

> In a country like Japan, so governed by ceremonials of all kinds, it was necessary to guard with the strictest etiquette even the forms of speech; and it was found that by a diligent attention to the minutest and apparently most insignificant details of word and action, the desired impression was made upon Japanese diplomacy; which, as a smooth surface requires one equally smooth to touch it at every point, can only be fully reached and met by the nicest adjustment of the most polished formality.[26]

The "smooth surface" of Perry's strategy manifested itself in parodic heights of civilized pageantry—refined gift-giving receptions, theatrical entertainments (including blackface minstrelsy), and militaristic display, all performed under the assumption that "so ceremonious and artificial a people as the Japanese" would consent only to a military policy of spectacle.[27] The other option was to use outright force, but this explicit course of colonialist aggression would not conform to a component of the national self-image that nineteenth-century Americans increasingly referred to as Manifest Destiny.

Perry's 1853–1854 opening of Japan prepared the ground for the convergence of spectacle and trauma that would characterize Japan-U.S. relations up to and through the shock-and-awe bombings of Hiroshima and Nagasaki that were seen as necessary to force the 1945 surrender of "so ceremonious and artificial a people as the Japanese." Perry's landing and its attendant spectacles serve as both the "original traumatizing scene" that obscures material violence throughout the history of Japanese-American relations, and as what Michel de Certeau calls the "inaugural scene" that historicizes Western narratives of discovery and conquest.[28] Diana Taylor derives from de Certeau's "inaugural scene" the notion of a "scenario" that scripts intercultural encounters; each consisting of "a paradigmatic setup" and "a schematic plot," these scenarios "exist as culturally specific imaginaries—sets of possibilities, ways of conceiving conflict, crisis, or resolution—activated with more or less theatricality" throughout the history of these ongoing encounters.[29] As the traumatic scene is replayed in the repetition compulsion, and the inaugural scene prepares the ground for the restaging of familiar spectacles, the logic of Perry's landing was reenacted by the U.S. government and mass media in the political spectacles staged in the wake of Japan's 7 December 1941 attack on Pearl Harbor. In chapter 1, I will start with this original traumatizing scene of the Perry spectacle in order to trace what I call a "theatricalizing discourse" constructed by the West (particularly America) around Japanese "cultural" (racial) difference. In the remainder of the book, I will focus on the scenario's particular reenactment in the events of the Japanese American internment.[30]

Spectacle

When I use "spectacle" in this book's title, I mean to invoke the spectacular mode's propensity to disengage its audience—to render even its participants as passive spectators. Although numerous possibilities always exist for spectacle to be used as a tool for active, critical engagement (in the manner that Bertolt Brecht and his many followers intend), for the most part spectacle can be defined as the staging of an event and arrangement of an audience that rewards passive consumption and deters engaged witnessing, most often through what twenty-first-century Americans increasingly recognize as a strategy of "shock and awe."[31] When resistant spectacles seek to challenge their audiences' passivity and encourage some mode of critical participation—as I will argue that Japanese American theatrical performances in the internment camps did—the term "spectacle" needs to be modified and qualified, not in a way that undermines this general definition, but instead so that the space for resistance can be recognized as always already in negotiation with what Debord calls the society of the spectacle's imposition of a normative "social relationship between people that is mediated by images."[32]

Debord's 1960s formulation of the consumerist spectacle has different emphases but was prefigured by the witnesses to the 1930s and '40s political spectacles of Italian and German fascism. Recently, Henry Giroux has identified these two moments in the formulation of spectacle as "the spectacle of fascism and the spectacle of consumerism," labeling them "two different expressions of what I call the *terror of the spectacle*." According to Giroux, the terror of the spectacle inheres in its demand for "a certain mode of attentiveness or gaze elicited through phantasmagoric practices, including various rites of passage, parades, pageantry, advertisements, and media presentations [which] offers the populace a collective sense of unity that serves to integrate them into state power." Where the spectacle of consumerism that Debord writes about uses visuality to obscure the material underpinnings of commodity capitalism—causing consumers to "miss" their own exploitation and disenfranchisement—the spectacle of fascism uses visuality to distract the populace from the political reality underwriting the regime's ideology. Giroux concludes of both twentieth-century manifestations of spectacle: "Politics and power are not eliminated, they are simply hidden within broader appeals to solidarity." [33]

Rey Chow has identified yet another reason that fascist ideology relies so heavily upon the visuality of spectacles. In her essay "The Fascist Longings in Our Midst," Chow departs from critics such as Louis Althusser and Roland Barthes who have attempted to explain fascism's rending of civilized internal feelings (morality, empathy, sociability) from external manifestations of atrocious behavior (racial persecution, witch hunts, genocide). On the contrary, Chow argues that fascism has no inside—or rather that under fascism the external becomes the internal—and that fascist regimes deploy spectacle as the ideal metaphor for a cognitive system that wholly consists of surface. She defines fascism as "a term that indicates the production and consumption of a glossy surface image, a crude style, for purposes of social identification even among intellectuals." The simultaneous ascendance of film technology and fascist ideology was no coincidence for Chow; rather, in the age of film, "If individuals are, to use Althusser's term, 'interpellated,' they are interpellated not simply as watchers of film but also as film itself. They 'know' themselves not only as the subject, the audience, but as the object, the spectacle, the movie." Under fascism, then, the motto for subjectivity is "to be is to be perceived" because the fascist spectacle positivistically proclaims that all judgments can be made based on the interplay of surface images. Difference and danger can be seen/scene just as certainly as unity and national security can be scene/seen. [34]

Although the Japanese American internment took place between these two moments of spectacle's formulation, it should be clear that the U.S. government and mass media's spectacles staged around the internment event capitalized on the spirit and power (if not always the precise ideology) of both consumerism and fascism. In addition to theorizing the fascist spectacle, Rey Chow represents an important intellectual strand within Asian diasporic studies that emphasizes how "Asia" (as a Western-constructed conglomeration to begin with) has been spectacularized by the West. In her essay "Where Have All the Natives Gone?" Chow argues of Western racialization, "When that other is Asia and the 'Far East,' it always seems as if the European intellectual must speak in absolute terms, making this other an utterly incomprehensible, terrifying, and fascinating spectacle. . . . As such, the 'native' is turned into an absolute entity in the form of an image (the 'empty' Japanese ritual or 'China loam'), whose silence becomes the occasion for *our* speech." Moreover, for Chow, the image of Asian difference "is always distrusted as illusion, deception, and falsehood," leading to an anxious Western fixation that masks the implication of the West's own identity. Instead, the logic of the spectacle renders East-West difference absolute, insofar as "the production of the West's 'others' depends on a logic of visuality that bifurcates 'subjects' and 'objects' into the incompatible positions of intellectuality and spectacularity." [35] Chow's theorization of the West's construction of Asian spectacularity allows us to see how "a social relationship between people that is mediated by images" underwrote (and continues to underwrite) an entire U.S. policy for containing the threat of Asian American difference by making the Asian other into an expressionless, dehumanized spectacle—pure surface, all image, so of course silent—undeserving of the protection of Western intellectuality and U.S. constitutional law. While this volume focuses on the manifestation of this spectacularity within the internment policy, spectacle is a traumatic structure potentially applicable to and resonant with many other instances in Asian American history and cultural studies.

Trauma

As a hidden psychic injury that results from the temporal delay occasioned by the shock and inexplicability of an atrocious event, the "trauma" of my title requires an interdisciplinary methodology to understand its history, structure, and ongoing repercussions. [36] Caruth poses trauma's scholarly challenge by saying "It brings us to the limits of our understanding: if psychoanalysis, psychiatry, sociology, and even literature are beginning to hear each other anew in the study of trauma, it is because they are listening through the radical disruption and gaps of traumatic experience." [37] Theatre and performance studies need to be added to this list of interdisciplines because of our intimate understanding of the operations made possible by the spectacular structure of trauma (as a repeated scene) and of the analytical richness of spectacle as an arrangement that seeks to reify Western binaries (such as mind-body, subject-object, reason-emotion, and actor-audience) but cannot live beyond the borderland in between. Diana Taylor focuses on the liminal quality of spectacle's visuality when she writes, "*seeing* also goes beyond us/them boundaries; it establishes a connection, an identification, and at times even a responsibility that one may not want to assume." [38] Even though spectacle is most often characterized by a failure to assume the responsibility of seeing—a refusal to actively witness or be personally implicated in the spectacularity—theatre and performance scholars are aware of spectacle's potential to unfold otherwise and of a lasting impact on actors and audience alike that outlasts the apparent ephemerality of the live event. These scholarly concerns have much to add to the interdisciplinary conversations happening around "trauma."

Likewise, scholars in Asian American studies have increasingly argued that racialization is a *national* trauma (even when the word "trauma" is not used) whose understanding exceeds the oppressor-oppressed and perpetrator-victim binaries. In *The Melancholy of Race,* Anne Anlin Cheng rejects the concept of trauma in favor of "melancholia," arguing that "trauma, so often associated with discussions of racial denigration, in focusing on a structure of crisis on the part of the victim, misses the violators' own dynamic process at stake in such denigration. Melancholia gets more potently at the notion of constitutive loss that expresses itself in both violent and muted ways, producing confirmation as well as crisis, knowledge as well as aporia. . . . It is this imbricated but denied relationship that forms the basis of white racial melancholia." [39] Melancholia thus becomes an analytic through which Cheng can highlight the mournful but compulsively repeated structure of racialization in the United States from outside the limits of the violator-victim stratification. As compelling as Cheng's book is, I would argue that racial trauma can also be understood as a dynamic *national* process that particularly underwrites the racialization of every "American," regardless of the individual's proximity to whiteness. For instance, Felman reminds us that compulsive repetitions of "the unexpectedness of the original traumatizing scene" are not only experienced on an individual level but can also act as the fuel feeding the engine of history; in her reading, "Freud thus shows how historical traumatic energy can be the motive-force of society, of culture, of tradition, and of history itself." [40] The spectacle of Japanese American internment emerged as a traumatic repetition and reenactment transmitted from the "historical traumatic energy" reverberating throughout Japan-U.S. relations since Perry's 1853 landing at Tokyo Bay. In this "original traumatizing scene" of coerced contact (what Taylor might call the inaugural scenario) Perry established a transmittable energy for both spectacularizing the Asian other and self-consciously performing white privilege across the East-West divide; this traumatic scenario repeats itself in various moments of Asian American encounter throughout U.S. history, including the Japanese American evacuation and internment of World War II.

Racial Performativity

Even as these national traumas repeat themselves in various moments throughout U.S. history, the traumatic structure of spectacle does not manifest itself untouched by its particular historical context. The "racial performativity" in my subtitle refers to a two-faced mode for imagining American national belonging; the United States deployed such a mode during World War II in order to distance its "racial problems" from the fascist persecutions occurring throughout Europe and especially from the Nazi policy toward Jews. Within gender theory in particular, performativity (after Judith Butler) has been defined as the unconscious repetition of a repertoire of codified acts that render their performer legible within a given society's normative gender roles. To be a "real" man, society tells us, involves a scripted set of gestures, behaviors, and physical mannerisms that the performer internalizes and society scrutinizes. For more than a decade, scholars have pondered the applicability of gender performativity to our understanding of racialization, with the key stumbling block being the extent to which race is biologically inscribed onto one's skin rather than culturally available for performative construction.

Butler herself has emphasized the primacy of the visual realm in racialization, suggesting that racial performativity is a conditioned mode of perceiving visual evidence that spectacularizes the other—in other words, the unconscious (or even conscious) enactment of codified acts would seem to have little impact because race will be predetermined through the reading practices of the interracial observer. In an essay on the 1992 Rodney King beating and the not-guilty verdict awarded to the Los Angeles Police Department (LAPD) officers caught on videotape, Butler makes clear how little the intentionality of the African American motorist's gestures of supplication meant when viewed by the white jurors at the trial. She writes of the verdict: "That it *was* achieved is not the consequence of ignoring the video, but, rather, of reproducing the video within a racially saturated field of visibility. If racism pervades white perception, structuring what can and cannot appear within the horizon of white perception, then to what extent does it interpret in advance 'visual evidence'?" The LAPD officers' defense attorneys edited the "visual evidence" of the explicit videotaped beating into a series of still images—including a close-up of King's hand raised in surrender, which was instead reinterpreted as raised in aggressive threat—and thereby converted the witnessing video into pure spectacle, pure visibility, by eliminating the accompanying soundtrack containing the officers' anti-black racial slurs. By thus spectacularizing the black body and activating a racialized mode of visually reading the other, the defense easily (and, for Butler, explicably) won a not-guilty verdict. In a subsequent interview, Butler extended her analysis of the King verdict to a tentative theorization of racialization through performativity:

> There is a performativity to the gaze that is not simply the transposition of a textual model [Austinian iteration] on to a visual one; that when we see Rodney King, when we see that video we are also reading and we are also constituting, and that the reading is a certain conjuring and a certain construction. How do we describe that? It seems to me that that is a modality of performativity, that it is racialization, that the kind of visual reading practice that goes into the viewing of the video is part of what I would mean by racialization, and part of what I would understand as the performativity of what it is 'to race something' or to be 'raced' by it.[41]

Consistent with Butler's hypothesis of a "racially saturated field of visibility," U.S. history clearly demonstrates the extent to which national belonging has been legislated to follow a strict brand of biological racism that uses a visual basis to exclude "non-whites" from full citizenship. Nonetheless, at various moments the nation-state has required a level of unity and patriotism possible only through the circulation of what I call "the myth of performative citizenship." [42] Karen Shimakawa has recorded the extent to which visually perceived racial characteristics have operated in the U.S. courts' upholding of restricted notions of citizenship—often posited on the assumed intentions of our Constitution's white forefathers—including the racial prerequisite laws and the adjudication of citizenship by birthright and by naturalization. [43] These legislative and judicial decisions repeat their national traumas in the afterlife they live in the U.S. official archives, dramatically manifesting what Jacques Derrida calls the *mal d'archive*. [44] In his reading of Derrida's *Archive Fever*, Herman Rappaport suggests that *mal* (usually translated as "fever") could also be interpreted as trauma: "where there is regularity and efficiency in Foucault's archive, there is trauma in Derrida's. The trauma in the archive is what, I think, Derrida is referring to when he speaks of there being a *mal d'archive*." Rappaport goes on to argue that for Derrida, "*mal d'archive* concerns a forgetting or obliteration of the trauma that the trauma itself instantiates in its being repeated as discourse." [45]

Actively attempting to forget the trauma of racial spectacularization that has underwritten the adjudication of U.S. citizenship since the founding of the republic, the American myth of performative citizenship publicly circulates in the place of this repressed history. The myth proclaims that American citizenship is officially and effectively conferred upon any individual, regardless of race or national origin, based simply upon the performance of a codified repertoire of speech acts and embodied acts, ranging from the recitation of the Oath of Citizenship to public participation in patriotic pageantry and even enlistment in the armed services. What this myth obscures is the extent to which citizenship has been officially denied to various racialized groups and, when conferred, has lacked efficacy in terms of the unequal enforcement of its privileges based on proximity to whiteness. [46] Historian Nayan Shah highlights similar concerns through his concept of the "citizen-subject," a term that attends to both the citizenship privileges of liberal democracy and the subject-formation produced by modern disciplinary institutions such as public health initiatives (the focus of his book, *Contagious Divides*). Analyzing San Francisco's Chinatown from the mid-nineteenth century through World War II, Shah finds that "The outcome of the Chinese American community's claim to citizenship and cultural belonging depended upon the performance of normative hygiene and heterosexual family forms." The performative dictates of U.S.

citizenship demanded that unsightly members of the "community" (especially Chinese bachelors) be rendered obscene (literally, "offstage"): "The terms of incorporation into American society redefine certain Chinese immigrants as citizen-subjects by their demonstrations of respectable domesticity, economic stability, and proper conduct." Shah makes the important point that Chinese American "demonstrations" of their fitness for national incorporation ended up excluding entire segments of their community, and even when such performative demonstrativeness succeeded in conferring citizen-subject status upon some Chinese Americans, it always "also emphasize[d] their perpetual difference from 'true' white American citizens."[47]

While Shah is interested in how the "repertoire" of public health acts variously impacted Chinatown's inclusion in notions of American national space over the course of a century, here I am interested in demonstrating how performative citizenship became an exclusionary discourse widely circulated on the American home front during World War II.[48] During the war, when America relied upon a constant cycle of patriotic pageantry that was often visually indistinguishable from that associated with fascist aesthetics abroad—and U.S. home-front policies such as the internment policy and the military policy of segregated armed forces bore an uncomfortable resemblance to the ideology of racial purity that underwrote fascism—the widespread circulation of the myth of performative citizenship became crucial to the manufacturing of consent and the spreading of national unity among the American public. As Henry Giroux describes European fascism, "In the 1930s, the fascist spectacle was embodied in the theater of giganticism with its precisely scripted pageantry around 'the mass of groups of people' . . . art glorifying racial purity and uniformed, white men."[49] So instead of foregrounding racial purity, American wartime pageantry leveraged the performative citizenship myth, which appeared to incorporate racially diverse groups based on their patriotic demonstrativeness. The publicizing of this myth bolstered the illusion that the internment policy resulted from the suspicious behavior of Japanese Americans (their lack of demonstrativeness) rather than from a historical ideology of biological racism that tied U.S. democracy to European fascism. Therefore, the *other face* of performative citizenship is what Butler describes as a performativity of the gaze that racializes the other through visual reading practices that bear much greater resemblance to the traumatic operation of the spectacle than to the self-determined constructions usually associated with performative identity. "Racial performativity," then, refers in this book to the two-faced discourse of American national belonging, the public presentation of which focuses on the myth of performative citizenship but whose *mal d'archive* testifies to the performativity of the gaze at work in spectacularizing the racial other. In this book, I use the methods of theatre and performance studies as well as historical ethnography to portray both faces of the wartime internment, in large part by reading between the lines of archival materials such as government documents, mainstream media accounts, and camp newspapers.

While the first part of this book considers the operation of the anti-Japanese spectacle, the second part considers the resistant potential for internees' own camp performances to call attention to the two-faced promise of American citizenship constantly dangled in front of Japanese Americans during World War II. As Esther Kim Lee notes in *A History of Asian American Theatre*, "Internment camp theatre has been dismissed and even forgotten mainly because of its controversial emphasis on assimilation and accommodation." [50] I argue that the emphasis of camp performance on U.S. principles of assimilation and accommodation does not translate to acceptance of these terms; rather, in foregrounding these issues, Japanese American performers revealed the contradictions inherent in American national belonging by putting both faces of racial performativity onstage. Guy Debord wrote that "spectacle's culture sector gives overt expression to what the spectacle is implicitly in its totality: *the communication of the incommunicable*." Without romanticizing internee theatre, I wish to consider these performances as productions of a "culture sector" capable of seizing upon the internal contradictions that characterized the spectacle of Japanese American trauma. Although Debord may have meant his formulation of cultural work to convey less optimism for resistant potential, my analysis of camp performance is meant to amplify his promise: "Culture is the meaning of an insufficiently meaningful world." [51]

In chapter 1 I argue that the spectacularization of Japanese (Americans) has been reenacted through what I call a "theatricalizing discourse" in formation since Commodore Perry's military and diplomatic coercion launched the Meiji era (1868–1912) of Westernization in Japan. In the Euro-American imagination, the rapidity of this Western-inspired modernization was immediately interpreted as symptomatic of the uncommon imitativeness of Japanese people, with the concomitant implication that their Westernization was only a surface imitation that was not truly assimilated into Japan's "feudal soul." Eight decades later, the internment policy would replicate this logic by insisting that Japanese Americans' claims to U.S. citizenship were merely surface imitations of Americanization that disguised their deep-seated loyalty to the Japanese Empire. I trace this theatricalizing discourse circulated by thinkers in the West about the natural-born actors of Japan from the 1850s up to the present, in which many Anglo-Americans still blithely repeat the long-standing racist stereotype that those of Japanese descent are inherently theatrical people prone to hide their true motives behind a screen of aesthetic display and disguise.

I trace the theatricalizing discourse about Japanese people to Western encounters with traditional Japanese performing arts (including Kabuki and other Japanese theatrics) and to scholarly accounts of Japan propagated by social scientists, culminating in anthropologist Ruth Benedict's famous wartime misreading of Japan, *The Chrysanthemum and the Sword*. During the war, Benedict deployed Japanese Americans to stand in for the enemy abroad through her "culture-at-a-distance" methodology; while it was necessitated by wartime, Benedict never questioned how her interviews with a spectacularized ethnic minority in the United States might have preconditioned her findings that the Japanese Empire was populated by self-conscious, shame-ridden, and theatrical people. Moreover, the theatricalizing discourse for which Benedict's text seems to stand as fountainhead in fact preceded the outbreak of hostilities between Japan and the United States, as decades of Western writings on the perceived peculiarities of Japanese culture constructed an airtight case for Japanese theatricalism. *The Chrysanthemum and the Sword* should thus be understood as the repository of this theatricalizing discourse, which hermetically questioned the existence of a sincere essence beneath the aesthetic constructions of Japanese culture and, when deployed to manage the home front in World War II, disallowed Japanese Americans access to the performative promise of U.S. citizenship.

After the critical discourse analysis of chapter 1, the remaining four chapters of the book pursue a historical ethnography of the spectacles and counter-spectacles performed by the internment's various players. Chapter 2 demonstrates how this theatricalizing stereotype of "the Japanese" was seamlessly transferred onto Japanese Americans and how Commodore Perry's inaugural scenario was repeated through the FBI's spectacular raids on Japanese communities in the wake of Pearl Harbor. The FBI spectacles anxiously asserted the duplicity of Japanese American suspects by attempting to pacify the American public with polished, choreographed containment of "the enemy" at home. These raids were very much the stage upon which the FBI sought the American public's approval for consolidating its national power. But the mimicry between the spectacularity of the FBI's highly constructed raids and the theatricalized identity of the Japanese American suspects met with dissatisfaction from domestic anti-Japanese factions, who pushed past the FBI's partial containment of roughly one thousand Japanese Americans by agitating for the wholesale removal of all those of Japanese descent.

Chapter 3 reconstructs the patriotic pageantry that the Hearst media empire staged in its newspaper pages and on city streets across the United States and argues that these pageants downplayed the coercive spectacularity of their stagings by showcasing the myth of performative citizenship. I demonstrate how William Randolph Hearst, as a metonym for the centralized power and influence of media magnates in this era, staged his own patriotic spectacles so as to exclude Japanese Americans from such assertions of loyalty to the

United States and reiterate instead the other's theatrical duplicity. The interplay between the myth of performative citizenship and the spectacularization of Japanese suspiciousness—a dual movement I have defined as racial performativity—yielded a repetitive melodrama in the Hearst pages throughout the six months in which the military evacuated Japanese Americans from the West Coast. I show how Hearst's wartime coverage of the West Coast's so-called Japanese problem punctuated his five decades of anti-Asian propaganda and deployed melodramatic film techniques gleaned from Hearst's Pathé studio in order to offer a compelling narrative in favor of the internment of Japanese Americans. Once the internment was under way, Hearst's pages constructed the evacuation as a benign field trip for Japanese Americans, a farcical spectacle that insisted upon the playfulness of U.S. internment camps, in contrast to the racist seriousness of Nazi concentration camps abroad. Such coverage disappeared the internment's violent import and traumatized Japanese Americans by compelling them to "miss" the event of their own disenfranchisement.

Chapter 4 explores the self-conscious construction of Japanese American identities and the internment experience in the internee-run *Manzanar Free Press*, which epitomized the camp newspapers independently published in each of the ten relocation centers. In the face of political spectacularization and racist media slander, internee journalists drew attention to what I call a "spectacle-archive," recording the ambivalent scrutiny imposed upon them from all sides. At the same time, internees staged intercultural performing arts festivals that defied the U.S. government's mono-Americanist assimilation policy, which pitted second-generation Nisei against their "Japanesey" Issei parents and criminalized displays of Japanese culture. Cultural performance festivals that brought together *odori* (traditional dance) and baton-twirling, Noh theatre chanting and swing musical stylings, opted out of the spectacle-archive by meriting few mentions in the *Manzanar Free Press* publicity machine. At the same time, for internee audiences these intercultural performances made visible the contradictions of American racial performativity. Unfortunately, the fact that this performed resistance lives on mainly through embodied memory has meant that progressive narratives of America's triumph over adversity—epitomized by the U.S. National Park Service's celebration of internees' festivity at Manzanar National Historic Site—have appropriated only the "model minority" interpretation of camp performing arts as rehearsals for assimilation and accommodationist endorsements of U.S. policy.

Chapter 5 uncovers the transnational performing arts (theatre, dance, and music) of internees at the "other" California relocation center, Tule Lake, which served from 1943 to 1946 as a segregation center for Japanese Americans deemed especially "disloyal" to the United States and loyal to Japan. Manzanar and Tule Lake are generally understood to have very different, even diametrically opposed, histories of internee compliance and resistance, but closer examination of the performance histories of Manzanar and Tule Lake reveal the nuanced and similar ways that internees "talked back" to theatricalized stereotypes about Japanese culture, the spectacularization of Asian American assimilation, and the scrutinization of Japanese American loyalty. Significantly, these transnational performing artists rejected the myth of performative citizenship outright by denying that the enactment of either Japanese or American culture necessarily correlated with their loyalty to either nation. The intercultural politics of such internee performances have not survived in the traumatized reenactments. The Western psychological realism of postwar "camp plays" particularly contributed to this amnesia, as realist dramas became staples of Asian American theatre companies in solidarity with the dramatic Commission on Wartime Relocation and Internment of Civilians (CWRIC) hearings that toured the United States in the early 1980s and produced the 1988 Civil Liberties Act's reparations for surviving former internees. But before turning to the performing arts staged by interned Issei and Nisei, I will start with a genealogical approach to the "natural-born actor" discourse that intuitively adheres to "the Japanese," in order to begin to explain why spectacularizing Americans of Japanese descent seemed to U.S. authorities the most natural and effective strategy to accomplish this ethnic minority's abjection from the U.S. body politic.[52]

CHAPTER 1

"A Race of Ingenious Marionettes"

Theatricalizing the Japanese, 1853–1946

O, it offends me to the soul to hear a robustious periwig-pated
fellow tear a passion to tatters, to very rags, to split the ears of
the groundlings, who for the most part are capable of nothing but
inexplicable dumbshows and noise. . . . It out-Herods Herod: pray
you, avoid it.
> —Hamlet to the Players, Act III, Scene ii [1]

This achievement of mine I consider an important event in my life.
The Pageant was magnificent, and I am the only Christian that has
ever before landed peacefully on this part of Japan or any part without submitting to the most humiliating degradation.
> —Commodore Matthew C. Perry, in a letter to his wife after
> the "opening" of Japan (1854) [2]

The polite but thoughtful [Japanese] patriot, perceiving that his
temples are regarded as bric-à-brac, his race as a race of ingenious
marionettes, protests in vain against the unwelcome flattery of sur-
prised admirers. "To this kind of people," wrote Mr. Fukai, one of
the ablest journalists in Tokyo, "our country is simply a play-ground
for globe-trotters, our people a band of cheerful, merry playfellows."
> —Osman Edwards, *Japanese Plays and Playfellows* (1901) [3]

The first phase of the U.S. East Asia Squadron's bloodless opening of Japan—
reputedly ending two centuries of the island nation's isolation "without
firing a shot"—proved so strategic in containing Japanese resistance that its
leader, Commodore Matthew C. Perry, resolved that the expedition's second
phase must either reprise his initial reliance on overwhelming spectacle or else
forego the spectacular altogether. Resolving his all-or-nothing strategy while

docked in China in the 1853–1854 period between the squadron's two landings in Japan, Perry wrote in his journal that for "the sequel" it was necessary "in conducting all my business with these very sagacious and deceitful people . . . either to set all ceremony aside, or to out-Herod Herod in assumed personal consequence and ostentation."[4] History clearly shows that Perry settled on the latter strategy, and Perry's biographers agree that the commodore's taste for self-dramatization and self-important pageantry at least partly predetermined this outcome. Still, historians in Japan and the United States alike have not found it nearly remarkable enough that Perry should have quoted a line from William Shakespeare's *Hamlet* on the occasion of deciding the best line of attack in pacifying the Japanese nation. Perry's reference to "out-Herod Herod" has generally been understood as conjuring the ostentatious proclivities of Herod the Great, the brutal ancient king of Palestine whom the New Testament blames for the massacre of the Innocents at Bethlehem. Certainly this interpretation is consistent with the phrase's colloquial usage throughout the West. But Commodore Perry proposed a military strategy that would "out-Herod Herod" with extreme awareness of his government's mandate that he *not* appear to be brutal or coercive like European colonialist missions had; instead, Perry was offering a model of American diplomacy based on the use of spectacular mediation ("the exhibition of great pomp") to manufacture consent in encounters with exotic others. Hamlet's mention of Herod refers not to the actual historical figure but to his theatrical representation on the stage; as one literary scholar explains of Shakespeare's play, "when Hamlet tells the traveling actors not to out-Herod Herod, he is alluding to the traditional rant of that character in the Corpus Christi [medieval mystery] plays. Spectacle was provided; hell yawned and devils vomited smoke."[5] Directing the traveling actors on the most effective manner of performance to elicit a guilty response from his murderous uncle and his adulterous mother, Hamlet instructs the players to avoid overacting and spectacular effects, "saw[ing] the air" as he puts it, or "chewing the scenery," as modern theatre people might call it. Perry rhetorically inverts Hamlet's advice, professing that "with people of forms" like the overly stylized Japanese, overacting is the best means to convey dominance and gain passive consent. This becomes a variant of "when in Rome, do as Romans do": when in Japan, set aside the artless realism that ostensibly prevails in American society and instead deal in the spectacular ceremonies that ruled what a later observer of Japan would call "the most esthetic nation in the present world."[6]

In this chapter, I am interested in how the discursive construction of Japan as "the most esthetic nation in the present world" became the commonsensical understanding that structures Western encounters with "the Japanese." To say that Japanese people are inherently theatrical, natural-born actors would raise little debate even today, even among Japanese themselves—and it may even be supportable with empirical evidence—so my point in what follows is neither to refute this taken-for-granted understanding of Japan nor to prove that Japanese difference does not exist. Rather, I trace how a *theatricalizing discourse* about the Japanese became ingrained in U.S. foreign policy and entrenched in the Western imagination, starting with Perry's spectacular opening of Japan in the mid-nineteenth century. This theatricalizing discourse insisted that Japanese people had long ago traded sincerity for artifice and focused their social and political interactions on the visible, superficial level of highly aesthetic ceremonies and spectacles—what Perry would call "forms." I characterize this discourse as "theatrical" because it contended that all Japanese operated as actors ("playfellows," "marionettes") whose inner motivations were constantly hidden or even absent, producing a stereotype that dovetailed easily with a generalized Western vision of "oriental" nationalities as deceptive and inscrutable. Contributors to this discourse caricatured Japanese people as behaving in a theatrical manner even off the stage; many writers relied on the spectacularly available difference of Japanese theatre in order to extrapolate a systematic explanation for Japanese society, politics, and psychology. Such discursive moves invariably set Japanese non-realist acting against Western realist acting, amending the *theatrum mundi* philosophy of previous eras to divide the East from the West.

In its particular Japanese iteration, I demonstrate that this theatricalizing discourse became what Diana Taylor calls the "given-to-be-seen"—Japanese theatricalism became the focal point and organizing rationale of U.S. spectacles used to control and then contain the perceived Japanese threat, starting with Perry's use of spectacle in 1853–1854. Taylor draws upon Debord to point out that spectacle's given-to-be-seen generally obscures the atrocities, disenfranchisements, and exploitations that undergird such spectacularity and thus they are rendered "given-to-be-invisible." [7] Likewise, Perry instituted a persuasive strategy for deploying spectacle to manage Japanese people based on the given-to-be-seen logic that Japan was a nation of forms, while obscuring the material violence undergirding U.S. policies. This spectacular obfuscation succeeded to such an extent that the East Asia Squadron continues to be overwhelmingly celebrated by Americans to this day as a peaceful mission accomplished "without firing a shot." [8] Americans celebrate the fact that their forefathers (Perry, along with Presidents Millard Fillmore and Calvin Coolidge) escorted Japan out of its isolated feudal past and into the modern era. But the relationship between Japanese modernity and American modernity has also yielded a strong sense of ambivalence that becomes evident in the mimetic logic behind Perry's founding scenario and its twentieth-century revivals (including the internment itself). This initial attempt to access Japanese modernity (forcefully introducing modern international trade and industrial advances to "backward" Japan) through theatrical language and spectacles of diplomacy established an indelible link between modernism and mimesis that remains intact in the internment spectacles I reconstruct in the remaining chapters of this book. But first I will parse these twin strands of the theatricalizing discourse by tracing how Japanese difference has been constructed in Western accounts of Japan's apparently schizophrenic relationship to modernity (usually described as a surface imitation of Western ways that seems to out-West the West but actually harbors a traditionally Asian, feudal soul) and in aesthetic modernists' appropriation of the use value presented by Japanese arts. The aesthetic modernists' fascination with all things Japanese is well known through the visual arts movements of Japonisme that swept fin de siècle Europe, but far less attention has been paid to understanding the appropriation of Japanese performing arts by Western theatrical modernists; this appropriation will constitute my focus here. In both socioeconomic and aesthetic discussions, we will see that Japan is constructed as the diametric opposite of the West, particularly of America, and that it is both a dangerous and instructive opposite at that. In the U.S. context that most concerns this book, the persistence of such oversimplified difference should be understood as a projection and externalization of America's anxieties about its own modernity when brought in contact with the Japanese other.

Perry's Spectacular Opening of Japan

Prior to embarking on his expedition with the East Asia Squadron, Commodore Perry gathered all extant sources on Japan, most of which had been produced within the Dutch trading compound that had been operating since 1641 on the small Japanese island of Deshima. As the only Westerners to have established trade relations with Japan, the Dutch had accepted what Perry considered utterly degrading subjugation by the Japanese shogunate. In his expedition account, in order to demonstrate this subjugation, Perry quoted extensively from a German physician by the name of Engelbert Kaempfer who practiced at the Deshima compound. According to Dr. Kaempfer, the Dutch who lived in Japan

> willingly underwent an almost perpetual imprisonment . . . and chose to suffer many hardships in a foreign and heathen country; to be remiss in performing divine service on Sundays and solemn festivals; to leave off praying and singing of psalms; entirely to avoid the sign of the cross, the calling upon Christ in the presence of the natives, and all the outer signs of Christianity; and, lastly, to patiently and submissively bear the abusive and injurious behavior of these proud infidels towards us, than which nothing can be offered more shocking to a noble and generous mind.[9]

Instead of performing the Christian ceremonies dictated by their own culture and their deeply held faith, the Dutch voluntarily submitted to a repertoire of "humiliating" (the word is used repeatedly throughout these accounts) and "heathen" performances that demonstrated their inferiority to the Japanese. "To amuse the Shogun," one account puts it, the Dutch "had been ordered to jump, dance, sing, act drunk, clown, and kiss each other. If they wanted to continue trading, they had to do whatever stunts the Shogun wished." [10] The voluntary aspect of these performative subjugations offended Perry the most, and he "resolved to adopt a course entirely contrary to that of all others who had hitherto visited Japan on a similar errand—to demand as a right, and not to solicit as a favor, those acts of courtesy which are due from one civilized nation to another." [11] At risk, of course, was American dignity and exceptionalism, since Japan had taken on the attitude of a "civilized nation" with presumed superiority over a Western colonial power (the Netherlands). However, it was a necessary risk because Japan "lay athwart the major future rout to China," as John Curtis Perry explained it; like Hong Kong, Japan's coal-rich ports offered an irresistible opportunity for American steamships to refuel en route to and from America's valuable new trade partners, the Chinese. [12] Once California had been settled in 1848, the Pacific nations seemed tangibly close to the United States, and as one captain quipped, Japan laid "directly on the line from San Francisco to Shanghai." [13]

Japan's strategic location may have seemed a simple, straightforward matter, but to Perry the Japanese government's reliance on performative degradations and elaborate ceremonies was infinitely complicated—and posed a dangerous threat to the United States. Perry insisted that Japan's national isolation and feudal stagnation had created a culture that prohibited innovation: "All must proceed exactly as it has done for centuries; progress is rendered impossible," which explained, for Perry, Japan's refusal of "communication with other nations." As Perry understood it, in order to ensure the maintenance of the status quo and the untouched quality of their way of life, the Japanese operated under constant internal surveillance, which "pervades the entire polity of Japan," as mandated by "a government of spies" in which even the most powerful men are accompanied by secret informers. Thus for Perry Japanese reliance on performative displays to effect power arrangements became the natural outgrowth of a national climate in which "Every body is watched." Although he depicted this system of surveillance as pervasive and hermetic, Perry also spared ordinary Japanese people the blame for their implication in "official deception." Although they went about their daily lives constantly aware of being watched, most Japanese did not engage in what Perry called "the systematic falsehood and duplicity exhibited, and often without shame, by the high Japanese officials and public dignitaries." Instead, Perry notes that extant sources on Japan nearly unanimously agreed that Japanese people were "naturally frank in manner, communicative and open in speech on ordinary topics, and possessed of a very high sense of honor . . . far superior to any other civilized eastern nation." This characterization of ordinary Japanese people as possessing the same artless honesty usually self-ascribed to Americans would not outlast Perry, as subsequent Western accounts would increasingly indict the Japanese masses along with their "government of spies" as unanimous in their natural inclination to "lie and practice artifice to save themselves from condemnation by higher powers." [14]

Realizing that his presence would enter into this system of watching and being watched—and intent on transcending the circumscribed Dutch position of "playing the fool"—Perry concocted a performative strategy of his own that would ensure he was treated as one of these "higher powers" and thus able to command respect. (His official chronicler more benignly summed up this strategy, writing that for Perry, "the pageantry was often an important part of the history of the negotiation itself, with a people so ceremonious as the Japanese.") [15] Perry relied upon Japan's ignorance of U.S. hierarchies and military ranks in order to make his naval position (a fairly middling commodore) appear higher than it was; he did not realize the extent to which the Japanese gullibility in this respect matched his own ignorance of Japan's military government, including his key oversight of the ineffectual power of the emperor relative to that of the shogunate. In order to render his assumed VIP status efficacious within the presumed Japanese "economy of looks and looking" (to borrow Diana Taylor's description of the society of the spectacle), Perry decided to strictly control his own visibility by dramatically delaying his first appearance on the deck of his resident steamship, the USS *Susquehanna*. [16]

Although Perry's Black Ships (as they came to be called) had been sighted immediately upon their arrival on Japanese shores on 9 July 1853, Perry did not allow the Japanese people to see him until six days later (15 July 1853), when he "donned his full-dress uniform despite the heat" and surrounded himself with an imposing entourage of three hundred sailors and marines and forty musicians to finally escort him onto Japanese soil. In the intervening six days between his arrival and his spectacular revelation to the Japanese people, Perry had remained hidden below deck, refusing to allow himself to be seen by any Japanese official who was not of the highest rank available. According to George Feifer, Perry's "seclusion had earned much native curiosity as well as respect. Japanese eyes laid on him for the first time strained to read what they could from his appearance." [17] But one element of Perry's spectacle must have struck Japanese eyes right away: the entire retinue marched fully armed, with an array of Western-manufactured firepower and gleaming pikes and cutlasses, and Perry's first steps were accompanied not only by the naval band's rendition of "Hail

Columbia" but also by the reverberations of a thirteen-gun salute fired from the flagship. Although a member of Perry's crew snidely recorded his impression that "the precise, colorful spectacle had to be 'outlandish and insolent'" for its Japanese audience, the intended reaction of awe and intimidation must have worked on a great number of the shocked spectators as well.[18] Indeed, not a single one of the five thousand Japanese samurai lining Reception Bay made the slightest movement to resist the landing party; the soldiers-turned-spectators seemed too stupefied by the scope of the American display to contemplate defending their shore, even though, as their contemporary, Kayama Eizaemon, described the scene, Perry's men acted "just *as if* they'd been marching into enemy territory" instead of disembarking for a diplomatic meeting.[19]

The "as if" quality of Perry's performative display framed an overtly military landing as a spectator sport rather than an act of "real" aggression. That the opening of Japan still carries the aura of having been accomplished "without firing a shot" points to how effectively this inaugural scene operated *as spectacle* in obscuring the imperialist violence underwriting every step Perry took.[20] In reality, a great many shots were fired, including the USS *Powhatan's* firing of an imposing twenty-one-cannon salute "in honor of the Emperor," followed by "a salute of seventeen for Hayashi Daigaku-no-kami, the high commissioner"—all by way of opening the March 1854 treaty negotiations at Kanagawa.[21] Ostensibly, of course, the use of such firepower was to be understood as merely decorative, a demonstration of hospitality that might counteract the fact that the Americans were forcefully making themselves at home as they steamed, uninvited, into Japanese bays. At the same time, accounts of Perry's expedition point out that such martial displays were both "for show and for real"—ceremonies performed "merely for effect" but also strategically enacted as a preemptive measure to cow the Japanese forces (and Japanese civilians), which frighteningly outnumbered the Americans.[22] To quote Guy Debord, "The spectacle, though it turns reality on its head, is itself a product of real activity. . . . Reality erupts within the spectacle, and the spectacle is real."[23] Thus, "for show" and "for real" converge since the "effect" remained the same in either case: Perry hoped to bring about Japanese passivity through overwhelming spectacles. This spectacle strategy proved remarkably successful, as Perry admitted in a letter to his wife after the 1854 Treaty of Kanagawa was signed: "This achievement of mine I consider an important event in my life. The Pageant was magnificent, and I am the only Christian that has ever before landed peacefully on this part of Japan or any part without submitting to the most humiliating degradation."[24]

Indeed, the East Asia Squadron recorded the steady dwindling of Japanese military presence along the crowded shores between the July 1853 and February 1854 landings. At first, the Japanese attempted to participate in or at least respond to Perry's spectacles with martial displays of their own, including the erection of banners and flags of rich scarlet and the arrangements of regiments of soldiers in fixed order, "evidently arrayed to give an appearance of martial force," the official record for 14 July 1853 states. But Perry refused to allow co-participation in his spectacles; rather than being "duly impressed with the military power of the Japanese," from his hidden perch beneath the *Susquehanna's* deck, he condescendingly dismissed these initial Japanese displays by saying the "whole effect, *though not startling,* was novel and cheerful." [25] Perry's arrangement of events guaranteed that "startling" performative effects were his sole prerogative, and the Japanese quickly realized they were relegated to spectators at the scene of their own traumatic opening to the West. When Perry returned to Japan in February 1854, he steamed ten ships into Uraga Bay (six more than the initial Black Ships); these ten ships represented one-quarter of the American Navy and therefore the "most powerful" squadron the U.S. government "had ever sent on a mission abroad." From a Japanese perspective on shore, the American martial display was so imposing that the ten ships seemed to fill the "the whole bay." With satisfaction, Perry would notice that "tens of thousands of spectators . . . ignored the [Japanese government's] prohibition in order to crowd the beach," and he congratulated himself that these Japanese spectators crowded round not out of hostile resistance but "in order to enjoy the music of the Black Ships' bells, bands, and sentry calls." [26] Although he remained somewhat wary of a people he considered deceitful, by the time they signed the Treaty of Kanagawa, Perry had contented himself that his squadron had pacified Japan by turning them into overawed spectators, resigned to watching in passive wonder as their era of national isolation came to a decisive end.

Later chroniclers of Perry's brand of diplomacy stress the benign neutrality of his insistence on performative displays. One of these is Perry biographer John Schroeder, who stated that "Perry understood that ceremonial events, lively entertainment, wine and spirits, and good food played a part in naval diplomacy." [27] But most fail to acknowledge that for Perry, such diplomatic "entertainment" operated only in a single direction. In addition to dismissing Japanese martial display as "novel and cheerful," Perry expressed utter disgust at one of the few performances with which the Japanese reciprocated. Perry's official chronicler (reproducing Perry's journal largely verbatim) included three pages of the commodore's disgustedly thick description detailing a sumo wrestling display performed by twenty-five "over-fed monsters." The account exudes apparent relief at the sumo's conclusion: "From the brutal performance of these wrestlers, the Americans turned with pride to the exhibition—to which the Japanese commissioners were now in their turn invited—of the telegraph and the railroad. It was a happy contrast, which a higher civilization presented, to the disgusting display on the part of the Japanese officials. In place of a show of brute animal force, there was a triumphant revelation, to a partially enlightened people, of the success of science and enterprise. The Japanese took great delight." [28] In part, the politics of this juxtaposition replay a familiar dynamic between the other and the West, in which the backward barbarism of the non-Western "native" is scrutinized as an ethnographic exhibit in absolute opposition to the refined viewing position privileged by Western modernity.

But there's a twist, a particular wrinkle that will pervade U.S. policy toward Japan up to and through the internment of Japanese Americans: faced with what Diana Taylor calls the apprehension of the "natives" as "perpetual performers," Perry sought to completely upstage Japanese performativity and control the visual field with his own dominant spectacles. [29] In addition to the spectacles of modernity occasioned by the American presentation of a miniature railroad and train set (upon which Japanese guests unexpectedly took a childlike ride) and a working telegraph machine, Perry attempted to "entertain" his Japanese audience through several performances of blackface minstrelsy. Since blackface minstrel shows arguably remained the most popular (and the first truly American) form of theatre throughout the antebellum U.S., Perry's decision to include the so-called Ethiopian Minstrels—actually a group of white sailors with an amateur training in "negro minstrelsy"—is not as surprising as it might initially seem. The official account boasts that Perry's actor-sailors, "blacking their faces and dressing themselves in character, enacted their parts with a humor that would have gained them unbounded applause from a New York audience even at Christy's," referring to one of the most successful resident professional minstrel troupes in antebellum New York, led by Edwin Pearce Christy. [30] At first Perry's pride at his men's virtuoso performance of a debased (though popular) art form seems baffling, to say the least. But as Anne Anlin Cheng reminds us: "As Ralph Ellison once wrote, 'When American life is most American it is apt to be most theatrical.' Pointing to the Boston Tea Party [16 December 1773] and the rebelling colonists' donning of Native American masks as an originary moment in American founding, Ellison tells us that the tradition of masking, especially the adopting of racial masks to both veil and authenticate whiteness, has played a persistent role in the process of Americanization." [31] Racial masking has become a means of asserting American exceptionalism, in terms of both the dominance of whiteness (in a competitive multiracial field unique to a "nation of immigrants") and the contradictions of modernity (which leverage non-white labor to sustain industrial production and a market economy that primarily benefits whites).

If Ellison and Cheng are right that the Boston Tea Party stands as the "originary moment" of racial masking operating toward U.S. nation building, Perry's deployment of blackface minstrel performance at the opening of Japan certainly operates as another early negotiation of American national identity through the spectacularization of race. But the historical record remains rather mum on the strategic motivation behind Perry's deployment of blackface performance. Of the 27 March 1854 minstrel show performed at a banquet aboard the USS *Powhatan*, the official account merely celebrates "the general hilarity provoked by the farcical antics and humorous performances of the mock negroes," insisting that the Japanese guests seated in the first row enjoyed the sailors' "blackened faces, banjos, tambourines, and silly dancing" as much as the Americans did.[32] At the port of Hakodate—one of those opened to American trade in the new Treaty of Kanagawa—Perry treated the Japanese officials to another onboard minstrel show. According to Rhoda Blumberg, "The audience seemed amused, and Perry was satisfied that he was leaving them with a good impression."[33] The accounts uniformly suggest that in the case of Perry's blackface performances, sometimes entertainment is just entertainment.

Despite the lack of significance ascribed to these blackface performances, their strategic import becomes clearer when compared with other instances of African American racialization displayed by Perry for his Japanese audience. Perry's squadron employed a number of African American men. Knowing the Japanese had never laid eyes upon this race before, Perry selected two "jet-black" stewards to act as spectacular bodyguards when he first presented himself to the natives on 15 July 1853. The official account describes the resultant spectacle: "On either side of the Commodore marched a tall, well-formed negro, who, armed to the teeth, acted as his personal guard. These blacks, selected for the occasion, were two of the best-looking fellows of their colour that the squadron could furnish. All this parade was but for effect. The procession was obliged to make a somewhat circular movement to reach the entrance of the house of reception. This gave a good opportunity for the display of the escort."[34] This self-conscious display of American race relations seemed intent upon reinforcing the notion that the Japanese had been relegated to spectators, cowed by a strange American spectacle of dominance and difference. Indeed, Perry was pleased to see how the black bodyguards fascinated and startled the Japanese audience, not to mention how these tall African Americans—fully armed and bearing American flags—strikingly towered over "the more effeminate looking" Japanese.[35] The passivity of Japan seemed assured by such confident demonstrations of American racialization.

So the palpable development becomes how Perry's total relegation of the Japanese to passive spectators and his apparently generous-minded insistence that ordinary Japanese people remained frank and artless despite their "government of spies" and its "official deception" led to the now commonplace characterization of Japan as "the most esthetic nation in the present world." Certainly the perception of Japanese as natural-born actors—socialized from birth into an economy of looks and looking—remained latent as the East Asia Squadron's rationale behind its strategy to "out-Herod Herod." More important, the Perry expedition essentially launched Japan into social, political, and economic modernity by introducing modern nationalism (if only as a way of uniting Japan's feudal hamlets against a common foreign enemy) and paving the way for the unprecedented Westernization accomplished during the Meiji Era. According to George Feifer, "No country in the world would learn the military lessons of the Industrial Revolution better than Japan, whose history from Perry's arrival to the conclusion of World War II can be summarized by its leaders' determination to 'Modernize! Industrialize! Build Big Guns!' The country could be saved from Western domination only by acquiring all the means for producing Western weapons, which the gritty Japanese spirit would put to better use." [36] Other telling slogans in Meiji Japan included "Japanese Spirit, Western Things" and "Eastern Ethics, Western Science." Likewise, Japan's headlong leap into Western-style colonialism under the slogan of a united "Greater East Asia Co-Prosperity Sphere" seemed a dramatic about-face from its pre-Perry isolationism. "Japan's victory over Russia in 1905 had catapulted Japan into the role of East Asian hegemon. Japan was now seen through the optics of a new, technologically sophisticated and capitalist-oriented imperialism. . . . Japan's victory over Russia and its progressive annexation of parts of East Asia made it a formidable foe, especially as regards the United States' own interests in East Asia. Under these circumstances, the issue of whether the Japanese should even be considered as Asian arose." [37]

Most Westerners managed the threateningly fast modernization and Western-style imperialist aspirations of a non-white other by interpreting Japanese modernity as merely a surface imitation accomplished by the uncommon adaptability and ape-like mimicry possessed by the Japanese as a people. This mimetic understanding of Japanese modernity translated to an anxiously repeated assertion that Japanese were not on par with Westerners but instead were just very good actors (adaptable to new contexts of modernity, able to mimic the trappings of modernization but without internalizing these developments). The apparently unchanged abundance of "forms and ceremonies" in Japanese traditional culture, including of course the spectacularly available difference of non-realist Japanese theatre like Kabuki and Noh, became the perfect metonym to characterize Japan at large as pure surface, emptied of a modern soul.[38] These anxious repetitions constitute what I am calling a theatricalizing discourse about "the Japanese."

Although Perry's characterizations of Japan became notorious, before and after his expedition a more generalized stereotype of Asiatic nations as duplicitous and inscrutable circulated in the United States independent of the Japanese. Rey Chow, for instance, describes how Asian difference "is always distrusted as illusion, deception, and falsehood" and how East-West difference is rendered absolute because "the production of the West's 'others' depends on a logic of visuality that bifurcates 'subjects' and 'objects' into the incompatible positions of intellectuality and spectacularity."[39] Nevertheless, as David Palumbo-Liu points out, the American notion of an Asian "Yellow Peril," invading the United States through immigration and other types of penetration, needs to be specifically understood based on the particular ethnicity/nationality in question and the historical context in which these stereotypes become (re)activated.[40] In particular, Nayan Shah argues that "from the mid-nineteenth century to World War II, white politicians and social critics characterized Chinatown as an immoral bachelor society of dissolute men who frequented opium dens, gambling houses, and brothels, and the few visible Chinese women were considered to be prostitutes." Moreover, Shah writes, "The Chinese were characterized repeatedly in terms of 'excess'—of their number, of their living densities, of the diseases they spawned, and of the waste they produced."[41] Palumbo-Liu shows that South Asian immigrants in the early part of the twentieth century were subjected to similar stereotypes as the Chinese "mass" but that South Asians' particular colonized status manifested itself in many whites' "special annoyance" and distrust at the presumed superiority of their "Anglicized behavior," which threatened through its seemingly conscious mimicry of the British colonizers' manners, dress, and speech. Filipinos, on the other hand, possessed a hybrid racial status (combining "Hispanic, Asian, and white blood") and a liminal national status (alternately controlled by Spain and the United States), which produced a threatening mix that manifested itself in an American fear of their "particularly malicious sexuality," targeted at miscegenation with white women.[42]

Aligned with this project of specifying the particular mutations of the Yellow Peril, the remainder of this chapter will be concerned with historicizing the post-Perry citation of Japan as "the most esthetic nation in the present world" and with tracing the Western perception that people of Japanese descent are natural-born actors—regardless of their nation of residence or citizenship status. Two forms of Euro-American bias fueled this theatricalizing discourse about Japan: Orientalism and antitheatrical prejudice. A few years after Edward Said published his groundbreaking *Orientalism,* Jonas Barish released his own tome, outlining another deep-rooted prejudicial system of Western thought: *The Antitheatrical Prejudice.* Said had defined Orientalism as a system of knowledge constructed by European and American imperialists about their colonial holdings in the East. Most important, as Said put it, this system is citational: "Every writer on the Orient . . . assumes some Oriental precedent, some previous knowledge of the Orient, to which he refers and on which he relies." These views of the Orient have "distributive currency," so that even as Orientalist writers disagree, they continue to cite and recirculate concurring assumptions about their distant, exotic other in order to constantly reinforce Orientalism's systematic conception that East-West cultural difference creates "a battlefront that separates them" and an imperative for "the West to control, contain, and otherwise govern the other." [43] Likewise, Barish traced the antitheatrical prejudice's citational network all the way back to Plato's powerful if contradictory critiques of mimetic arts as debased copies of reality that lull audiences into forgetting their true, pious selves. From the Western classical tradition onward, Barish traces a scholarly, religious, and popular discourse that reached its peak in the seventeenth and eighteenth centuries, when the criminalization of actors as dangerous dissemblers led to crackdowns throughout Europe, including the closing of theatre districts and the refusal of burial rights for professional theatre artists.[44] But in the United States, public policy decisions based on an institutionalized belief in the hypocrisy and deviant sexuality of theatrical performers and performance extended well beyond the eighteenth century. Indeed, this prejudice died hard here: state ordinances against theatrical practices remained in effect until almost the nineteenth century, much later than in Europe.[45] As historian Jean-Christophe Agnew notes, while they enjoyed touring performances, Americans held theatre apart as a non-native art form in order to distance U.S. national identity from its perceived threats; Agnew also attributes the distinctly American strain of the antitheatrical prejudice to the stubborn remnants of Puritan asceticism.[46]

Although the Western antitheatrical prejudice historically may not have had the international policy impact that Orientalist thought provided for Western imperialism, I want to suggest that these two forms of Euro-American bias—against the Protean illegitimacy of theatrical practitioners on the one hand and the decadent, inscrutable exoticism of "Oriental" nationals on the other—converged in American attitudes toward Japanese people after Perry launched Japan headlong into modernity. While the antitheatrical prejudice repeatedly criminalized the shape-shifting potential of theatrical acting, both discourses bolstered Western chauvinism by posing the other as theatrical in a deviant, soulless fashion. I will begin and end with the most influential World War II repository of this theatricalizing discourse: celebrated liberal anthropologist Ruth Benedict's *The Chrysanthemum and the Sword: Patterns of Japanese Culture*, which found government distribution prior to Japan's surrender but was published only in 1946. While it will become clear that Benedict's characterization of the Japanese "national personality" as riddled by dualism and insincerity shares a great deal with an overarching methodological trend in American liberal anthropology and sociology [47]—and continuities can be found between Benedict's assessment of Japan and contemporaneous accounts of other national others like the Russians—in what follows, my concern will be to point out a particular citation that threads through Western explanations of Japanese modernity and Japanese aesthetics. The citation's utilization in *The Chrysanthemum and the Sword* has particular salience for the internment because of its circulation within high levels of the U.S. government (and thus its impact on wartime policy) and owing to the manner in which its conclusions were overdetermined by Benedict's reliance on Japanese American informants to bolster the "culture-at-a-distance" methodology necessitated by her inability to conduct fieldwork in Japan.

Benedict's Elders: Mapping the Theatricalizing Discourse

When Benedict was commissioned by the U.S. Office of War Information (OWI) in June 1944 to explain Japanese behavior (despite possessing no prior expertise on Japan), the startling means of Japanese war waging and the sweeping will to fight to apparently impossible victory were foremost on the American list of baffling cultural differences in need of explanation. Anthropologist Jennifer Robertson describes the "implicit theatricality" apparent in how the Japanese Empire managed the "natives" under its colonial rule (for instance, exporting Japanese theatrical productions as a way of inculcating imperial values), as well as the "thespian tactics" deployed by the Japanese military in warfare against Allied troops. Robertson gives the telling example of Japanese soldiers dressing as Malays during their invasion of Malaya in order to capitalize upon British troops' racial confusion for their strategic advantage.[48] Indeed, the Japanese military successes inaugurated by Pearl Harbor and continuing for several months into 1942 seemed ample confirmation of the American public's widespread belief, after Pearl Harbor, that the Japanese were not just treacherous but theatrically so. Even before the United States entered the conflict, the stockpile of "thespian tactics" used by the Japanese military in World War II also contained incidents like the unabashed 1937 enactment of mass atrocities (soldiers raping and beheading tens of thousands of civilians) in Nanking, China, and spectacular battlefield displays of self-sacrifice like kamikaze bombings. Rey Chow refers to "the aesthetics of Japanese brutality . . . not in the narrow sense of principles of beauty or good taste, but in the broader, Kantian sense of principles of perception and cognition, principles that are in turn manifested in outward behavior, as behavioral style."[49] The apparent investment of the Japanese military in staging such atrocities according to a monstrous aesthetics or outward style struck its intended audiences as coldly calculated spectacles and self-conscious national fashioning.

Benedict did not set out to explain the aesthetics and behavioral style of military tactics but rather the mundane aspects of everyday Japanese life, in order to link these apparently idiosyncratic behaviors in a coherent pattern that could be used to bring about Japan's defeat and manage its postwar occupation by conquering the minds of the Japanese masses.[50] However, the exigencies of war meant that Benedict could not travel to Japan to pursue the fieldwork privileged by anthropologists; instead, as Benedict herself put it, "In studying Japan, I was the heir of many students."[51] Benedict offset her inability to conduct fieldwork by compiling her own library at the OWI offices in Washington, D.C.; her primary and secondary sources consisted of published texts and archival manuscripts on Japan written by Europeans, Americans, and Japanese themselves. Relying on this citational network, which recycled and reconfirmed a theatricalizing discourse about people of Japanese descent, Benedict confidently asserted all-encompassing cultural diagnoses about a country she had never visited, and she posited far-ranging policy recommendations to conquer an ethnic group she had encountered only in the diaspora. The *Patterns of Japanese Culture* of Benedict's subtitle, which earned Japan the designation of "the most alien enemy the United States had ever fought," were to be understood as diametrically opposed to American customs because they were theatrical in terms of being both repressively scripted and aesthetically arranged for an ever-present audience. Benedict's appraisal of the Japanese national personality would gain popularity in the U.S. government, American popular culture, and Japanese media circles alike. Most famously, Benedict called Japan a collective "shame culture," shame (*haji*) being an external morality system regulated by the sanctions of the group; it was compared with guilt, an internal morality system answering only to an individual's conscience. By contrast, Benedict characterized the individualistic America as a "guilt culture" and deployed theatrical terms to illustrate the difference, arguing that absolutely inverted notions of "sincerity" lay at the root of the Japan-U.S. culture clash.[52] She posited that the management of shame in Japanese life was inherently theatrical because the efficacy of shame "requires an audience or at least a man's fantasy of an audience," and she proceeded to locate the root of this consciousness of a judging audience in the Japanese mother's repeated staging of "little plays" that deceived her children into believing that not following cultural sanctions would cause them to be disowned. Practices of child rearing were the lynchpin of anthropological analysis in Benedict's era, so it is significant that she opened her chapter "A Child Learns" with the warning, "Japanese babies are not brought up in the fashion that a thoughtful Westerner might suppose." She proceeded to narrate one of the repeated "little plays" that ritually marked Japanese childhood: "When the child of one or two has been noisy or has failed to be prompt about something, the mother will say to a man visitor, 'Will you take this child away? We don't want it.' The visitor acts out his rôle. He starts to take the child out of the house. The baby screams and calls upon its mother to rescue it. He has a full-sized tantrum. When she thinks the teasing has worked, she relents and takes back the child, exacting its frenzied promise to be good. The little play is acted out sometimes with children who are as old as five and six." "Such experiences," Benedict solemnly stated, "are rich soil for the fear of ridicule and of ostracism which is so marked in the Japanese grown-up."[53]

Yet Benedict did not consider cruel these little plays of Japanese child rearing; for her, they emanated from a basic difference between the Western conceptualization of sincerity and the Japanese conceptualization of sincerity (*makoto*). Benedict's Westerners expected people to "act 'in character,'" whereas her Japanese people possessed the ability to "swing from one behavior to another without psychic cost," an apparent schizophrenia she dubbed "right-about-face" and "situational realism." The logical coherence or pattern explaining these changes of character—donned and doffed with as little psychological confusion as an actor playing different characters onstage—emerged from what Benedict identified as the distinctly Japanese meaning of "sincerity" as "the zeal to follow the 'road' mapped out by the Japanese code and the Japanese spirit."[54] Intent on demonstrating the "road" that purportedly scripted Japanese behavior and thus inverted the Western notion of "sincerity" (natural, individual, spontaneous, original), Benedict was in fact dutifully following a map from her own culture through her unquestioned, highly conventional reiteration of tropes culled from decades of theatricalizing discourse that likewise attempted to contain "the most alien enemy the United States had ever fought."

Working in the enforced ivory tower of wartime anthropology, Benedict drew upon many published English sources on Japan, but she provided no bibliography to acknowledge these sources. One text she probably consulted and obliquely references in her introduction is British theatre critic Osman Edwards' *Japanese Plays and Playfellows* (1901). Benedict refers to the long lineage of Japan observers who summed up the Japanese national character using litanies of paradoxes like "the chrysanthemum and the sword." Although she assumes a somewhat skeptical attitude toward such citations, in the end Benedict equivocally endorses them in her book's title and statements such as "All these contradictions, however, are the warp and woof of books on Japan. They are true."[55] Suggesting a link in this lineage, the first chapter of Edwards' book, which details his knowledge of Japanese theatre after six months spent in Japan, introduces the idea of the two-faced "Japanese Janus."

In what seemed a speedy conversion from national isolation to Western-style imperialism, Japan had opened Korea in 1876, annexed the Ryukyus (now Okinawa) in 1879, defeated China in the 1894–1895 Sino-Japanese War, and then quickly taken Taiwan and Korea in full (the latter would be annexed as a protectorate in 1910). As a British man writing on the heels of these stunning feats of Asian expansion, Edwards manages Japan's threat to Western modernity (with its own investment in East Asia) by emphasizing that a traditionally feudal nature resided just beneath the superficial modernization of the Japanese people. Edwards sees Japanese people as two-faced because they balance a litany of paradoxes in their national character, paradoxes that follow in turn from "a profoundly narrow patriotism" that results from physically ending two centuries of isolation but mentally harboring the need "to restrict at all costs 'Japan to the Japanese.'" The Japanese paradoxes Edwards identifies include the surface "imitating" of foreign traders' methods by the mercantile classes—while they meanwhile "dread and dislike the invading trader," nursing all along "the intention of ousting him as much as possible from their markets"—and the intellectual class' "appreciation" of Western science and government—which brings it "none the nearer spiritually through their acquisition." Edwards is careful to note, however, that these inconsistencies remain neatly compartmentalized between the Japanese surface and the Japanese soul, noting, "even the [foreign] victim of [Japanese] patriotic manoeuvres is hardly ever exposed to personal malevolence. The politest nation in the world would certainly not be guilty of any overt discourtesy." Japanese people, Edwards suggests, are excellent actors in everyday life, seamlessly performing for outsiders "the impress of democratic ambitions," while underneath preserving "feudal obedience to a common call." In short, for Edwards, populating Japan is "a race which remains, the more it changes, the more indissoluably [sic] the same." [56]

At first, Edwards' book title seems to indicate his intention to move beyond what Said identified as the Orientalist's miniaturizing impulse of "turning the Orient into a theater for his representations of the Orient." He even sets up a cautionary tale against Westerners who underestimate the power and overstate the quaintness of the tiny island nation. The "Playfellows" of *Japanese Plays and Playfellows* comes from a quotation by "one of the ablest journalists in Tokyo," a Mr. Fukai, who decried the theatrical miniaturization of his people by Western visitors, for whom "his temples are regarded as bric-à-brac, his race as a race of ingenious marionettes." Much as Benedict would four decades later, Edwards caricatured the (presumably Western) tourists derided by his native informant in order to distance himself from those intercultural dilettantes who would theatricalize everyday Japanese life:

> A foreign country for most travellers is very like a theatre. They arrive in a holiday mood, resolving to be pleased. Should their choice have fallen on Japan, be sure that eulogistic notices from the pens of Sir Edwin Arnold and M. Pierre Loti have prepared them to enjoy the daintiest of comediettas. They reach the enchanted shore. They pass swiftly from one aspect of fairyland to another. Nothing happens to shake their preconceived conviction that in the Land of the Rising Sun Nature began and Art completed a yellow paradise. . . . The picturesque unreality of common things abets illusion. Surely these dolls' houses

of wood and paper, these canopies of rose bloom and curtains of purple wisteria, the gigantic cryptomeria, the tenacular pines, the azure inland sea and snow-streaked Fuji itself—surely all these compose a superb mise en scène for poetic comedy![57]

Edwards signals his distance from the naïve traveler's interpretation of Japan as "the daintiest of comediettas" through the outrageousness of his tone and his identification of an early Orientalist network of writing on Japan (emerging from "the pens" of Arnold and Loti). However, in the remainder of the chapter he merely substitutes the common understanding of everyday Japan's comedic *mise en scène* with a different theatrical genre—the "problem-play"—of which he proceeds to peer "behind the scenes." Edwards embarks on what he considers a revolutionary project: revealing the sociopolitical "intrigues of the greenroom," foregrounding a backstage space that most Western observers of Japanese aesthetics seemed content to leave to obscurity in favor of the surface light comedy.[58] For Edwards, these intrigues display a dark side to the otherwise "dainty" Japanese, mostly owing to Japan's attempts to be taken seriously as a modern, imperialist nation in a global order oriented toward the West.

After a respectful but brief foray "behind the scenes," Edwards devotes the rest of *Plays and Playfellows* to the theatre proper, but although he promises to "forget the intrigues of the green-room, in which we have happily no concern" and give his "undivided attention" to plays themselves, his initial sociopolitical assessment of the "Japanese Janus" ghosts the aesthetic analyses that follow.[59] Edwards proceeds to characterize the Japanese as "a race of artists," an apparent accolade whereby the author collapses all distinctions between the fictionalized world of theatrical representation and the real lives of Japanese people and between the profession of theatrical acting and the manner in which all Japanese people manage their identities in everyday life. As a typical node on the theatricalizing discourse's network, Edwards rejects an interpretation of Japanese popular and traditional theatre as art for art's sake; here I depart sharply from Kojin Karatani, who argues that Orientalist fascination with Japan should be called "aestheticentrism" because it "brackets" Japanese aesthetics off as unrelated to Japanese politics and other material realities of Japanese life.[60] Instead, Edwards, like other theatricalizing writers on Japan, saw Japanese theatre as the most important "political instrument" for "indoctrinating" and preserving the feudal soul he detected in Japan.[61] As noted, Edwards believed that Japanese people harbored a feudal soul beneath all their external manifestations of Westernization, democratization, and modernization. Japanese theatre thus becomes a powerful metaphor for the secretly feudal society of Japan. Moreover, Edwards felt that Japanese theatre espoused feudal allegiance to duty and the past through both its form and its content, communicating its political message in *what* got represented on the stage and *how* these themes were represented.

"Enter a Tokyo theatre to-day," Edwards promises his readers, "and you will find yourself in old Japan, among resplendent monsters, whose actions violate moral sense, yet exhibit a high and stern morality by no means outmoded through the advent of modern ideas. Beauty and duty are the hall-marks that stamp as authentic the plays which delight and instruct the Japanese." Despite the obvious "beauty" of the Japanese *mise en scène,* Edwards testifies that feudalism trumps aesthetics in Japanese theatre: "However clear the call of beauty, duty's voice is louder still—duty, not as we Westerns conceive it, a half-hearted compromise between our own interests and those of others, but complete moral and mental suicide. No lesson was more impressively preached to the people by the dramatists in hundreds of historical plays than the duty of obedience at any price. . . . The cultivated *samurai* were not allowed to enter the theatre, but the masses were melted to tears and heated to transports of patriotic subservience by the representation of heroic self-sacrifice." [62]

Imagining the populist audience to Kabuki performances as passively rehearsing a nationalist duty to enact "complete moral and mental suicide," Edwards enlarges Japanese theatre's implications exponentially beyond simple popular entertainment. Elsewhere in *Plays and Playfellows,* Edwards illustrates how Japanese acting itself cultivates the feudal soul of Japan. For instance, Edwards estimates that one in ten Japanese dramas requires the Japanese actor to perform *hara-kiri,* or ritual suicide, onstage, and he describes in detail the acting methods used to achieve this scene: "The actor writes a letter, generally in blood, to explain why his honour requires self-slaughter, and then with great deliberation draws a knife across his stomach, until his admirably twitching limbs are covered with gore." Equally important is the reaction of the Japanese audience members (including "Japanese babies"!), who do not share the squeamishness of the Western tourist at such gory theatrics. By stoically bearing apparently frequent scenes of *hara-kiri,* Edwards argues, Japanese people learn "that superb indifference to death, that supreme attachment to honour, which no other nation displays to the same degree." [63]

Likewise, Edwards identifies a "mingled ferocity and devotion" in Japanese popular plays and stage acting, which he theorizes as appealing to "the devil and the angel cohabiting the human heart" (referring exclusively to the Japanese heart, having a few lines earlier described Westerners' alienation from such techniques). He raves about certain examples from the *shimpa* (twentieth-century realist theatre) company of Kawakami Otojiro and his wife, Sada Yakko, whose Kabuki-infused acting offered an exotic sensation in turn-of-the-century America and Europe. Writing of Kawakami's performance in *The Loyalist* in England, Edwards sums up the acting as an easy shuttling between extremes of emotion: "Alternately fierce and pensive, agile and immobile, [Kawakami] played the part of Takanori with such force and feeling, that *yamato-damashii*, the fervent temper of Japanese chivalry, lived and moved before us, a visibly realised ideal." Similarly, in the infamous temple bell scene of *The Geisha and the Knight,* Sada Yakko is seen as mastering transformation and, thus, the audience: "At this moment, with bare arms and dishevelled hair, she thrills and dominates the audience: the fairy has become a fury; the comedy is at once attuned by this tragic figure to ghastly seriousness." [64] With such descriptions—especially given Edwards' side note that virtuoso displays of acting like *hara-kiri* and swings in emotion have ample real-world counterparts in Japan—the genesis of Benedict's assessment four decades later that Japanese people are able to "swing from one behavior to another without psychic cost" becomes entirely obvious. [65]

Beyond its impact on Benedict, Edwards' *Japanese Plays and Playfellows* can be understood as the forefather of much of the repetitive assessments of Japanese theatrical culture proffered by radical voices of the European avant-garde. [66] Whether or not these directors and philosophers read Edwards, he set the tone for future discussion of Japanese theatre and acting, both in his continuous cycling between everyday life and stage behavior and in his linking of theatrical form and content with feudal indoctrination. These Western assumptions would remain remarkably consistent for the rest of the twentieth century and throughout their interdisciplinary and international circles of dispersal. [67]

Japanese Acting and Western Modernism's Theatrical Avant-Garde

Two particular strands of the Western theatrical avant-garde found special inspiration in Noh, Kabuki, *bunraku,* and other Japanese performing and visual arts. High modernism, personified by theatre artists such as Irish poet and dramatist W. B. Yeats and English director Edward Gordon Craig, encountered Japanese theatre in the historical context unfolding during and after the unlikely victory of the new "East Asian hegemon" in the 1904–1905 Russo-Japanese War. [68] Yeats and Craig are perhaps the most famous Western admirers of Noh theatre, but their main source on it came from American poet Ezra Pound (who published the posthumous fieldnotes of American economist/Japanophile Ernest Fenollosa). On the other end of the modernist spectrum are the Marxist avant-garde figures of the 1930s and 1940s, who observed Japanese theatre from the vantage point of Japan's early Pacific War aggressions, notably the 1931 invasion of Manchuria and the 1937 invasion of China (the Berlin-Rome-Tokyo Axis would not coalesce until September 1940). While the modernists' anti-humanist concerns (sometimes bordering on fascist, in the case of Craig, and elitist, in the case of Yeats) primarily drew them to the fourteenth-century aristocratic form of the Noh theatre, the second wave of avant-garde interest in Japan—including artists like Soviet director Vsevold Meyerhold, Soviet theatre-director-turned-filmmaker Sergei Eisenstein, and German director and dramatist Bertolt Brecht—embraced more of the variety of Japanese theatre. From the radically popular Kabuki and its exaggerated makeup to the aged, conservative, masked Noh, the second wave of avant-garde directors appreciated these forms' applicability to their interest in defamiliarizing the theatrical event and casting audience members in a more active, empowered role.[69] Central to both sub-movements, however, remained the impulse to isolate Japanese acting as a useful aesthetic enemy poised to combat Western theatre's mimesis, naturalism, and individualism.

Much like Osman Edwards' pioneering position in the history of Western research on Japanese theatre, Edward Gordon Craig presents a precocious instance of Western modernists' appreciation of Japanese acting. In his theatre journal, *The Mask*, Craig published numerous articles on Noh and other Japanese performing arts between 1908 and 1926. Increasingly, scholars now attribute Yeats' initial interest in Japan to Craig's early example rather than to his fellow poet Ezra Pound, as had been originally thought. (Yeats never traveled to Japan nor witnessed an authentic performance of its traditional theatre, so his textual contact with *The Mask*—of which he owned every issue and to which he contributed his own articles—is of primal importance.)[70] In her book on Craig's journal, Olga Taxidou resists the temptation to overstate her subject's influence: "Craig's journal, together with Pound's highly personal completion of the first major translation of Noh plays into English, constituted the first substantial attempts to initiate western audiences to this highly abstract and ritualistic theatrical practice. The contribution of *The Mask* in spreading the Noh cult among the more literary Modernists is very important."[71]

Craig saw in Noh acting and in *bunraku* puppet manipulation (in which the puppeteers are visible to the audience but efface their presence through various means, including black face covering) practical applications of the dehumanization and depersonalization he valorized in his actor-as-*Übermarionette* theory. As Taxidou points out, Craig also admired Japanese acting that he could locate in the "exotic theatre of the past" and theatre that prohibited women from appearing on stage—he severely disapproved, therefore, of the contemporary tours of Kawakami and Sada Yakko—and for these reasons he disdained *shimpa*. For the latter reason, Craig was able to find value in Kabuki's *onnagata*, or female impersonator, even though Kabuki was itself fairly contemporary, populist, and unmasked. Beyond the apparent obliteration of the actor's subjectivity through face covering, Craig embraced the "rigid stylization" of the Japanese actor's dance-like movements because they substituted conventions of rhythm for individual psychology. For instance, in *The Mask*, Craig praised Japanese theatrical dance for "its strict ritual, its noble conservatism which still preserves traditional posture without change, or modification, its obedience to a fine tradition, its perfect control of its material." All these qualities referenced Craig's approval of what he saw as the feudal history of Japanese theatre, an appreciation that Taxidou connects to his fascist aesthetic leanings. "Hence," she maintains, "what he terms the grand past of the Orient can fuel and serve as justification for his fascist tendencies."[72]

Fulfilling the request of Ernest Fenollosa's widow, in 1916 Ezra Pound compiled and published the American economy professor's Noh drama translations and theatre essays. The resultant volume, *Noh, or Accomplishment* (titled *Certain Noble Plays of Japan* and *The Classic Noh Theatre of Japan* in subsequent editions), influenced many Westerners' perceptions of Japanese theatre, including Yeats'. According to Pound, "Fenollosa has been credited with singlehandedly persuading the Japanese to preserve their cultural heritage" by "stop[ping] the aping of Europe." The "aping of Europe" implicitly referred to early-twentieth-century Japanese *shimpa,* a theatre movement that embraced Western realist aesthetics and other foreign theatre innovations (paving the way for the more successful *shingeki,* or new theatre). Fenollosa disapprovingly observed the insurgent *shimpa* movement during his time in Japan and felt that the anti-mimetic qualities of Noh, which so confused most "modern" (read: Western) audiences, were worth preserving. As Pound put it, the value of preserving the ancient Japanese form lies in "how far [Noh] is from the conditions of the Occidental stage." Moreover, Fenollosa wrote in 1906 that Noh presented an instance of Japanese people's "special art-life"—in other words, the Japanese aestheticization of nature "into one continuous drama of the art of pure living."[73] The uniqueness of Noh that made it the polar opposite of Western theatre thus had to be preserved. Fenollosa also seized upon and more explicitly repeated Edwards' subtext that everyday Japanese life and Japanese theatre were "continuous" or indistinguishable, thus making conjectures about Noh applicable to Japanese society as a whole. The Western theatrical avant-garde recycled and cited this theatricalizing discourse on Japan for the next three decades.

William Butler Yeats learned about Noh through his friendships with Craig and Pound and refined his vision for his own Noh plays on Irish nationalist themes (*At the Hawk's Well, The Dreaming of the Bones,* and two others) through a later friendship with a Japanese modern dancer living in London, Michio Ito. At the same time, as noted, Yeats never saw a performance of Noh theatre. Therefore, his readings of Craig and Pound/Fenollosa carried much of the burden for forming his opinions. In an introduction he wrote for one edition of Pound and Fenollosa's *Noh*, Yeats maintained that "with the help of these plays . . . I have invented a form of drama, distinguished, indirect, and symbolic, and having no need of mob or press to pay its way—an aristocratic form." Yeats rationalizes that the "half-Asiatic" composition of ancient Greek theatre dictated his turning to Japan "for a stage-convention, for more formal faces, for a chorus that has no part in the action and perhaps for those movements of the body copied from the marionette shows of the fourteenth century." Moreover, mimicking the Noh convention of masking "will enable me to substitute for the face of some commonplace player." As a high modernist of Craig's ilk, Yeats unabashedly embraced the aristocratic roots and techniques of Noh and expressed his impatience with theatre for the masses, arguing that "Realism is created for the common folk and was always their particular delight," the outgrowth of "their pretence that ignorance can understand beauty." While Edwards compared the indoctrinating power of Japanese traditional theatre to the Greek Church in service to the czar, Yeats chose a different state-religion analogue, writing that Noh, as an art form patronized by the Japanese military aristocracy since medieval times, "has taught more men to die than oratory or the Prayer Book." The modern imperialist expansion of Japan and its recent military victories proved the salience of any tradition perpetuated by the Japanese, and for his own agenda of Irish nationalist revolution, Yeats found great value in what he saw as the Japanese traditional theatre's continued indoctrination of each audience member's "role in life" and "acceptance of death" in the name of a higher cause.[74]

In another revolutionary milieu, Vsevold Meyerhold's political theatre aimed at a "revival of conscious theatricality" that would recall past eras, turning the contemporary theatre away from individuated naturalism to its "communal-religious origins." In so doing, Meyerhold hoped to move the spectators to action by involving them in a participatory experience that recalled the Dionysian "ecstasy of the sacrificial ritual." Inherent in these aims was a triumph of the theatrical over the literary that emphasized physiology and plasticity of movement through stylization rather than naturalism's focus on psychology and the spoken text. Meyerhold saw in "true theatricality" the potential for revolution, a potential partially fulfilled for him by the violent demonstrations that met his jarringly anti-realist 1906 production of The Fairground Booth.[75] So in keeping with the avant-garde's strategic rebellion against stage naturalism through a return to the theatre's roots, Meyerhold turned to many "ancient" sources, including the traditional Japanese theatre. More immediately, Meyerhold found many paradigms for his theory of rhythmical movement in the 1902 Russian tour of Kawakami and Sada Yakko.[76] By the time he witnessed an "authentic" Kabuki troupe tour in Russia in 1928 (headed by Ichikawa Sadanji), Meyerhold had already formed most of his impressions of Japanese theatre from other sources.

Edward Braun maintains that Meyerhold's dedication to and influence from Noh and Kabuki were considerable, going beyond just the form to the content of Japanese theatre, as evidenced by his 1909 project of translating the Kabuki play *Terakoya* from an existing text in German to his own Russian. In his writings, Meyerhold refers to the perceived qualities of Japanese theatre with almost obsessive repetition, an interest Braun sees as "Meyerhold's assimilation of the spirit and techniques of the Kabuki and Noh theatres, which lent his style at once a new freedom and a new discipline." [77] Meyerhold repeatedly characterizes Noh and Kabuki as subordinating the dramatic text to movement, sacrificing the individual to the group pattern, repressing emotions and psychology to the typology of the mask. He uses words like "decorative" and "architectural" to describe these same tropes—perhaps stimulating French playwright Jean Genet's later comparison of Kabuki actors to "human pieces of architecture." [78] Moreover, Japanese theatre seemed also to act as a mirror for Meyerhold, as he saw his key concepts converge in Noh and Kabuki; indeed, it is difficult to ascertain which came first: did his interpretation of the Japanese theatre inspire his theories, or did his theories inspire his interpretation? Such a chicken-before-the-egg question has no simple answer, but it lies at the very heart of the theatricalizing discourse's system of knowledge, especially in terms of its circulation among the avant-garde. The way in which the techniques of Noh and Kabuki mirrored back most of Meyerhold's key concepts for him was remarkable. Around 1911, Meyerhold cited the Japanese theatre as *the* example of an "art of the grotesque" that "aims to subordinate psychologism to a decorative task." [79]

Meyerhold was quite candid about the techniques he "plundered" from the Japanese theatre (to quote Eisenstein on his colleague's appropriations; see below). According to Meyerhold, he appropriated Noh's total actor concept (singer, dancer, and dramatic reciter all at once) for his actor training programs, especially for his "biomechanics," because he felt that such rigid stylization, refined ceremony, and proximity to the audience transported Noh spectators "into a world of hallucination." Meyerhold also borrowed Kabuki's use of the *kurogo* (black-costumed stage assistants who make no attempt to disguise their stage business), adapting this figure for his theatre's "little blackamoors." [80] The Japanese theatre's use of highly stylized, controlled, and choreographed movement was also an important reservoir for Meyerhold: this "decorative" movement inspired his idea of dance-like blocking enacted independent of emotional motivation or speech. He applied this idea in his production of *Hedda Gabler* (1906), in which he believed that stylization would reveal the hidden essence of human relationships better than a sanctification of the dialogue. It also seemed to foreshadow his crucial theory of pre-acting, in which a motion before speaking reveals the character's true substance; pre-acting is also reminiscent, of course, of the *mie*, a Kabuki actor's character-expressing pose struck upon entering or exiting a scene or at a climactic moment.

Through such close association with Meyerhold's revolutionary theories, the Japanese theatre appears as dehumanizing (or to use his own word, "depersonalizing"). Meyerhold repeatedly refers to the Noh actor's movement in relationship to his own theories of movement—theories that utilize terminology such as "hieroglyphs" and "the plasticity of the statue." Meyerhold's critics proclaimed that his Japanese-inspired theatre—as used, for instance, in the production of *The Death of Tintagiles* (1905)—"reduced the artist to a mere puppet."[81] More contemporary theatre critics like Nick Worrall have referred to the "collective synchronization of movement" used by Meyerhold in *The Magnificent Cuckold* (1922) to organically integrate the individual into the collective stage architecture. According to Worrall, in this non-individualistic process, the actors "obliterate their particular selves and become a unified whole."[82]

Sergei Eisenstein found similarly anti-psychological and collectivist inspiration in the overt theatricalism of Kabuki, especially the 1928 Ichikawa company's tour (in response to which Eisenstein dismissed the idea that "there's nothing new here," even though most of his colleagues assumed that "Meyerhold has already plundered everything of use from the Japanese theater!").[83] Not surprising for a pupil of Meyerhold, Eisenstein's theories in *Film Form* reflect many of the same assumptions about Japanese culture. However, unlike Meyerhold, Eisenstein had studied the Japanese language prior to the Kabuki visit: he memorized hundreds of Japanese *kanji* characters during his time in the Red Army and at the General Staff Academy in Moscow. Such linguistic expertise may have prompted a member of the touring Ichikawa troupe, who observed Meyerhold's enthusiasm and commitment as an audience member (Meyerhold attended every Moscow performance and regularly found his way backstage to talk with the touring company) to remark upon "Eisenstein's insight into Kabuki; he did not see it as an exotic art, but was able to grasp its essence at a single glance." Eisenstein also expressed a strong desire to travel to Japan but was barred for political reasons.[84]

Unfortunately, Eisenstein's prior exposure to Japanese culture perhaps freed him to make sweeping generalizations about the "cultural peculiarities" of Japan. For instance, after expounding on Kabuki for a while, Eisenstein leaves particularities behind, extending his theory to "not the Japanese theater, alone, for these fundamental features, in my opinion, profoundly penetrate all aspects of the Japanese world-view." He belatedly adds the caveat, "Certainly in those incomplete fragments of Japanese culture accessible to me, this seems a penetration to their very base." Simply put, Eisenstein finds Japanese culture to be the polar opposite of hegemonic Western culture, particularly useful in relation to the Marxist artist's rebellion against capitalist rationality. In another plunge from the specific to the sweepingly general, Eisenstein launches from a discussion of Japanese haiku poetry into the following statement:

> This original archaic "pantheism" [of images] is undoubtedly based on a non-differentiation of perception—a well-known absence of the sensation of "perspective." It could not be otherwise. Japanese history is too rich in historical experience, and the burden of feudalism, though overcome politically, still runs like a red thread through the cultural traditions of Japan. Differentiation, entering society with its transition to capitalism and bringing in its wake, as a consequence of economic differentiation, differentiated perceptions of the world—is not yet apparent in many cultural areas of Japan. And the Japanese continues to think "feudally," i.e., undifferentiatedly.[85]

Such a generalizing tendency is described by Said as part of the power of the Orientalist system of thought: even for the liberal/sympathetic Westerner, "Orientalism overrode the Orient" and "always rose from the specifically human detail to the general transhuman one."[86] Both Meyerhold and Eisenstein worked from the implicit presumption that Japan was homogenous, unchanging, and easily knowable because it was the West's mirror opposite—distancing the threatening mimicry posed by Japanese economic modernity by asserting instead the persistence of a feudal soul expressed through Japan's traditional culture.[87]

So for Eisenstein Japanese theatre becomes the instructive inversion of extant Western arts and a challenging paradigm for the then undiscovered territory of the sound film because of its perceived qualities of conventionalism and undifferentiated unity. He uses the term "monism of ensemble" to describe what he considers Kabuki's resistance to the naturalistic theatre (epitomized by Stanislavsky's Moscow Art Ensemble) and its emotive ensemble. In other words, while the Western theatre toils over the psychologized individual, Kabuki apparently achieves a unity of theatre by subordinating the individual to a collective purpose. In effect, this theatre functions as a single body within which the Kabuki actor—traced back to "mechanical puppets" with "no consciousness at all" by Eisenstein via Heinrich von Kleist—is merely an organ or appendage that cannot function outside the collective. Eisenstein explains the conventionalism of Japanese theatre by reference to the feudal past of the Japanese because he is confident that this "well-known absence" of differentiation in Japanese thought constitutes an agreed-upon discourse for his Western readership. Eisenstein goes on to compare this perception to the naïve displays of children's art as well as "people cured of blindness," reflecting Orientalism's standard depiction of non-Western people as primitive, immature, and diseased. He uses the anecdote of a child who illustrates the subject "lighting the stove" by drawing larger-than-life matches (dwarfing the human pictured alongside them), which reflects the matches' instrumental role in the action but overlooks their disproportion to the rational order dictated by naturalist accuracy.[88]

Echoing Meyerhold's deployment of Japan as a revolutionary arsenal against naturalism, Eisenstein's relation of Kabuki to his revolutionary cinematic principle of montage yields the familiar discourse of Japan as a useful but dangerous enemy. For instance, Eisenstein mixes military and sporting metaphors in his vivid endorsement of the Kabuki artist as both sensual and calculating, describing the Japanese as "brilliantly calculating the blow of their sensual billiard-cue on the spectator's cerebral target."[89] Even Japanese theatre's most fervent followers in the Western avant-garde were compelled to characterize all Japanese people as alike theatrically and thus alike in their feudal conventionalism (despite their superficial mimicry of economic modernity); the added implication that this militantly powerful culture presented a useful aesthetic enemy for the West mirrored the very real military aggression seen in Japan's East Asian expansion.

The Prewar Students of Japan and Their Postwar Legacy

Before Benedict sought to explain Japanese national behavior in order to facilitate their management in defeat, many American writers with varying degrees of social science accreditation offered their own explanations of a Japanese people rapidly ascending to a position that threatened U.S. power and Western hegemony. Although these prewar writers each reflected the historical developments surrounding their particular moment of composition, even in works on Japan from three different authors writing in three different decades leading up to *The Chrysanthemum and the Sword,* we find a remarkably coherent discourse on "the Japanese" that draws from the same storehouse of tropes about Japan. For instance, Percival Lowell opens his 1911 book, *The Soul of the Far East,* with a laundry list of "upside down" Japanese qualities that position Japan in diametric opposition to the West. Ten years later, in *Mysterious Japan* (1921) Julian Street unselfconsciously repeats this literary conceit by describing the "list of things which according to our ideas the Japanese do backwards," a list he began recording immediately upon arriving in Japan.[90] Likewise, in his 1934 book, *Challenge: Behind the Face of Japan,* Upton Close echoes Lowell's 1894 *Occult Japan or the Way of the Gods* through the shared indictment of Japan as a "feminine-mined nation" or "the feminine half of the world," embodying qualities of extreme emotionalism, imitativeness, and aestheticism.[91] Benedict drew from this repetitive network in her study of Japan as an Axis enemy, quoting Close at length and implicitly citing his predecessors; all deploy theatrical metaphors as explanatory models for the Japanese national character. While all three authors use theatrical framing devices for their books—implicitly quoting Edwards' technique from his 1901 *Japanese Plays and Playfellows*—they also share even deeper assumptions that gather strength in the decades leading up to World War II. Taken together, this theatricalizing discourse might be understood as the realization of Japan as the problem play that Edwards had predicted would replace the dainty comedy of tourist Japan. Needless to say, in walking their readers through this Japanese problem play, impending danger is never hidden far beneath the "Japanese mask."

In order to make his case that "Japan is the feminine half of the world" and that such gendered national subjectivity is dangerous, in *Occult Japan* Lowell makes a telling recourse to one of the great villainesses of Western drama: Lady Macbeth. Lowell compares Meiji-era Japan's ostensible casting off of feudalism and its assimilation of Western ways to the transformation of Lady Macbeth into a murderous instigator in Shakespeare's *Macbeth*: "When a woman once lets go her old rules of conduct, she will go pretty much any lengths in the new. . . . Impulse possesses her for its own. There is in her a capacity for self-abandonment to an idea impossible to man. Lady Macbeth, once started, outdoes any lord in crime. She knows no hindering regard for self, no ghostly shapes of other thoughts to rise and cry to this one 'Halt! enough!' So Japan." [92]

Although Lowell does not explicitly carry this comparison through to equate the Japanese national character with Lady Macbeth's crazed possession by her own guilt and eventual death from madness, most of his book (as his title, *Occult Japan,* suggests) deals with the purportedly Japanese ease of bodily possession. While this characterization is certainly consistent with sexist assumptions of female permeability and openness to external forces—signaling a common Orientalist feminization of the East—I am more interested in how Lowell depicts Japanese people as insincere actors in everyday life. At the end of the nineteenth century, many Americans could be heard commenting on "the uncommon imitativeness of the [Japanese] race," but Lowell was one of the few to suggest that Japanese imitation of foreign customs stemmed from hypnosis. "It is hardly exaggeration," Lowell maintained, "to say that Japan at this moment is affording the rest of the world the spectacle of the most stupendous hypnotic act ever seen, nothing less than the hypnotization of a whole nation, with its eyes open." By declaring Meiji modernization to be a national "spectacle" and an "act," Lowell accused the Japanese of overblown staginess and consciousness of an international audience's attention. But comparing this imitativeness to over-easy hypnosis and pointing out "the instant unassimilated character of the imitation"—a process he also calls adoption without adaptation—he further suggests that this national mimicry remains at the surface level.[93] In short, Lowell characterizes Japan's modern behavior as an insincere parlor trick.

Although Lowell opens *The Soul of the Far East* with his notion of Japan as the opposite of the West, his argument actually centers on the notion of a racial and geographic continuum. This continuum extends from the highly developed selfhood of the "blonde" West to the "impersonality" of the Far East and finally to the unnamed character of "black" nations. According to Lowell, the races and nationalities that populate the earth *"grow steadily more personal as we go west."* His exposition of "this gradation of spirit" is worth quoting at length:

> It is as marked as the change in color of the human complexion observable along any meridian, which ranges from black at the equator to blonde toward the pole. In like manner, the sense of self grows more intense as we follow in the wake of the setting sun, and fades steadily as we advance into the dawn. America, Europe, the Levant [modern-day Lebanon, Israel, and parts of Syria and Turkey], India, Japan, each is less personal than the one before. . . . If with us the *I* seems to be of the very essence of the soul, then the soul of the Far East may be said to be Impersonality.

The last on a list of diminishing individuality, Japan becomes emblematic of "impersonality" because of both its geographic location and its effete culture. Impersonality translates to an effete culturation (versus the artless naturalism of the "blonde" nations), as Lowell declares of Japan's land of "politeness" and "delicacy": "culture there is not the attainment of the few, but the common property of the people."[94]

Lowell's image of artful proclivities pervading the Japanese masses foreshadows Upton Close's characterization of Japan as "the most esthetic nation" the world has ever known—a characterization with which Benedict was undoubtedly familiar. Close's judgment of Japan's artfulness was unequivocal: "I am convinced that the Japanese nation is the most esthetic nation in the present world, and, more than that, the most esthetic this world has ever produced. I do not forget ancient Greece. Only the top crust there had commerce with beauty. In no society other than Japanese has the cult of beauty seeped so far down into the mass."[95]

Such sweeping generalization slipped past the censor of the liberal conscience, which ostensibly plead for a less biologically deterministic position on Japanese difference than that which pervaded popular opinion. But dubbing Japan "the most esthetic [nation] this world has ever produced" merely substituted Japanese culture into the deterministic slot usually filled by racialized biology. For instance, Julian Street boasted a less biologically deterministic position on Japanese difference in his 1921 book, maintaining that despite Japan's opposite approach, Japan and the United States should not be understood as natural enemies but rather as bred for conflict by very different cultures. Japan, after all, "is a land of customs" that dictate the individual's patterned response to stimuli. According to Street, "Thus it often seems that every little word and act of a Japanese can be accounted for in some curious, complex yet essentially logical manner—that every thought in the Japanese mind has, so to speak, a genealogy, which, like the genealogy of the Japanese Imperial Family, reaches back into the mists of antiquity." Americans, by contrast, generally have only the present and their own individual inclinations to answer. Echoing many other Westerners writing on Japan, Street finds the anti-realist acting of Japanese theatre to demonstrate the impersonality of Japanese culture. For instance, in Japan, "Action in the theatre is modelled not on life but on the movements of dolls in marionette shows, and in the classic Nō drama the possibility of showing emotion by facial expression is eliminated by the use of carved wood masks." The lack of direct reference to human life and the absenting of the individually expressive human face both point to the assumed impersonality, or what theatrical avant-gardists would call "depersonalization," of Japanese people. Street later stresses the synecdochic character of the impersonal Noh by mentioning the ancient theatre as one of the key paradigms to understanding Japan as a whole.[96]

When they existed, the apparent idiosyncrasies and ideological departures made by each individual author and text only strengthened the appearance that this citational network consisted of serious, respectable research on Japan. But in fact, these gestures at estrangement—exemplified by Edwards' caricaturing of the "the pens of Sir Edwin Arnold and M. Pierre Loti"—usually facilitate the earnestness with which the theatricalizing discourse is repeated by making it seem new. Instead, this theatricalizing discourse insists upon a knowable, static, and artificial Japan that remains the same as a comforting counterbalance against the increasing threat of the Japanese Empire. Although Close set out "to see the face behind the mask," his 1934 text presented the most sustained use of theatricalizing terms to do so, and by dispelling the infamous inscrutability of the Japanese, he seemed to gain the most conviction about their dangerous essence, breaking what he found "behind the mask" down into various sinister "faces" of Japan. Close designated Japan "most esthetic" in order to remark of the East Asian hegemon that long ago "the love of beauty became an essential part of patriotism," thus reiterating the theatricalizing discourse's founding assumption that the seepage of Japanese artfulness into everyday life and its mingling with politics made Japan dangerous to the West. "Japan, like most nations that can afford diplomats, censorships and propaganda services, wears a mask," Close declares early in the book. "It is always possible, with more or less persistence and perhaps risk to the observer, to see the face behind the mask. But we are going behind that again—the lineaments of the face indicate to us the sublimely indomitable, insanely egoistic spirit which is Nippon." By positing the reality behind the surface artifice as itself fractured and dangerous—"indomitable" and "insanely egoistic"—Close rejects the possibility of rendering Japan understandable "behind the mask" and instead delivers the theatricalizing discourse's stock message that Japanese masking and disguise constitute the nation's essence and thus its essential danger. In fact, the "challenge" in his title refers to the threat that Japan's hidden face(s) presents to "the unfolding drama of the human race." Moreover, Close minimizes the proximity of modernity to Japan's plight (thus minimizing the proximity of Japan to the West) by declaring that Japanese masking represents the inevitable "outgrowth of the fifteen centuries that have gone before." [97]

In the section of *Challenge* titled "Emotional Faces of Japan" Close is particularly insistent in asserting the danger of the Japanese once their infamous inscrutability is parted. Close insists that Japanese are supersensitive, if childishly so, because sensitivity to the suffering of others fails to occur to them: "the Japanese for the most part tends to view life, when he is not himself concerned, objectively like a fatalistic play, fascinating the understanding; interesting, regardless of how cruel." Viewing the external world as a "fatalistic play" strikes Close as childish playacting, not dangerous psychosis, except when the Japanese applies such theatrical distance to his own life. "Once he has given himself over to the supreme ecstasy of his soul," Close writes, "he can view his own life in the same detached manner. It is then that he is dangerous." In other words, when such theatrical alienation bleeds into Japanese everyday life, Close sees it as threatening to the West (the dangers to which he refers throughout the book relate to Japan's threat in an economic and military sense since his book was published during Japanese militarization and on the eve of World War II). Likewise, Close complicates but reinforces the Meiji-era image of Japan as a mere mimic of Western modernity, insisting that Japanese people are not just imitative but also inventive. But in mitigating the sense of Japanese mimicry, Close substitutes a more threatening lack of conformism in terms of international law and humanity. He relates "the Japanese penchant for nonconformism" to a militaristic "love of a surprise blow," noting that "every war of modern as well as ancient Japan has been opened by a surprise blow, not by formal declaration or a diplomatic nose thumbing." [98] This identification of Japan with the surprise blow would of course be born out in the Japanese attack on Pearl Harbor, which the United States received as damning evidence of Japan's utter rejection of Western textuality and diplomacy in favor of suspense and spectacularity.

One of the "Emotional Faces" chapters of *Challenge* details "The Hysterical

Face" of the Japanese, diagnosing Japan with a psychological disorder historically associated with the feminine constitution. Defining Japan as a feminine nation in contrast to the U.S. masculine nation, Close details Japanese hysteria's "spectacular outbursts of this patriotic emotion," most notably *hara-kiri* and other forms of suicide or self-mutilation. He links these apparently hysterical displays to "the cautious, cold, steady scheming" of government officials, categorizing the latter as yet another manifestation of hysteria, resonating significantly with Perry's idea of "official deception" but extending this notion into a wholesale indictment of systemic histrionics in Japan. For Close, Japanese hysteria is quite simply the legacy of Japan's feudal past, and it is at this nexus that he identifies another site of Japanese danger or "challenge": "This medieval Japanese emotionalism is T.N.T. in the modern world of population pressures, trade wars, international rivalries and naval competition," Close warns in a typical Orientalist's temporal displacement of the purportedly timeless other.[99]

Despite his obvious recycling of extant tropes about Japan, Close framed his explanation of Japanese people as an emergent theory that called into question prevailing American attitudes. While popular opinion rendered Japanese people theatrical, prone to concealment and playacting, Close complicated such consensus by locating their otherness in the realities discernible only behind the theatrical and beneath the mask. For example, in moments of unguarded privacy, Close depicts Japanese people as no less prone to constructing performances. "A Japanese friend writes that during his long residence in America he came near to being converted to the American idea that his own people are inscrutable and artificial," Close relates. "Then he strode through Japanese parks and came upon a group indulging in the national sport of picnicking. Spontaneously two elderly women rose, took fans in their hands and did a graceful amateur dance, and the crowd looked on and applauded in childish delight." The "unceremonious" qualities of Japanese people are revealed to be no less aesthetically charged and even more instrumental in their improvisational quality, in contrast to other Asian nationalities such as the Chinese, who "have become too old a race to dance."[100]

Decades of such theatricalizing discourse on Japan seemed confirmed by the events of World War II and were lent scholarly and diplomatic credibility by the publication of Benedict's influential book. What followed was a glut of such works that emerged from 1945 to the present. Over and over again, even authors who sought to challenge prevailing stereotypes had to engage the theatricalizing discourse in order to debate it; often this very engagement seemed to reinscribe the stereotypes. A cursory glance at these repetitive titles demonstrates how theatrical terminology became shorthand for Japanese identity. Two books with nearly identical titles—David Matsumoto's *Unmasking Japan* and Fumie Kumagai's *Unmasking Japan Today*—came out in 1996, making oblique reference to Ichiro Kawasaki's *Japan Unmasked* (1969) and Robert Craigie's *Behind the Japanese Mask* (1945). Likewise, Hal Porter's *The Actors: An Image of the New Japan* (1968) set a postmodern tone of loosely linked vignettes, which William Bohnaker's *The Hollow Doll* (1990) echoed both in structure and in pointed reference to Japanese stage performers (hollow dolls connoting marionettes).[101]

Although these postwar texts emerged from very different disciplines and from both popular and scholarly presses, they sound uncannily like one another and like Benedict. Robert Craigie was British ambassador to Japan from 1937 to 1942 and writes *Behind the Japanese Mask* from the standpoint of diplomatic experience, but he opens the book with a personal anecdote culled from his early childhood in various parts of Asia. He remembers the Japanese being very polite, "courteous, considerate people bent on making us comfortable," but remarks, "And yet—and yet—even in those days I realized that one never seemed to get below the surface of smiling politeness. Nowhere in Japan did I make a friend in the way I promptly did of Ah Choy, the Chinese servant whose special job it was to look after me while we were out East. Here [in Ah Choy] was a real human being."[102] Australian literary critic Hal Porter constructs his image of Japan as *The Actors* in part from fragments of extant works on the Japanese, framing this unanimous pastiche with an opening quotation from Jean Raspail that begins, "Japan has no use for Westerners who are too sincere. They interrupt its play-acting. Japanese life is an elaborate comedy."[103] American expatriate William Bohnaker taught for some time in Nagoya and outlines in his book the "formulaic" and "scripted behavior" of Japanese people but maintains that he refers to collective conduct rather than individual actions; after all, for Bohnaker, with Japanese "it may seem to be the individual who is acting and speaking, [but] it is in fact a double illusion of the ventriloquist; in this case it is the hollow doll who throws its voice and pulls the human levers."[104] Homi Bhabha is certainly right to notice the unstable quality of Western stereotypes about the other, but the resultant compulsion to constantly repeat stereotypical assertions also tends to erect a hermetic discourse that anxiously requires that even those writers seeking to subvert, say, Western suspicion of Japanese "artificiality" must reinscribe the terms of the discourse along the way.[105] The theatricalizing discourse about Japan has thus maintained a tight grip on Western thinkers to the present day.

Benedict's "One Great Research Weapon": Surrogating the Japanese Enemy in the Diaspora

Benedict's *The Chrysanthemum and the Sword* deserves center stage in this theatricalizing discourse, not only because the text operates both as a repository of prewar citations and the fountainhead for postwar recitations that delved "behind the Japanese mask." At the pivot point, Benedict's book also stands as a World War II artifact that records the manner in which those of Japanese descent living in the wartime United States—American-born citizens and immigrants alike—were spectacularized by this discourse. Cultural anthropologists like Benedict cherished the ability to conduct fieldwork, and in the absence of this chosen method, as Ezra Vogel put it in the 1989 foreword to Benedict's book, "her one great research weapon was interviewing Japanese immigrants in America."[106] By casting Japanese Americans as stand-ins for the Japanese enemy, Benedict unselfconsciously reproduced the logic of her government's conflation of the Japanese abroad with ethnic Japanese in the United States and its subsequent evacuation and internment of all 120,000 residing on the West Coast, regardless of their citizenship status. Both seamlessly translated the "uncommon imitativeness" of Meiji-era Japanese seeking Western modernization with the American dreams of Japanese immigrants and their citizen children. But more than that, Benedict failed to realize how profoundly her methodology, predicated on ethnic surrogation, predetermined her assessments of "the Japanese." After all, the U.S. domestic policy during World War II drew upon the theatricalizing discourse in order to justify Japanese American internment and, in turn, rendered this ethnic group's exclusion from the body politic spectacular in order to manufacture public consent. At the center of this overdetermined theatricalization of Japanese ethnicity, Benedict researched and wrote the most influential Western assessment of Japan whose conclusion circulated to the highest levels of power in the U.S. government, military, and academy.

Benedict's severe scrutiny of her Japanese American informants both collaborated with the U.S. government and mass media's spectacularization of ethnic Japanese and diagnosed the foreign Japanese's constant "fantasy of an audience" by observing an American ethnic group that found itself spectacularized before a hostile audience by wartime domestic policies.[107] In *The Chrysanthemum and the Sword*'s foreword, Ezra Vogel recalls "some of these informants telling me what it felt like to talk with Benedict over lunch, day after day." Although Benedict's Issei and Nisei informants all lived in Washington, D.C., in 1944–1945, and thus were no longer interned at the time of the interviews, to hear Vogel tell it, a decidedly compulsory air surrounded Japanese Americans' cooperation in the study: "They admired the thoroughness of her questioning, but they lived in dread of her excruciating effort to delve into every little aspect of their feelings and experience. It seemed to them as if she wanted to hear every detail they could possibly remember, over and over again. They recalled the exhaustion and relief they felt as they were allowed to leave when the meal ended."[108] Benedict may not have had previous experience with Japanese people, but she had been utilizing a similar methodology since June 1943, when she became head analyst at the Overseas Intelligence Division of the OWI. In this wartime capacity, the government called upon Benedict to contribute to "psychological warfare" plots in Thailand, Romania, and the Netherlands by preparing national character reports culled from extant national studies and interviews of these countries' descendants in America. By June 1944, this method of studying culture-at-a-distance, while not ideal, must have seemed to Benedict a viable substitute for fieldwork during the exigencies of world war.[109]

Although the position in which she placed Japanese Americans may strike present-day readers as, at best, uncomfortable, Benedict shared with her social science colleagues the methodological justification that such anthropological marginality and cultural self-consciousness could be a beneficial condition in an increasingly globalized world. As Christopher Shannon has observed, such self-conscious detachment from one's own culture was precisely "the experience of marginality with respect to one's own culture that Benedict deems necessary to living in a world made safe for differences. In such a world, marginality must be central; it must be the representative experience of individuals within cultures."[110] In short, Benedict saw herself providing a valuable service by rendering her informants and readers veritable anthropologists themselves. She shared this valorization of marginality with her colleague, Chicago School sociologist Robert E. Park, who coined the term "marginal man" to describe the condition of racial minorities (particularly "Orientals") who self-consciously observed themselves from an alienated position between two cultures and thus fully participated in neither.[111]

In his work on Park's scholarly milieu, David Palumbo-Liu wonders, "Why does it surprise these sociologists that racially marked people might have a particular intuition of being watched?" Palumbo-Liu reinterprets these white sociologists' ideas of ethnic schizophrenia through W. E. B. DuBois' concept of "double consciousness," which shifts the blame for racialized minorities' "sense of always looking at one's self through the eyes of others" from individuals' racial pathology to the contemptuous treatment doled out by a racist system.[112] Recognizing that for many scholars "double consciousness" easily slipped into "dual personality"—repathologizing the sense of inauthenticity experienced by racial minorities—Palumbo-Liu set out instead to demonstrate how DuBois' theories were borne out in institutional practices like the Chicago School of sociology. In much the same way, the World War II iterations of the theatricalizing discourse about Japanese people must be shifted from its dominant interpretation as a politically liberal, psychologically nuanced diagnosis of what Benedict called "the most alien enemy the United States had ever fought" to a more materialist understanding of this discourse as structural evidence of the constant scrutinization and spectacularization enacted upon Japanese Americans by the U.S. government and media through the internment policy.

The Chrysanthemum and the Sword's discussion of the Japanese battle maxim "the eyes of the world are upon you" presents the most compelling example of how Benedict's institutional methodology constructed "the Japanese" as theatrical through her unselfconscious assessment of Japanese Americans' "intuition of being watched." In her chapter on "The Japanese in the War"—a suitably ambivalent heading whose referent floats between Japanese Americans on the home front and the enemy abroad—Benedict maintains that a "constant theme in the Japanese conduct of the war" should also be understood as "a concern deeply imbedded in Japanese culture": citing Japanese military broadcasts, she declares that Japanese "continually spoke of how 'the eyes of the world were upon them.'" Later in the book, Benedict clearly articulates a dominant notion of Japanese American unassimilability, remarking that her immigrant informants "sometimes contrast the difficulties of their own adjustment to American life with the lesser difficulties of Chinese or Siamese they have known." Ventriloquizing her informants, Benedict declares, "The specific Japanese problem, as they see it, is that they have been brought up to trust in a security which depends on others' recognition of the nuances of their observance of a code. They cast about to find similar meticulous properties according to which Westerners live and when they do not find them, some speak of the anger they feel and some of how frightened they are."[113]

Benedict maintained that the untheatrical United States, which lacked a shame culture's ever-present audience, not only diametrically opposed the Japanese enemy's "eyes of the world upon you" worldview but was also incompatible with diasporic Japanese attempts at American assimilation. Harking back to Perry's assessments of nineteenth-century Japan as an economy of looks and looking, Benedict accentuated the absolute difference between Japanese and Americans by claiming that a shame culture's constant awareness of an audience could not be reconciled with or integrated into a guilt culture to yield a Japanese-American hybrid. Damning as this assessment was, Benedict's diagnosis of Japanese unassimilability was also circular in its logic, owing to the fact that the trope of "the eyes of the world are upon you" also emanated from the internment camps themselves. As I noted in the introduction and will show in chapter 4, the Manzanar internment camp prisoners published their own newspaper, the *Manzanar Free Press,* because they recognized that, as one early headline put it, "Manzanar, the eyes of the world are upon you," and they needed to bear witness to their scrutinization and spectacularization by the U.S. government, media, and public. Manzanar internees thus reproduced and commented upon mainstream assessments of their unassimilability through the pages of their camp newspaper, a resistant tactic practiced in each of the ten Japanese American camps (all of which published newspapers).

Instead of reflexively realizing that her conclusions might be predetermined by the assumptions of her own patterned culture, Benedict attributed the conflicts at the center of the internment camps—and, by association, at the center of the internment policy itself—to the theatrical logic of Japanese cultural difference. Perhaps the most stunning example of the theatricalizing discourse being used to justify the internment policy in Benedict's book is her explanation of the intergenerational strife that ran rampant in all ten internment camps. Benedict explains the strife not as institutionalized by U.S. policies (which in fact criminalized the elders' Japanese culture and peddled American assimilation through their citizen children) but rather as emanating from "the basic Japanese sense of *makoto*, or sincerity. She claims that the Japanese meaning of *makoto* dictates an entire "logic" of behavior that is "opposite to American usage" and that became activated by unassimilated Japanese elders in the internment camps. Rather than relaying an anecdote from the camps themselves to illustrate that such an inverted notion of sincerity supposedly led to conflict between "the pro-Japan Issei" and "the pro-United States Nisei"— impossible since she had not conducted research in the Japanese American camps—Benedict fell back upon what she had read much about: Japanese theatre. She proclaims that usage of *makoto* "in the Japanese Relocation Camps during the war was exactly parallel to that in *The Forty-Seven Ronin*," referring to the eighteenth-century *bunraku* and Kabuki drama of *Chūshingura*, which is an archetypal showcasing of feudal values that had had multimedia retellings in most every genre of Japanese storytelling in the intervening two centuries. Surrogating Kabuki theatre characters with interned Americans, Benedict argues that what Japanese American elders meant when they accused their fervently assimilating children of lacking *makoto* was that the Nisei did not enact a "zeal" to follow Imperial Japan's script and instead earnestly threw themselves into patriotic acts like joining the all-Nisei 442nd Regimental Combat Team.[114] In this way, Benedict not only aestheticizes and homogenizes all Issei as blindly faithful to their native Japanese script but she also insinuates that Nisei demonstrations of American patriotism lacked "sincerity" (albeit an inverted Japanese notion thereof). By activating a theatricalizing discourse in formation since the United States opened Japan in 1853–1854, Benedict collaborated in the U.S. government's spectacularization of Japanese Americans by linking them to the enemy aesthetics of their ancestral culture and to anxieties about the mimicry presented by Japan's economic modernity and imperial expansion. In chapter 2, the FBI's post–Pearl Harbor raids against Japanese American communities will serve to illustrate the convergence of these two strands of the theatricalizing discourse (interweaving aesthetic modernism and economic modernity) in U.S. anti-Japanese domestic policy. The FBI's criminalization of ethnic Japanese and its resultant raids not only theatricalized suspect Americans—as indeed the Bureau theatricalized all its "criminal-actor" targets regardless of race or ethnicity—but also reenacted the scenario of the 1853–1854 opening. Reviving Perry's strategy of out-Heroding Herod to achieve a spectacular containment of the Japanese, the FBI resolved to use tightly choreographed nationwide spectacles to pacify ethnic Japanese and manufacture the American public's consent. But as we will see, the FBI's recourse to spectacle butted up against the theatricalizing discourse's anxious insistence upon the absolute difference between Japanese theatricality and Western naturalism.

CHAPTER 2

Spectacularizing Japanese American Suspects

The Genealogy of the FBI's Post–Pearl Harbor Raids

> The FBI is well-known today in spite of spectacular happenings, not because of them.
> —J. Edgar Hoover, *Persons in Hiding*[1]

> It used to be everybody wanted to write a play. Suddenly [in the "riptide that followed Pearl Harbor"] everybody wanted to catch a spy.
> —Frederick Collins, *The FBI in Peace and War*[2]

> Under the guise of an emergency and pretended threats to national security, the citizenry was denied the known facts, public opinion skillfully manipulated, and a cruel and massive government hoax enacted.
> —Michi Nishiura Weglyn, *Years of Infamy*[3]

Within hours of the 7 December 1941 Japanese attack on Pearl Harbor, FBI agents had snapped into spectacular action that resulted in the arrests of 1,395 purportedly dangerous Japanese Americans, newly classified as "enemy aliens" and "non-aliens," in New York, California, and around the country.[4] Headed by infamous director J. Edgar Hoover, the FBI raids on Japanese American communities in the wake of Pearl Harbor, and the subsequent detention of those of Japanese descent suspected of harboring intentions for sabotage or espionage, initiated a chain reaction that three months later led to the mass evacuation and internment of all West Coast Japanese Americans (120,000 citizens and aliens alike). The U.S. government and mass media would eventually cast these Japanese American evacuees, especially the roughly two-thirds of them who were American citizens, as willing players in a happy "lark" in order to frame the internment as a benign counter-spectacle to the Nazi persecution of Jews, for an international audience observing the U.S. treatment of its own minorities.[5] But before that racial farce entered the wartime repertoire, Japanese Americans were compelled to make their debut on the national stage by Hoover's calculated decision to spectacularize the post–Pearl Harbor raids for various historically and ideologically situated reasons.

As the first non-white, transnational subjects of the FBI's decade-long discourse indicting "actor-criminals" and their dangerously perverse use of theatrical disguise in real life, these Japanese suspects demanded spectacular containment—in Hoover's logic—to quiet public anxiety. In the 1930s, when the FBI's gallery of suspects contained only white Americans, Hoover instituted a public relations and surveillance strategy that encouraged vicarious participation on the part of the American audience. The FBI staged what Robert Gid Powers calls "crime pageants," focusing the American people's attention on the "Public Enemy Number One" of the moment so they could be co-participants in the Bureau's crime fighting.[6] G-men (which stands for "Government men," a catchier word for FBI agents) fan clubs popped up among various groups around the nation; in these fan clubs ordinary Americans could learn the tricks of the FBI's trade and envision themselves as amateur arms of the Bureau. As Powers points out, the FBI's focus on participation through publicity echoed President Franklin Roosevelt's early New Deal public mobilization. (The "fear itself" of Roosevelt's famous 1933 inauguration speech cast public demoralization as more dangerous than the direct economic impact of the Depression.) The American public may have been cast as audience to much of this publicity, but this audience was not understood as passive. Instead, ordinary (innocent) Americans were co-participants along with suspect (criminal) Americans because FBI crime pageants were performed even for the benefit of criminals themselves. After all, Hoover believed "the theory that the best way to defeat crime is to impress upon criminals the surety of apprehension and punishment."[7]

While the participatory crime pageants and other G-men pop culture rituals of the 1930s may have been the proper audience arrangement to win the peacetime public away from the seductiveness of gangster glamour, Hoover completely overhauled the FBI's publicity program for the World War II context in order to finally realize the starkly modernist vision he had always had for his Bureau and to render the spectators to the Japanese counterespionage campaign as passive as possible. Much as Diana Taylor has argued about Argentine policing during the Dirty War, the FBI "needed disguises to infiltrate the *other's* space, the space of the 'weak'" but it emphasized the enemy's theatrical tactics "while denying that the military used the same tactics."[8] Hoover devised a "modern version of counterespionage" for the war that relied upon spectacle through painstakingly rehearsed and tightly scripted raids, which repeated the U.S. founding scenario for encountering Japanese modernity through pacifying spectacles.[9] But his Bureau's resultant reliance on theatrical tactics encroached upon the abject difference ascribed to Japanese artificiality by the theatricalizing discourse, which had gained anxious resonance as Japan gained economic and imperialist power that threatened Western modernity.

Despite the FBI's attempts to deny its own use of drama and disguise, and its concomitant attempts to stress the exceptional theatricalism of ethnic Japanese suspects, an uncanny reflection appeared in Hoover's post–Pearl Harbor spectacles that both called into question the FBI's authorization as enforcer of wartime "us-versus-them" binaries and vividly embodied the purported threat posed by Japanese immigrants and Americans of Japanese descent. Published photographs of the FBI raids against Japanese Americans displayed the mimetic gazes exchanged between the captors and their captives, as the suspects and Hoover's men appeared to mimic each other in an ambivalent competition of the visual field. While by and large Japanese Americans were *in fact* arrested for their "cultish" attempts at ethnic cohesion and cultural nationalism, Japanese American arrestees, their families, and the communities at large were *spectacularized* in FBI raids that inadvertently showcased the danger and questionable motivations of their proximity to Western modernity. The FBI's spectacularization of this inaugural moment of the national "Japanese problem" thus misidentified the material conditions of Japanese America and missed the point by utterly obscuring the underlying disenfranchisement of Japanese Americans that followed Pearl Harbor.

Despite the fanfare with which Hoover introduced the post–Pearl Harbor raids as the premiere spectacles of his Bureau's new "modern version of counterespionage," since the war the FBI has officially distanced itself from any active role in the containment of Japanese Americans and shifted the raids to the margins of its institutional history. FBI accounts downplay the importance of its raids on Japanese American communities in order to pose the Bureau as a bit player whose moderate actions pale in comparison to the massive upheaval of constitutional rights perpetrated by the military's evacuation and internment of all West Coast Japanese.[10] This revisionist account has persuaded most internment scholars, including those who wrote the official U.S. government history of the period, *Personal Justice Denied.*[11] These raids on Japanese American communities must be reinserted into the FBI genealogy in order to bring their spectacularity back into focus, both as part of the FBI's now infamous excesses and as a transitional moment in the FBI's unprecedented publicity program.[12]

The FBI's Antitheatrical Assault on Criminal Melodramatics

During World War I, Hoover's first position at the Bureau of Investigation (the FBI's earlier incarnation) was as head of the Enemy Alien Registration Section, where he skillfully "scapegoated the ethnic alien as the source of social disorder."[13] The "source of social disorder" later shifted from the ethnic alien to the "moral alien" (the native law breaker) and came full circle with the World War II raids on immigrants and citizens of Japanese descent. Regardless of the "source of social disorder," Hoover saw his agenda as consistent: to render visible the deviance of these various "aliens" by exposing their aptitude for disguise. In *The Burden of Representation,* John Tagg demonstrates how the Foucauldian microphysics of power under Western economic modernity called for a police force "capable of making all visible, as long as it could remain invisible." Beyond the fixed surveillance of the punitive panopticon, "The institution of the police offered just such a means of control which could be present in the very midst of the working population, under the alibi of a criminal threat itself manufactured across a set of new apparatuses ranging from the penitentiary to crime reporting and the crime novel." Moreover, as capitalist democracy advanced in the United States in the 1920s and 1930s, new means of mass production and new demands for social consensus "changed the basis of political communication and made publicity central to the political process."[14]

At the same time, Hoover's initiation into criminal surveillance as head of the Enemy Alien Registration Section indelibly marked his ideological origins in what Nayan Shah shows to be the link between racialization and criminality in the U.S. public health movement. Shah argues that government health inspectors criminalized the early Chinese American bachelor society by promising to render visible the "ocular and olfactory proofs" of Chinatown's diseased degradation by "visiting and surveying Chinatown" and inviting the public to conduct its own tours. Shah notes the anxiety in such spectacularization of Chinese immigrants: "Despite all the confidence that visual scrutiny would provide proof, [public health] investigators simultaneously held a keen appreciation that the 'truth' of Chinatown was hidden from public view. The most revealing journeys, then, had to be conducted at night, when the 'true character' of the quarter—with its gambling houses, opium dens, and brothels—revealed itself."[15] Government initiatives around criminalilty and racialization thus presumed to improve upon everyday perception, using the newest technologies of surveillance to peer behind public appearances and reveal the "true character" of the threats to American health and innocence.

Hoover stood as heir to the promises of both policing and alien registration, combining both lineages by promising to render criminality visible through the educated participation of a sympathetic public. His FBI would eventually realize this promise through what one scholar calls "perhaps the benchmark governmental publicity drive of this country's history." [16] In her book on the FBI's Racial Conditions in World War II (RACON) program, Roberta Hill states without hesitation that "public relations was the first priority of the Bureau's work in law enforcement and intelligence surveillance." [17] In fact, most FBI scholars agree that Hoover focused a large part, if not the largest part, of his Bureau's energies on public relations and that he sought complete control over this publicity through measures such as the refusal to hold press conferences (which contained too much unscripted improvisation) and the production of his own comics, films, and radio shows, which manufactured his own version of the criminal threat. [18]

In Hoover's version of this threat criminals were natural-born actors who preyed upon the childish credulity—the willingness to suspend disbelief—of the untrained American public, as well as its childish tendency to imitate criminal behavior as if it were harmless play. A typically paternalistic Hoover statement would read: "Greater . . . than the fault of the criminal or of the parent, is . . . the gullible and lethargic attitude which is common to practically all our citizens, and which aids crime, even while it pleads that crime be eradicated." [19] The FBI sought to train and then deputize the general public in order to destroy such gullibility and disabuse American citizens of the "childlike faith" that allowed them to unquestioningly believe such thinly veiled disguises as those donned by criminals on the run from the law. In the 1930s, glamorous criminals (think Bonnie and Clyde) enthralled many Americans and staged spectacular crimes and getaways in order to awe the public, spreading a pro-crime public opinion that thought nothing of its young boys playing gangsters rather than cowboys. [20] Hoover was not amused by such playacting and remarked that "Because every street corner is filled with boys playing at being [machine-gun] bandits," he would buck popular sentiment and go after gangsters, warning that the alternative was truly frightening: "either that or have a lot of those boys grow up to be real criminals. If it's undignified, then I'll be undignified. I'm going to tell the truth about these rats." [21] Underlying Hoover's statement are the beliefs that Americans at large cannot discern "the truth" themselves and that tolerance for "playing at" criminality could have the disastrous result of creating even more crime—in short, that overly sympathetic spectating and playful imitation produced deadly real outcomes.

As in the public health initiatives aimed at Chinatown, early FBI discussions of crime established the danger of "appearances" in this climate of gullibility and imitation; the deeply Protestant Hoover repeatedly yearned for crime fighting and the revelation of hidden criminal behavior to be rendered more visible in order to upstage the seductive spectacles of evasion used by the criminal masters of disguise. The "spectacular cases" of criminal actions that "occupied public attention" in the 1930s were denigrated by the FBI as uncreative repetitions of a highly conventionalized criminal "formula" that remained "the same, whether the place be New York, San Francisco, New Orleans or Chicago" and regardless of the individual criminals involved.[22] But these repetitive criminal acts nonetheless captivated the populace. Hoover mused, "Were crime more visual, if a siren sounded every time there was a murder or an assault or a burglary, and we all rushed out and became personally interested in each affair, then we would understand indeed that lawbreaking is something which is very dangerous to all of us."[23]

Instead, as the FBI-endorsed book *Ten Thousand Public Enemies* put it, criminals "look, act, and seem like the rest of us," while the gullible public expects them to "look like criminals," as they do "when they are dressed in prison gray." Moreover, "the dangerous part of the underworld carries no banners announcing its occupation. Its members do not scowl fiercely. . . . They go about as good citizens go about, well dressed and buoyant." Hoover decried the melodramatic proclivities of an American populace that "believes that all criminals are labeled," and he caricatured the public's attitude as aligning with the fictive tropes of melodrama's villains: "Crooks are supposed to be low-browed, evil-eyed, bearded, poorly clothed, and to carry dark lanterns."[24] According to Robert Gid Powers, "Whenever the bureau wanted to show the relationship between big-time crime and the ordinary citizen, it dredged up the case of [gangster] Eddie Doll, who had used the disguise of respectability to lure a 'legitimate woman' into crime." Hoover asserted that the story of this fallen "legitimate woman," Doll's widow, Doris Brown, was highly typical: "She, like so many others, believed that a criminal was someone who could be detected a mile off, by his face, his manners, his clothing, his conversation. But Doris Brown learned differently, as so many thousands of other persons must learn."[25] Impotent to direct criminal performance, unauthorized by definition, Hoover aimed at the public and worked to change its relationship to criminality, or the relationship of spectator to spectacle. He empowered his Bureau through a particular twist on the old adage of appearances existing only in the eye of the beholder; the FBI version insisted, "Appearances run that way. . . . Your own mood accounts greatly for the manner in which you see a thing."[26]

The FBI sought to change the public's "mood" about criminals by deploying an antitheatrical prejudice to describe criminal performance. In order to show up the phoniness of gangster folk heroes, Hoover harped on the actorly qualities of criminals, a constellation of attributes that was sometimes signaled with the hybrid term "actor-criminal." "If you want to understand the criminal brain," Hoover warned his FBI fan base, "you must become a momentary actor" (the threat contained for members of the audience by the fact that they would only momentarily become actors, whereas criminals were natural-born, perpetual performers). He also compared outlaw leaders to divas: "as temperamental as any stage or motion-picture star." In sharp contrast to the upright, manly stoicism of the ideal G-man, FBI discourse rendered criminal disguises in effeminate terms and accused their wearers of catering to the public's melodramatic tastes by using cheap ocular tricks like hair dye and cosmetic surgery. On the lam, the wife of George "Machine Gun" Kelly appears in FBI accounts with "her old clothing, her red wig, and a twelve-year-old child as . . . camouflage" and meets up with her fugitive husband, "now with blondined hair and eyebrows." [27] The John Dillinger gang is described in repetitions of the same formula: "All the old attributes were there—dyed hair, newly grown mustaches, mutilated fingers [to avoid fingerprints], dark spectacles, lifted faces, wigs." [28] Hoover and his colleagues barely concealed their disgust with such self-conscious manipulation of criminals' physical appearance. Kelly, for example, with his newly "blondined hair and eyebrows," supposedly accompanied his wife "on a trail which covered thousands of miles, during most of which time . . . she sneered at her husband's fright." [29]

Much as stage actors have been compared to women, children, and animals throughout Western history's antitheatrical discourse, Hoover's FBI feminized, infantilized, and even dehumanized criminals by comparing them to actors. Hoover, for instance, wrote, "It must be remembered that the true criminal, being nearer to the beast than others of us, also necessarily is nearer to the instincts by which beasts live—the predatory habits of depredation and seizure, plus the inherent instincts of escape. In animal life these take the form of visual camouflage. In the criminal, the transposition is mental. He changes his viewpoint to suit his desires." [30] Thus, for Hoover, criminal dissembling was worse than animal deception because only humans mentally incorporate their disguises to the level of deluding themselves. If not an animal, the criminal was at least to be treated as a child, owing to the fact that the "guilty man in trouble does not care whom he uses. . . . His psychology is exactly that of a child who will fasten a family infraction on his own sister if he, himself, can evade a spanking." [31]

After spending so much FBI rhetoric sharpening his critique of the "actor-criminal," Hoover was very concerned about the corrupting potential of undercover detective work for his agents. But the FBI decried the average American murder trial's "crime-opera rules," dictated by jury boxes full of "the usual hand-picked collection of oversentimental nitwits," and claimed that the threat to justice posed by such gullibility "necessitates subterfuges" by law enforcement to keep up with criminal deceit.[32] So the FBI had to strike a delicate balance between its necessity for disguise and its antitheatrical criminal discourse, yielding an ambivalent tone that pervaded FBI policy from the 1930s and into the 1940s. Hoover drew from the two-pronged emphasis on visibility and invisibility, which both Tagg and Diana Taylor emphasize in relation to systems of surveillance. Taylor writes that the Argentine military donned disguises in order to hunt subversive elements, leveraging precisely the same ambivalence: "The military, while flaunting its visibility, also laid claim to invisibility, appropriating the tactics of the weak, those who, as de Certeau puts it, can never control but only insinuate themselves into, invade, or disrupt the space of the powerful. . . . [The military] could see without being seen."[33]

The ambivalent coexistence of criminal visibility and powerful invisibility could be seen in FBI publicity of the late 1930s, when former FBI special agent Leon Turrou wrote most of the popular-press book *How to Be a G-Man* in the subjunctive mood, asking the reader to pretend to be a G-man but also providing an important caveat: "[In this surrogate scenario,] you are a soldier fighting an enemy army, but for you there aren't any fine uniforms, parades, or medals. You must do your work swiftly and secretly, dodging the spotlight and holding to the shadows."[34] Likewise, Hoover endorsed FBI historian Frederick Collins, for instance, because Collins researched the FBI's work "not only in its more spectacular phases but in its constructive ones." Official FBI books like Courtney Ryley Cooper's *Ten Thousand Public Enemies* (1935) explicitly privileged the invisible side of Bureau work, consisting of scientific research, months and years of waiting for resolution, and watching from outside public view.[35] In fact, as a disenchanted former circus man, Cooper positioned himself as uniquely qualified to "go behind the scenes" in order to "dispel illusions" of "spectacular" criminal escapades and reveal how these escapades were constructed—in short, to foreground their theatricalism in order to disenchant a public consumed with romanticism toward crime and criminals. But in order to disseminate the FBI's antitheatrical image, Bureau writers had to rely on publicity that ironically spectacularized these same methods.

In the decade leading up to World War II, Hoover's FBI needed a strong public relations program for three related reasons: (1) to gain public consent for expanding its jurisdiction and becoming a federal law enforcement body; (2) to reeducate public opinion about criminal behavior; and (3) to ideologically deputize lay Americans to assist the FBI with surveillance of their neighbors so as to make policing a nation's worth of criminals manageable. Hoover needed a sophisticated publicity program to manufacture consent for FBI expansion because such bureaucratic growth threatened the anti-federal, "individualistic, libertarian ideal" of mainstream American public opinion. As Matthew Cecil explains it, through publicity the FBI sought to "naturalize the unnatural": a centralized police force that virtually guaranteed at least some infringement on civil liberties, privacy, and individual states' autonomy.[36] Or as Turrou told his readers, "As a '*policeman of the nation*' you must be as familiar with all parts of the United States as a policeman is with his beat."[37]

Moreover, since ordinary, "innocent" Americans were seen as aiding crime through their willful ignorance of criminals on the street, their sympathy with criminals in the press, and their clemency toward criminals in the courtroom, FBI publicity attempted to arouse its audience from compassion to vigilance through reproach and recognition. The FBI openly espoused this patronizing attitude, insisting that guilty suspects routinely went free because of American public opinion rather than flaws in the juridical system. Cooper insisted, "judges give clemency because public opinion demands it. So, just like everything else, the blame [for criminality] settles right back to where it belongs—at the feet of you who happen to be reading this volume." In a slightly less reproachful and condescending manner, the FBI also sought to modify the newspaper coverage of crime, claiming that until Bureau work got "the right kind of newspaper publicity," the American press would continue to aid criminals by romanticizing crime, presenting local police and federal agents in competition rather than cooperation (the former being more melodramatic), and feeding criminals information useful in evading law enforcement.[38]

By the 1930s Hoover had refined a philosophy of intelligence work that centered on the idea that the FBI should not attempt the impossible task of wiping out lawbreakers single-handedly, but rather that it should lead the fight against crime and espionage by providing public examples for local law enforcement and laypeople to follow. In other words, "the FBI was doing its job only when it was in the news."[39] But even before he had refined the intelligence role of publicity, Hoover became so enamored with the largely positive response to the Bureau's mass raids in the 1920s that he started a scrapbook to archive newspaper clippings reporting arrests he had led.[40]

Despite Hoover's infatuation with raids, Jay Robert Nash insists that "Hoover almost never had his agents perform any undercover work for fear of corruption" and instead farmed much of this work out to local police officers, who were then robbed of crime-fighting credit in the press.[41] Eventually, though, Hoover's agents were forced to don disguises, so the politics of undercover mimesis were presented as patently different from the disguises used by criminals. Whereas criminal disguises were portrayed as melodramatic and reliant on ocular tricks like hair dye and plastic surgery, FBI disguises were instead represented as realistic and rooted in the agents' personal histories. Unlike the empty subterfuges of criminals, FBI agents supposedly possessed real-world experience that qualified them for the covers they undertook—for example, one agent had been raised on a farm and later used this "prior life" to go undercover as a farmhand; another agent improbably "had spent most of his life among Indians" and consequently "became a medicine man" in order to investigate a crime on an Indian reservation. Such reality-based disguises were used frequently, and the FBI maintained an index of all the past lives of its agents: as FBI mythology went, "almost daily Mr. Hoover calls upon his men to revert to the trades or professions which they once knew, that they may successfully track a law violator."[42]

While Hoover's index no doubt contained a wealth of possible disguises, FBI agents still faced situations in which they had to pretend to be someone entirely alien to their personal experience. So this FBI politics of mimesis dictated that G-men "must be sufficiently adaptable to play the part of a garage mechanic one week, a hobo the next and the playboy scion of a rich family the week after that. Not that they use false whiskers; impersonation is a matter of clothes, mannerisms, and familiarity with the part one is playing."[43] Emphasizing the virtue of invisibility, one FBI publicity piece told the reader, "Despite all you may have heard or read, G-men do not use disguises, such as flowing mustaches and false hunchbacks. They go to the opposite extreme and try to make themselves as plain as possible. . . . [The ideal cover is] a quietly dressed individual of medium build who is little different from scores of other people." The pinnacle of invisibility was reached through special agents' ability to "be just like the people around them" and thus avoid attracting "a second glance" while doing undercover work.[44]

But while FBI rhetoric insisted on the authenticity and realism of agent disguises, it instead positioned Hoover himself as utterly unactorly and seized by stage fright when called upon to speak in front of an audience. "Of the thousands of [speaking] invitations Mr. Hoover is able to accept about a dozen a year," one FBI writer dished, "for which he labors with almost pathetic seriousness; every speech is a horror of stage fright and nervousness, followed by a sleepless night. But he has become the voice of honesty against the crime world."[45] In short, Hoover stood at the FBI helm poised as the quintessential "straight man." The upright, manly stoicism of the stage-fraught Hoover demonstrated the latent gender dimension of the FBI's antitheatrical attitude toward crime. The distinctly American patriarchal norms of straight talk and masculine action found their other in the melodramatic effeminacy that belied popular criminal performances.

Significantly, the FBI scapegoated the wives and mothers of famous criminals as the true sources of social disorder, both because such women "coddled" their boys and because femininity was depicted as the ultimate training ground for self-conscious manipulation and cold-hearted deception. Hoover traced the criminal tendencies of the famed bank-robbing Barker-Karpis gang to the family matriarch, Ma Barker, and her over-pampering or "parental overindulgence" of her sons (the Barker father's absence is also key). Hoover attributed the criminal effect of Ma Barker's too feminine parenting to the fact that she "was one of the easiest weepers in the history of criminality." Moreover, she supposedly taught her boys lessons "in every phase of secrecy and the foiling of pursuit." The routines she would perform every time her undeniably guilty sons were brought to the local police station were utterly predictable: first, she would angrily denounce the charges against her boys; then "she would weaken, even to the weeping state, as she begged for clemency"; eventually, she would return home with her brood and berate them for getting caught by the police in the first place.[46]

The accusations of women's hyper-emotional displays, over-nurturing, and easy weeping have long been stock items in misogynist stereotypes, but they are also part of the Western lineage of antitheatrical attacks on actors. The FBI referred to the women behind the crimes as consummate actors; for example, Hoover wrote of Ma Barker's "sixth sense of deceit" and maintained that even near the end of her life (which came when the FBI gunned the old woman down), "hard-featured by this time, able to curse with the worst of her comrades, Ma Barker nevertheless was an actress. She could easily become a quiet, demure, round woman who smiled pleasantly and who took a great interest in quiet, respectable surroundings."[47] Hoover likewise insisted that it was not "Machine Gun" Kelly but his beautiful, apparently sweet wife who was one of the most dangerous criminals of her day. In fact, Hoover reasoned, "She was the best example I have ever encountered of the fact that present-day crime no longer bears a label to separate it from honesty. Kathryn Thorne Kelly was one of the most coldly deliberate criminals of my experience." By using stock misogynist tropes, he then described Kathryn through a ransom note she wrote: "the words, the construction, the imagery, the supersentimentality mixed with utter coldheartedness, could only have come from Kathryn Kelly." In the end, Hoover dubbed her "a cunning, shrewd criminal-actress" and called her "Kathryn Kelly, actress of crime, the kind of woman who could weep on one page and on the next condemn a person to death."[48]

The Racialized "Actor-Criminal" and the Gendering of Japanese "Vocational Disguises"

Although Hoover and his FBI colleagues certainly spared no venom in equating female criminals such as Ma Barker or Kathryn Kelly with cold-hearted actresses, if we compare these portraits of white women with their Japanese counterparts, it becomes clear that the FBI perceived a particular danger when "moral aliens" were compounded by "ethnic alien" alterity. Ma Barker and Kathryn Kelly may have had no redeeming qualities hidden beneath their weepy feminine disguises, but at least the FBI was confident that when they were not performing their roles, behind the mask could be found a heteronormative, predictable essence: a mother, wife, or girlfriend standing by her man. But the glamorous "girls" of the diasporic Japanese spy world presented a threat whose difference emanated from the inscrutability of transnational transformation and the departures from heteronormativity created by Asian immigration (which included, of course, the Chinatown bachelor societies traced by Shah). The FBI saw these Japanese immigrants as shedding their native identities, much as a snake would its skin, and utterly transforming themselves into diasporic identities that were of far lower status than their former lives but allowed them camouflage amid the ethnic enclaves scattered across the United States. The FBI's differential scrutiny of white and Japanese women can be mapped onto what Homi Bhabha has identified as the divergence between colonialist notions of "mimesis" and "mimicry." Whereas mimesis is a type of representation based on metaphoric stand-ins—the familiar and temporary donning of an often melodramatic role practiced by shrewd "criminal-actresses" like Kathryn Kelly—mimicry is a "metonymy of presence" whereby impersonators camouflage their difference (anxiously understood as subversive) by displaying "identity effects" that seem to assimilate hegemonic practices but (in the paranoid theatre of those in power) in fact disguise an inscrutable, if not altogether absent, essence.[49] FBI discourse accused white "criminal-actresses" of mimesis but, as we shall see, accused Japanese American "glamour girls" of the much more slippery theatricality of mimicry, whereby characteristics of U.S. performative citizenship—assimilative practices like upward, "by-your-bootstraps" mobility—were displayed as identity effects that mocked rather than symbolized American loyalty. Such mimicry of the American Dream was seized upon by the FBI as proof that Japanese Americans lacked a knowable essence, igniting a racist logic that internment agitators would later sum up in the impossibly tautological statement "A Jap is a Jap."

"Sachiko," for instance, was one of the first Japanese Americans arrested by the FBI in the wake of Pearl Harbor. One FBI work described her as the former "child wife of a high-ranking naval officer in Japan" who turned her back on her former life—though not on her blind adherence to the Japanese emperor—in order to transform herself "in the guise of a humble slavey." Sacrificing the elite status she enjoyed in her homeland for an unglamorous working-class life waiting tables at a Los Angeles Japanese restaurant, Sachiko parlayed her immigrant positioning to marry a Japanese American doctor in order to use his office and "the guise of a respectable wife of a prosperous physician" as a cover for spy activities. Sachiko's immigration-to-assimilation story is presented as a perversion of the American Dream's "rags to riches" myth because in Sachiko's version, temporary economic sacrifice is not the necessary step toward a better life in an America whose streets were mythologized (in Asia particularly) as "paved with gold," but rather a crafty cover for national treachery. Thus, FBI agents soon discovered that Sachiko's doctor husband's "second-floor 'patients' and third-floor dinner 'guests' were usually Japanese naval officers disguised as language students" in order to engage in espionage.[50]

In her domestic disguise, Sachiko hid the international allegiances that made her "indubitably the 'brain' of Japanese espionage on the West Coast," but the title of "real glamour girl of the Jap end of the spy axis" went to another alleged Japanese spy who remained nameless in FBI public accounts. Described in terms suggesting beauty to rival Kathryn Kelly's but not explainable through her romantic loyalty to one man, the promiscuity of this Japanese American "glamour girl" centered on her playing hostess to an endless stream of ethnic Japanese (men and women) engaged in covert espionage activities. According to the FBI, she served as hostess on several occasions for the Japanese ambassador to the United States at the time of Pearl Harbor, Kichisaburo Nomura, but it was her acquisition of master's and doctoral degrees from the University of Michigan that put her at the helm of a network of disloyal Japanese Americans. What the FBI skeptically called "her position as a scholar" proved especially valuable because she used her personal library as a cover for receiving and disseminating espionage information:

> All day long, into the thickly carpeted, book-lined room which was her domain, streamed little yellow men and women . . . a bit awkward in their Occidental clothes but scrupulously polite, each with a paper-covered book squeezed tightly between arm and ribs. . . . Without comment, too, she grasped the book in her quick, capable hands, and, still without comment, delivered to the supposed delver into Oriental lore an outgoing book. No one would have suspected—at least nobody but an FBI special agent—that, by these simple, routine maneuvers, she might be performing one of the most delicate operations known to international sabotage.[51]

While Sachiko supposedly perverted the rags-to-riches subplot of the American Dream in order to spy for Japan, the "real glamour girl" manipulated what would become a hallmark of the Asian "model minority" myth in the 1960s— the idea that American education, particularly at the undergraduate and postgraduate levels, guaranteed socioeconomic success in the United States, no matter one's ethnic heritage—by using higher learning as an occasion for exchanging national secrets.

Whereas the grotesquerie of white criminals' cheap melodramatic disguises marked out the manageable boundaries of their deception, suspicion of Japanese American deceit was boundless because of the perceived homogeneity of Japanese Americans and the overwhelming ordinariness of what the FBI called Japanese "vocational disguises." FBI discourse asserted the clannishness of Japanese American communities, insisting that "Our Japanese aliens organized for every conceivable purpose" and "thus created an interlocking network."[52] A post–Pearl Harbor memorandum from Hoover to Attorney General Francis Biddle made the FBI's stance clear, stating that it "is believed to be true" that "the Japanese worked as a homogenous unit." [53] This view of Japanese Americans handily justified what Bob Kumamoto calls "the racial intolerance that many Americans traditionally held in regard to Asians: it was widely presumed that the homogeneity and ethnic loyalty of the Japanese would lead to acts of sabotage against the United States." [54] The FBI endorsed the logic that the very gathering of Japanese Americans into a group guaranteed that suspicious activities would take place; in the FBI's words, most all of these organizations, regardless of their stated intents or activities, "masked" pro-Japan motives and were "mere fronts" for anti-U.S. espionage. The supposed political disinterest of religious organizations especially attracted FBI suspicion, as did "Americanization" campaigns originating within Japanese communities. And while white criminals hid behind corporeal disguises, the FBI assumed that resident Japanese instead deployed "vocational disguises" that hid spy activities behind apparently benign occupations, necessary because they could not hide the ethnic loyalty marked on their bodies: "Physical disguise was, of course, impossible; Japs carried their nationality in their faces." [55] Under this logic, Japanese Americans employed in any occupation could garner suspicion, especially if their work put them in situations that necessitated contact with large numbers of their own ethnic group.

While the negative connotations of racial "organization" grew out of generalized fears of powerful labor, the accusation that Japanese Americans were group-minded specifically related to a particular understanding of Japan itself as ever-feudal, homogenous, and totalitarian; such an understanding emerged from the theatricalizing discourse's anxious reaction to Japanese economic modernity. The confluence of anti-Japanese theatricalization and anxiety over competition with a non-Western economic power was clear when Collins and Hoover wrote of the Japanese espionage threat in the United States: "Each Jap agent was a cog in a machine which was run, for the most part, by important diplomatic and intelligence officials residing in this country, usually in the guise of 'language students.' It was a good system—and this is how it worked." [56] As we shall see, this begrudging respect for the advanced "machine" of the Japanese "spy system"—in stark contrast to the FBI's ceaseless ridicule of failed German espionage attempts like the U-boat landings on the Atlantic Coast—may have grown out of the FBI's own adherence to a "cog in a machine" philosophy of depersonalized crime fighting that uncannily resembled its suspicious characterizations of Japanese people.

Despite such partly avowed similarities, the FBI shored up its critique of Japanese organizations through the indiscriminate doubt it cast on all their practices. A 13 November 1941 FBI intelligence report to President Roosevelt's office told of the organized nature of West Coast and Hawaiian Japanese and considered the Japanese American Citizens League (JACL, which at that time denied membership to those lacking American citizenship) in the same breath as the Nippon Kaigun Kyokai (Japanese Naval Association, headquartered in Tokyo) in terms of their potential danger to an America at war with Japan. In fact, the FBI report ominously called the JACL "the most active Japanese organization in Northern California," even though it acknowledged that the organization was "made up entirely of Second Generation Japanese who are citizens of the United States." FBI officials found that Japanese American societies that espoused social, educational, and religious goals "masked their pro-Japanese activities behind campaigns for the 'Americanization' of their members." [57] The quotation marks offsetting this "Americanization" pointed toward the menacing mimicry perceived in Japanese American assimilation. But earnest ties to ancestral homeland institutions and practices also garnered FBI scrutiny: the FBI focused on Buddhist and Shinto churches and Japanese language schools especially as "too often mere fronts for espionage activities." In this way, the FBI indicted both assimilation and cultural nationalism, both Japanese American attempts to Americanize their communities through socialization and education and Japanese American attempts to preserve some traditions from Japan through repetition and through the reinfusion delivered by Japanese visitors engaged in "goodwill tours." [58]

All together, such boundless scrutiny criminalized the very idea of Japanese American culture, justifying the FBI's attempted "cultural extermination" of Japanese Americans after Pearl Harbor. [59] The cultural issue of language especially left Japanese Americans in a no-win situation: whether they were American-born citizens learning the language of their Japanese ancestors or Japanese nationals studying English at American institutions, the FBI considered their internationalizing acquisition of language skills to be a suspicious activity. In the January 1940 *American Magazine* article "Stamping Out the Spies," Hoover introduced "one 'Tani,'" who was, to all appearances, a mild, pleasant-mannered [English] language student at Stanford University," and claimed, "Actually, [Tani] was Lieutenant Commander Toshio Miyazaki of the Imperial Japanese Navy, a spy." Hoover told of how Miyazaki solicited information from a discharged naval officer named Harry Thomas Thompson and then mysteriously left the country after his informant was convicted. [60] Interpreted as an act of espionage hidden by cultural exchange, the FBI considered "the guise of 'language students'" to be remarkably effective for Japanese spies. [61]

All people of Japanese descent garnered suspicion in the FBI's logic of surveilling ethnic mimicry so long as their work put them in contact with other members of their ethnic group—and such contact described most Japanese Americans at a time when the vicious cycle of prejudice and language barriers kept them socially and economically segregated from whites. Justifying the 1,395 Japanese Americans seized in the post–Pearl Harbor raids, one FBI work insisted that it "could give . . . hundreds of other examples of immediately apprehended, apparently innocent Japanese [Americans] who were not what they seemed"; the listed examples of innocent-looking Japanese American spies and saboteurs included a seemingly innocuous dry cleaner, laundry owner, and photo shop proprietor—stock characters many urban Americans encountered in everyday life. By contrast, the resident Germans under surveillance since 1938 and arrested by the FBI after Hitler's declaration of war thinly "disguised their espionage activities under the veil of propaganda." [62] Another FBI writer described German disguise as relying on the same cheap theatrics as the white actor-criminals of the 1930s, noting that the German Abwehr submarine agents who landed on the U.S. Atlantic coast in 1942 had trained at a Nazi sabotage school in Berlin, where "Each man memorized the location of the targets, most of them aluminum plants, Ohio River locks and railroads. They rehearsed phony life stories as an actor learns his lines for a play. And these life stories were documented with false birth certificates, draft deferment cards, SS cards, and automobile drivers' licenses." [63]

In contrast to these easily detected actorly tricks, for the FBI, Japanese Americans were much more drastically "not what they seemed" and thus had much more fluid identities. Such logic led to glaring omissions of those of Japanese descent from FBI acquittals of "enemy alien" groups. For instance, in the August 1941 *American Magazine* article "Big Scare," Hoover declared, "The overwhelming majority of persons of German descent in this country are opposed to everything that symbolizes Nazism. The same applies to the loyal Americans of Italian descent." [64] The paragraph ended there, leaving a gaping absence where a similar endorsement of Japanese Americans should have been. While the majority of German and Italian Americans might be called loyal to the United States, for Hoover the majority of apparently innocent Japanese Americans were exactly the ones who merited a second look.

To further illustrate the point that resident Japanese were "not what they seemed," the FBI offered the tale of "two Jims," both of Japanese descent and both apparently making honest livings in the United States. Although the generic structure of "two Jims" suggested that one Jim would have some redeeming qualities to contrast with the inevitably evil Jim, once again, all Japanese were found to be hiding something. As the FBI told it, the first Jim, who owned a bar called Jim's Place, presented an imperfect performance of American masculinity through his effete posture and appearance:

> Back and forth, never hurried, seldom observed, but continually on the move, glided rather than walked a stocky, middle-aged, respectable-looking man of pleasing personality. His clothes were immaculately American, and his heavy black mustache was trimmed in the latest American tonsorial style, but his

lack of stature—he barely cleared five feet—and his complexion, which was slightly on the amber side, proclaimed him a Japanese. This was Jim. . . . This man, who concealed 58 years under a youthful manner and a dapper American wardrobe, had been a ranking officer in the Imperial Japanese Navy during the Jap-Russo war.[65]

Meanwhile, "Jim the Salesman" worked in a Seattle department store and hid the damning fact that he was "a cousin to [Japanese ambassador] Kichisaburo Nomura" behind his daily routine of wrapping packages for Japanese American clientele. Both Jims were supposedly engaged in espionage, a finding the FBI declared was indicative of countless instances of "individual Japanese doing very different kinds of espionage work under very different circumstances and against very different backgrounds." The commonality of these wide-ranging espionage covers rested in the opportunity each disguise presented for Japanese Americans to socialize with one another and exchange letters and packages unobserved. "In short," the FBI insisted, "what looked like sporadic activities by widely separated individuals must be part of a carefully considered and directed plan . . . [which] led inescapably to the conclusion that these supposedly unimportant people were not what they seemed."[66]

FBI Publicity from Participatory Rituals to the Japanese American Spectacle

Whereas much of prewar FBI strategy against white actor-criminals sought to "dispel illusions" and recruit the American public into enlightened co-participants, the Bureau's wartime containment of Japanese spies and their supporting "ethnic aliens" took a decidedly different tack. In preparation for America's entrance into World War II, Hoover shifted his public relations focus from what Powers characterizes as participatory *rituals* of "social unity" and "national solidarity," which engaged the audience in peering behind criminal disguises, to what I would call, by contrast, mystifying *spectacles* of counterespionage, which discouraged participation in favor of passive spectatorship.[67] More specifically, as World War II embroiled the U.S. allies in Europe and spelled out the nation's own inevitable entry into war, the FBI attempted to stage spectacles demonstrating its dominance over "enemy aliens" but that instead demonstrated its implied domination over the American public. Through this subjective slippage, the Bureau's wartime surveillance and its post–Pearl Harbor raids became for the public "spectacles of deconstruction," to borrow Baz Kershaw's terminology: they were performances of equivocation that open up space for audience members' rejection of their passive roles by rendering the paradoxes and human vulnerability of spectacle itself abundantly clear.[68] The FBI's wartime disavowal of its wildly popular "crime and punishment rituals" threatened its public ontology.[69] Hoover attempted to abruptly shift the public's experience of the FBI and its enemies from vicarious participation to passive consumption in part to gain control over a public no longer lenient but now increasingly inclined to engage in vigilante activity against suspected lawbreakers.

The FBI needed to curb such vigilante activity, as well as distance the Bureau from any possible resemblance to Nazi policing, a mimetic conflation still perceptible from critiques of its prewar raids. Presaging Antonio Gramsci's now classic critique of ideology and hegemony, a 1939 *New Republic* editorial accused the FBI of leveraging "gangster movies and ten-cent detective magazines" to gain the public's "voluntary support" for Gestapo-like tactics to which foreign governments must instead force their constituents to submit.[70] On 3 February 1940, FBI agents led arrests in Detroit and Milwaukee of Spanish Civil War veterans (former volunteers of the Abraham Lincoln Brigade). These midnight raids provoked public furor and calls for Hoover's dismissal because the FBI's methods were seen to resemble Gestapo tactics, as veterans were dragged from bed and chained together for transport. The FBI image also suffered from the embarrassing failure of the "greatest spy hunt ever" in the spring of 1938. Following the Nazis' coup in Austria on 16 February 1938 and the American outcry to reign in the German-American Bund, President Roosevelt ordered the army, navy, and FBI to cooperate in rounding up suspects of German descent. But "patriotic groups" like the American Legion and Martin Dies' House Rules Committee (later to become the House Un-American Activities Committee, or HUAC) were aroused rather than pacified by these jointly staged mass raids and took up vigilante activities and investigations beyond the FBI's control.[71] Even the much publicized Nazi spy trials of that summer failed to cool the public, teaching Hoover not only the lesson that there was indeed such a thing as bad publicity but also that his Bureau required total control over such spectacles of containment in order to also contain the public's reactions.

Therefore, at a time when many businesses and government agencies were rejecting or at least challenging the "centralized, rigid, static, closed, and machine-like" modernist systems characteristic of Taylorism's scientific management and were instead embracing "decentralized, flexible, dynamic, open, and 'naturalistic' systems" (as Jon McKenzie describes the shift), Hoover attempted just the opposite.[72] Although championed by Progressive Era engineer Frederick Winslow Taylor, scientific management's critics warned that the efficiency of such systems dehumanized the workplace and turned workers into automatons. By shifting the FBI's protocol and public relations frame to an even more rigidly modernist model, Hoover sought more control over the organization's image—a project that was impossible as long as the unscripted variable of public participation remained such a prominent part of the equation. Moreover, in the manipulation of the conventions framing the public's encounter with crime fighting and thus the denaturalization of this encounter, the artificiality and constructedness of the FBI publicity program became apparent, drawing the specter of the actor-criminal into uncomfortably close proximity to the Bureau's own public image.

The FBI had announced this transition in a series of *American Magazine* articles by Hoover published in 1940–1941. Cooper had contributed flattering features on the FBI to *American Magazine* since 1933 (twenty-four such full-color articles were published between 1933 and Cooper's death in 1940); the articles were "surrounded by formula adventures by Rafael Sabatini, Max Brand, Rex Stout, and Agatha Christie."[73] But three articles in the two-year period before Pearl Harbor presented a significant twist to the "FBI formula": "Stamping Out Spies" (January 1940), "Big Scare" (August 1941), and "War Begins at Home" (September 1941) worked in tandem to forecast the wartime strategy of the FBI. Although the United States remained officially neutral, in the pages of *American Magazine* Hoover's publicity machine wrote the American public's role as spectators rather than participants in the FBI's home front war. Powers characterized this new strategy as a mystification of FBI activity that for the first time in the Bureau's history drew a boundary between the amateur audience and the professional agents: "The spy-smashing publicity that Hoover orchestrated during World War II sought to discourage amateur spy-chasing by 'mystifying' counterintelligence. The FBI made counterespionage out to be a complex, highly sophisticated task best left to experts scientifically trained for the job—in other words, the FBI."[74] This mystification not only cast doubt on laypeople's ability to do anything about spies; it also called into question their freedom of speech and discredited their vision. In fact, the FBI's *American Magazine* public relations campaign that led up to Pearl Harbor espoused the virtues of doing nothing, saying nothing, and seeing nothing: cultivating the very apathy and passivity that its 1930s publicity had vilified. The message was that the FBI would let the public know when it was safe to look. However, the empowered American audience was not necessarily willing to revert to its earlier quietude or to embrace the FBI's latest public incarnation.

Beyond mystifying counterespionage, FBI writers suggested that any unsolicited public statements about suspected spies or suspicious activities, whether in the form of rumors, gossip, or even press accounts, could endanger the "highly sophisticated" work of the Bureau. By silencing the din of any other public discourse on crime, the FBI positioned itself to consolidate the nation's policing power entirely under its jurisdiction. In "Stamping Out the Spies," Hoover declared, "The citizen should consider his particular task fulfilled when he reports his suspicions to the nearest FBI office. After that they should not become gossip [*sic*]. Idle talk can hamper proper investigation." Hoover elaborated: "When apparently crackpot activities intrude upon our national defense, the citizen who becomes aware of them should neither condone, excuse, or judge them. Report them impartially to the FBI and allow experienced investigators to determine whether the actions are mere irrationalities or carefully concealed plotting. Now as never before the amateur detective should stay where he belongs: on the side lines."[75] Whereas 1930s FBI publicity criticized the citizen who failed to take notice of suspect activities and offered that citizen the unpaid job of FBI sidekick, 1940s publicity condemned the responses of a now alert public and encouraged audience members to silence themselves and report on any "questionable facts and rumors" generated by their fellow alert Americans.[76] The subtext of this directive feminized and disenfranchised the public, giving it the role of the sociopolitically weak wife to the FBI's omniscient and powerful husband. Likewise, the media "exposé" was cast as the gossipy female opposite the FBI's strong, tight-lipped male. The FBI criticized revelatory media reports as potentially resulting in the "premature exposure" of suspects the FBI had been stealthily tracking. "I do not imply that the public should not be fully informed," Hoover insisted in "Big Scare," "but spies, like criminals, love publicity when they can be told by print, radio, or the hue and cry of vigilantes that their whereabouts and activities are known."[77] What Hoover implied in these articles was reiterated by fellow FBI writers such as Frederick Collins. In his 1943 book on the FBI in World War II Collins insisted, "Not only should we *do* nothing about our suspicions until we consult the FBI, but we should *say* nothing—and we mean *nothing*."[78]

At the root of this enforced passivity was the FBI's apprehension that laypeople could not detect the staginess of Axis spies' disguises and covers, which were allegedly more realistic than the melodramatics of peacetime criminals. Collins reported being told by Hoover, "Real spies are selected for their cleverness and trained in the technique of concealment. They seldom do anything the average layman can spot."[79] Hoover continued to maintain that "everyone should be alert to the impersonator" and warned that "'peculiarities' are often used by enemies of this nation as a shield for vicious activities," but now the eyewitness accounts of ordinary citizens were discredited as overly emotional and in need of filtering through FBI channels in case the suspected actions turned out to be "mere irrationalities."[80] In other words, in Hoover's latently misogynist view, the American public could not see through the illusions created by enemy spies because it was prone to hysteria and lacked the ability to rationally differentiate between reality and representation.

In the FBI's gendered discourse, Hoover's men were poised to step in as patriarchal protectors, as "Big Scare" made clear. The article's subheading promised, "Here the director of the FBI exposes the menace of cooked-up hysteria, and shows how every American can help to protect himself and his neighbor from the ugly schemes of vigilantes and fearmongers," foregrounding the proximity of the emotional danger to the reader. The article's large, disembodied photographs of a wide-eyed, frightened woman in the foreground and a similarly feminized man in the background echoed this sentiment. Hoover implied that Americans were becoming more dangerously emotional, rather than evolving into the cynical public he had long sought to cultivate:

> Today, in the United States, astonishing as it may seem, war hysteria is already more widespread than it was twenty-three years ago [in World War I]. . . . I shudder to think what might have happened to [the innocent people reported to the FBI as probable spies] if their cases had been handled by hysterical mobs and bands of inexperienced and emotional vigilantes instead of by impartial and objective law-enforcement agents. Fortunately, the cases were reported to us. . . . If frightened citizens will report their suspicions to the proper authorities, we have nothing to fear from hysteria.[81]

There is nothing to be hysterical about except hysteria itself, the FBI riffed on New Deal public mobilization but for very different ends. Again, the amateurism and melodramatic tastes of laypeople were contrasted with the professionalism and detachment of the FBI, signaling that the days of participation and imitation by the American public were over and an era of enforced spectatorship had begun. Before the war, adults vicariously participated in crime fighting adventures like the sensational Lindbergh case, and children formed "Junior G-Men" clubs; by contrast, in a *Seattle Post-Intelligencer* article published one week after Pearl Harbor, First Lady Eleanor Roosevelt was quoted as saying, "The FBI is rounding up the people who are suspects. We should not try to become FBI agents ourselves."[82] The transition smacked of resignation and repression, but the FBI called it progress.

At the same time, the World War II era marked the first widespread public awareness of the FBI's performances as undercover or double agents. After U.S. authorities arrested thirty-three German agents in the summer of 1941, the fact that the FBI had penetrated the Nazi spy apparatus using double agents became headline news. The public also learned that the FBI had planted undercover agents in American defense plants to combat possible sabotage and had recruited laborers as informants. Considered less newsworthy was the fact that civil liberties were being overshadowed by the perceived fifth column threat. Indeed, at this time the spy menace and counterespionage efforts were considered such showstoppers that in 1942, 60 percent of the war features released by the motion picture industry focused on the spy threat. The public's fixation had became so great that in September 1942 the Bureau of Motion Pictures accused studios of creating "an exaggerated idea of this menace," prompting a significant decrease in espionage pictures (down to only 24 percent in 1943 and 16 percent in 1944).[83]

Perhaps the seepage of fiction into reality (the fantastic elements of FBI undercover operations) and of "reality" back into fiction (the omnipresence of spies in motion pictures) contributed to the American public's delay in realizing the war was real when it finally came to the United States. Anecdotes abound of people who thought that Pearl Harbor was a joke, modeled after Orson Welles' October 1938 "Invasion from Mars" radio show, which concocted a fictional drama of Martians invading New Jersey that was taken seriously by some listeners.[84] The inseparability of fiction and reality led to an incredulity about the seriousness of the Japanese threat that was common enough in the wake of Pearl Harbor to prompt articles such as the *Los Angeles Times*' "Public Believed First War Reports Only Gag: Reporter Finds It Difficult to Make People Grasp Facts of Japanese Hawaii Attack," which sought to assure the public of the reality of war. Another article, "Jap Spies Not So Funny—Joke's on Us," gave the *New York Post*'s "Far East Expert" a forum to declare, "Japanese spies always seemed funny, with a perpetual grin on their faces. We regarded them as jokes, and built up an entire literature on the subject, from fanciful murder mysteries to comic strips. Now, with a shock, we learn they are not so funny."[85] Even before war came home, journalists set themselves to the task of rousing Americans who believed that Japanese spies were entertaining, harmless figures rather than a real threat to be feared. In a March 1939 *Reader's Digest* article titled "So Sorry for You: Japanese Espionage Used To Be Funny—But No More," author Hallett Abend "aimed at increasing popular awareness of Tokyo's alleged Fifth Column prowess [but] conceded that 'the Japanese spy, even in the Orient, does have his comic as well as his highly exasperating aspects.'"[86]

The Spectacular Containment of Japanese Americans

Faced with an unpredictably skeptical public that was still taken in by criminal disguises—but now harbored aspirations to play FBI agents—Hoover turned to what he heralded as a "modern version of counterespionage" that would eliminate laypeople's roles altogether and relegate them to spectators on the sidelines. As its agents moved into Japanese American communities and arrested "enemy aliens" whose sincerity was in question, the FBI understood its post–Pearl Harbor raids as the first large-scale operation of this modern counterespionage. Now that the American public had been demoted from co-participant to passive spectator, not only were the FBI's duties more tightly under the control of Hoover as director, but these actions could also be choreographed down to the very last detail through advanced rehearsals and machine-like efficiency. Hoover and other Washington leaders found such restraint necessary to minimize hysteria among the populace and keep the U.S. home front on the gentlemanly side of martial law. Even before Japanese troops took to the high seas for their approach to Pearl Harbor, FBI rationales had been decided and plans for the enemy alien raids had been finalized.

Hoover staged the Honolulu raids against Japanese Americans as what FBI lingo called the premiere "performance," and it was then repeated across the mainland. FBI memoranda from the months before Pearl Harbor reveal that by 26 November 1941, Hoover and Honolulu's special agent in charge (SAC) had prepared detailed scripts for apprehending Japanese Americans under various contingencies.[87] These detailed plans served as the model for the other field offices around the country as they set about "duplicating, with the able cooperation of local law enforcement officers, the *performance* of the thirteen Honolulu squads in rounding up dangerous enemy aliens and citizens co-operating with them." Such coordination was later considered by the FBI to be the reason for the lack of "successful enemy-directed acts of sabotage at all, so far in World War II": "the faithful *performance* of a routine duty at a Honolulu switchboard . . . made possible the almost machine-gun rapidity with which the FBI went into action, not only in Hawaii, but in far-off Puerto Rico and Alaska and throughout the United States."[88] Repeating this same performance discourse about the post–Pearl Harbor raids a decade later, FBI writer Don Whitehead contended, "The roundup was a remarkable *performance* in speed and coordination. The careful advance preparation made it possible to take into custody 3,846 enemy aliens within the first 72 hours of the war with no violence."[89]

This recourse to the language of performance—and concomitant insistence upon its instrumentality in circumventing violence—repeated the scenario of Perry's founding raid upon Japan in 1853. But in the World War II context of Japan's ascendance as a dangerously modern enemy, Hoover's vision of "performance" took on a highly modernist tone that substituted the inefficiency of human impulses with the standardized efficiency of machines and machine-like coordination. Much as Perry's mission was celebrated for taking place "without a single shot," even though many shots were fired for spectacular "effect," the FBI staged a nationwide series of bloodless spectacles that nonetheless traded upon the effect of "machine-gun rapidity." Such an aesthetic of superhuman efficiency encapsulated both Hoover's and the public's perceptions of the post–Pearl Harbor raids. According to FBI accounts, in the hours and days after Pearl Harbor, "There was no lost motion, no lost time," an efficiency that presented a sharp contrast to the chaotic actions against the enemy aliens in World War I. This valorous efficiency was chalked up to bureaucratic minutiae: not only did the switchboards, telephones, and teletypes "perform," but also other office supplies took on heroic roles as each field office divided its special agents into squads and gave these squads "a specified number of previously prepared 3" × 5" filing cards, on which had been entered the name, address and citizenship status of each person to be picked up."[90] Such advanced preparation and omniscient machinery allowed FBI agents to apprehend the bulk of "suspicious" Japanese Americans within three hours of receiving their orders. And within a fleeting thirty-six hour period, the agents performed actions that had been written and rehearsed since 1939. The overall effect created a series of simultaneous spectacles that relegated the American public and mass media to awestruck spectators. American journalists marveled at the weeks and months of undisclosed planning that had preceded the quick FBI roundup of Japanese aliens on the West Coast, in New York City, and around the country. "These [raids] culminate months of intensive investigation by FBI agents here," the *Los Angeles Times* pointed out. Media analysts attributed the "quiet thoroughness" and sudden "striking" of the raids to the fact that FBI agents were "acting swiftly on the basis of lists of suspicious persons which have been under preparation since last spring." The FBI lingo for rounded-up Japanese was picked up by reporters, who referred in arch quotation marks to the "previously known suspicious aliens" arrested in the raids.[91]

These "previously known suspicious aliens" and their families found themselves trapped in FBI spectacles that were unabashedly scripted and predictable, thus short-circuiting any improvised reactions. Nisei Wilson Makabe remembered being aware of the surreal deliberateness of the FBI agents' actions as they searched his family home in Loomis, California, during dinner on 7 December 1941; at the same time he was stunned as he watched his father's seizure: "They started talking to us and my father. Then we went into the house. And that's when one of the most amazing things happened: a person who had never been in our house before knew just where to go to look for things. He pulled out correspondence that my father had from Japan. Some old papers from way back, twenty, thirty years before. So, he gathered some things up and he said, 'You come with me,' and he took my father."[92] Indeed, as Bill Hosokawa points out, Japanese Americans knew about FBI plans well in advance of Pearl Harbor because "as early as October 21, 1941, FBI agents visited Li'l Tokyo in Los Angeles, questioned officers of various Japanese organizations and seized records and documents for further study."[93] Many Japanese Americans developed the ability to anticipate the FBI's repetitive actions. After the FBI had picked up the majority of community leaders in his neighborhood, Issei Kenko Yamashita, a Buddhist minister in Southern California, seemed numb to the inevitability of the FBI's actions; he testified that he "thought the FBI would come and pick me up soon because of this. So I put my belongings into a suitcase and I prepared to go at a moment's notice. . . . I was ready for it from the beginning. But they came on March 13, 1942. I was tired of waiting for so long."[94]

Perhaps the FBI took so long to arrest Kenko Yamashita—and other Japanese Americans who were lying in wait—because Hoover and his fellow Washington leaders decided that FBI agents would direct each and every raid on Japanese American businesses and private residences in order to control these repeat "performances," despite the fact that many other federal government agencies and local law enforcement bodies had the physical capacity to round up the suspects. Instead of sharing the leadership role, as Francis MacDonnell puts it, "Hoover argued that the overlapping of responsibilities among competing intelligence bureaucracies on the home front undermined counterespionage, heightened public confusion, and opened the door to mass hysteria." [95] Hoover had long considered the emotional reactions of the American people to be part of his Bureau's purview, and only by controlling the execution of these spectacles could he do his job.

Hoover's aesthetic approach to these raids was supported by the predominant opinion in Washington—that is, FBI agents were most capable of preventing public hysteria over the local "Japanese problem" in the event of war because they were plain-clothed gentlemen rather than uniformed officers and because they had the ability to coordinate their efforts across the United States in order to stage an efficient onslaught on all Japanese communities simultaneously. An internal FBI memo about a week before Pearl Harbor noted that General Short, the commander of the U.S. Army in Hawaii, wanted "to have aliens taken into custody by Agents of the FBI in order to prevent confusion and hysteria that might result if uniformed soldiers were sent into certain localities of [Honolulu] to make arrests." The issue of appropriate costuming became key: although FBI agents functioned as police, they could appear less menacing to the American public because of their gentlemanly costumes. Honolulu Field Office Special Agent in Charge R. L. Shivers insisted that G-men's appearance of civility would win the passive trust of the public: "Special Agents of the FBI, in conjunction with some of the military personnel, could carry out these objectives with less disturbance to the civilian community and prevent a fear and hysteria psychosis in the public mind." [96] In other words, the soothing effect of what might be dubbed the FBI's *suits and simultaneity* would calm jangled war nerves and convince Americans that the problem was being handled while they sat back and watched. Officials wasted little concern on how this slick strategy would impact the Japanese Americans being raided, but it was obviously in the government's best interest if the arrestees became spectators as well, avoiding any messy resistance or improvised displays that might win the larger public's sympathy. At issue for Washington was the prevention of public hysteria, which threatened to court vigilante reaction and undermine the politically correct home front posture of calm cheerfulness. For all these reasons, the well-dressed, well-groomed, and well-behaved agents of the FBI seemed the ideal choice for ensuring public predictability, and Hoover embraced such a role for them.

Newspaper accounts of the FBI raids from around the country demonstrate that Hoover's goals were largely realized. The mainland raids began in San Francisco, where the front page of William Randolph Hearst's *Examiner* trumpeted, "Squads of Federal Bureau of Investigation agents and police ranged through San Francisco's Japanese section, taking into custody undisclosed numbers of 'suspicious aliens' considered as potential saboteurs." The reporter described how armed policemen quickly blocked off the city's "Japanese colony." Much of the article consisted of a breathless description of FBI agents' actions occurring in various suspicious locales "at the same time"; these repetitive actions were comprised of entering Japanese businesses and removing "enemy aliens" along with documents. The first installment of the article's spectacular sequence painted a surrealistic scene: "G-men and plainclothes officers, traveling in several cars, swung into action first at the Aki Hotel, 1651 Post Street, and took out a Japanese, while a Japanese Salvation Army band outside played 'Marching through Georgia.'" The reporter noted that the FBI took all the "Japanese" arrested in the raids to the Silver Avenue Immigration Station but insisted that the biggest events were yet to come: "They will be held pending further internment orders. . . . Developments on a much larger scale are expected today and during the next several days as the drive fans into the valley regions and other coastal districts to apprehend possible spies and saboteurs before they can do any damage." [97]

The next day, Hearst's Los Angeles paper described the drive as it fanned out into the Southland region: "Striking swiftly throughout Los Angeles and Southern California, civilian officials working under the direction of Federal Bureau of Investigation agents took 500 alien Japanese into custody yesterday . . . both men and women." By noon Monday, these Japanese Americans had been taken to the County Jail and then on to the Terminal Island Federal Immigration Station, all the while "held incommunicado for the FBI." [98] One Nisei who witnessed the raids remembers how "Swiftly, silently, [the FBI] sealed off the town, cut telephone lines to Japanese homes and spirited off a score of Japanese leaders. They left as swiftly and mysteriously as they had come, leaving behind a stunned community." [99] A wartime advocate for Japanese Americans, white activist Carey McWilliams similarly described the "swift, sudden, silent FBI raids and roundups following Pearl Harbor." [100] These spectacles rendered victims and bystanders alike as passive spectators, overawed and even mesmerized by the "swift, sudden, silent FBI raids"; indeed, the repetition of these imposing adjectives signaled the uniformly stunned reaction of everyone involved.

The *New York Times* also observed the stunning efficiency of the FBI as it arrested Japanese Americans on the East Coast, but even more remarkable to its reporter was the silence of the crowds and lack of resistance by those raided. The reporter first explained the methodical quality of the FBI's actions:

> The Japanese nationals were visited in their homes by FBI agents and detectives, told to take along a suitcase with traveling essentials, taken to a station house and booked as "prisoners of the Federal authorities," then removed in groups in patrol wagons and squad cars to the Federal Building at Foley Square. There, usually, their case histories were taken briefly, checked with official records already prepared, and then, in small groups, they were taken to the Barge Office at the Battery and to Ellis Island by ferry. A score, however, underwent extended questioning. . . . The FBI agents apparently acted according to a pre-arranged plan.[101]

Although the reporter snuck in one interview with a Japanese American detainee, "Later newspaper men were not permitted to talk to the prisoners," and "No information about the roundup was given by Federal or local authorities."[102] Unaware of Hoover's apparent will to control every aspect of these raids' presentation, a few New Yorkers at first attempted to participate in the raids by assisting the FBI's investigations; the reporter noted that in addition to Federal stenographers and clerks, "Telephone operators also had to be called in as the FBI switchboard was swamped with telephone calls from citizens giving the Bureau 'tips' on activities by Japanese and other nationals that they considered suspicious." Whether speaking from unofficial sources or offering his own suppositions, the reporter opined that all these "tips" were fielded, "although all, apparently, reflected overzealousness"—delivering a decisive verdict on laypeople's counterespionage talents (or lack thereof). The reporter also insisted on the passivity of the raid victims and audiences alike: "Some of the Japanese [arrested] were crestfallen, some were smiling, but none offered resistance. Crowds were not permitted to collect, so there were no demonstrations."[103]

Along the same lines, the *Chicago Tribune* noted the FBI's discouragement of local action and lay participation, but in the Midwest a more sympathetic picture emerged of the raids' impact on Japanese Americans. One writer dutifully reported, "United States attorneys were instructed to advise state and local authorities that all complaints against Japanese nationals were to be handled thru the FBI."[104] But another *Tribune* reporter presented a less closely controlled portrait of the raids from the perspective of the Japanese community. "Chicago's Japanese were gloomy yesterday as federal and local agents acted swiftly and secretly against their restaurants, gift shops, and business establishments," the reporter wrote and continued, "Few of those who could be found would talk and those who did affirmed their loyalty to this country and wanted to know when they could reopen their stores. . . . Most bewildered of all were the owners and waiters of the city's 25 Japanese owned lunchrooms and eating places, closed down by Mayor Kelly a few hours after the outbreak of hostilities. In the Tokyo Lunch, one of the largest restaurants, at 551 South State Street, a group of frightened Japanese huddled in a rear room." [105]

Hoover believed that the highly rehearsed quality of his Bureau's actions was the key to preventing public confusion. His Bureau repeatedly boasted of the fact that agents were so well rehearsed in the nationwide plans that they could be "ready in a few moments' notice" to enact these raids. The "notice" in question was to be a Presidential Proclamation declaring a state of war and thus activating the 1798 Alien and Sedition Acts, allowing for the apprehension, detention, and even deportation of any enemy aliens considered threats to national security. [106] Such a declaration of war, in the manner of Western textualism, was legible only in the form of a performative signing of documents serving as prerequisite to physical action. Therefore, when FBI agents waited in suspended animation for President Roosevelt to sign the document giving them the official power to enact their long-established plans, their watchful tableau vivant was meant to embody Western codes of honor. One article even pointed out that policemen working under FBI direction "permitted diners" at a Japanese restaurant in New York City "to finish their meals, and then escorted owners and their staffs to their homes" to wait out a curfew on Japanese Americans imposed by the mayor. [107] The FBI's actions in the hours after Pearl Harbor almost seemed to parody this idea of wartime gentlemanliness, obscuring the underlying cruel dread that filled many Japanese Americans, who witnessed the armed FBI agents staking out their homes in anticipation of "a moment's notice." But the FBI's restraint spectacularized the very rules that the Japanese government was seen to have flouted, thus establishing a binary opposition with the enemy's "uncivilized" treachery. [108]

The first teletype Hoover sent to his field offices upon receiving news of Pearl Harbor's attack commanded special agents in charge to create a state of readiness, but it called upon them to "postpone actual making of arrests until telegraphic authority received from Bureau." [109] After the fact, FBI publicity explained this suspended animation in more detail: "Each [FBI field] office knew precisely what to do when the order came for the roundup. But Hoover and his men couldn't move on this job until President Roosevelt had issued an emergency proclamation and Attorney General Francis Biddle had signed the necessary directives giving the FBI authority to act." [110] A *San Francisco Examiner* reporter noticed this "watching and waiting," and the resulting news report demonstrates how distracting the surface spectacle became, at the cost of questioning the material repercussions upon the Japanese Americans being raided: "While awaiting FBI squads at San Jose, deputies under Sheriff William J. Emig patrolled residential areas containing an estimated 4,000 Japanese. There was no protest against the patrols, but S. J. Hirano, president of the San Jose Japanese Association, which has about 2,700 members, said, 'We consider ourselves Americans. Our loyalties are with the United States.'"[111] Decades later, Elaine Black Yoneda, a white woman of Jewish descent married to a Nisei residing in San Francisco at the time of Pearl Harbor and who herself was later interned with her husband at the Manzanar Relocation Center, related her experience of "just" being watched and not being able to protest such spectacularized violations:

> About 7:45 a.m. on December 8, 1941, three FBI agents came looking for [my husband] Karl. I let them in without inquiring whether they had a search warrant, something I would have demanded if Japan's military attack on the United States had not taken place. When I informed them Karl had gone to his long-shore job on Pier 45 (he was a member of the ILWU), they were skeptical and had me call the Union Hiring Hall for confirmation. The agents searched our small four-room flat, taking nothing, and making snide remarks as they looked through some Chinese War Relief cards I was addressing for our Christmas and New Year's messages. They called them 'a good cover for pro-Japan activity'. . . . Soon after this they left. Later I was informed by two neighbors that additional FBI agents with submachine guns had been posted on roofs facing the front and rear entrances to our home.[112]

Although the gentlemanly FBI agents left Yoneda without arresting her or taking any evidence from her home, the violation of being unwillingly cast in the center of such a neighborhood spectacle (violating the respectable neighborly edict against "making a spectacle of yourself"), which newspapers and other media then broadcast for wider audiences, remained tangible to her forty years later. The spectacle of it all compelled Yoneda's passive reaction, particularly because the aesthetics of the staging pointedly mirrored and inverted the theatrical treachery of Japan's unwritten declaration of war. As Yoneda explains, "I would have demanded [to see a search warrant] if Japan's military attack on the United States had not taken place."

Japanese Americans found themselves trapped at the center of attention for these spectacles but also relegated to passive spectatorship as they watched the FBI constantly watching them—Hoover had scripted both roles as passive. Like Yoneda, Nisei Mary Tsukamoto, living in Florin, California, at the time of Pearl Harbor and later interned in Jerome, Arkansas, vividly remembered the feeling of being made a spectacle by the FBI and her ever-watchful neighbors: "The FBI was always lurking around. We were told we couldn't stay out after eight o'clock in the evening. Meanwhile, Hakujin [white] neighbors were watching us and reporting to the FBI that we were having secret meetings."

Likewise, after Nisei Amy Uno Ishii's father was arrested in Los Angeles, "The FBI came out regularly. They were coming out to the house almost like clockwork. We could see FBI people sitting in automobiles, just within view of our house. . . . It's very possible they could have been 'keeping us under surveillance.' It's a very uneasy feeling to know that somebody is out there watching your house and your movements twenty-four hours a day." White neighbor Virginia Swanson witnessed the FBI raids on Terminal Island and remembers that "movie men were all set with cameras outside the cottages, hoping to catch a picture of a struggling Japanese." [113] Scholar David Eng has observed that hegemonic U.S. discourse renders Asian Americans invisible in their contributions to nation building but hypervisible when their loyalty to the nation becomes suspect.[114] Lending further credence to Eng's observation, the post–Pearl Harbor raids' hypervisibility indicted Japanese Americans in a very mundane but pervasive manner; as Hosokawa puts it, "Whites who were aware that the FBI had swooped down on the mild, inoffensive Japanese who had been running the corner grocery store for twenty years, couldn't help but think the worst of all Japanese. If the truck gardener who grew that beautiful lettuce, the friendly fellow who operated the cleaning shop, and the meticulous little gardener all had been picked up by the FBI, could any of the Japs be trusted?" [115]

The FBI's Modernist Antitheatricalism and Japanese American Doubling

> I don't think these very fine young lawyers serving as FBI agents are just the ones to appraise the military value of information and parcel it out promptly to the Army and Navy.
> —Los Angeles Mayor Fletcher Bowron testifying at the Tolan Committee Hearings on the West Coast "Japanese problem"

Despite Hoover's prescripting, the FBI roundups in Little Tokyos and Japantowns did not uphold the binary between sincere Americans and theatrical Japanese that was passed down by the theatricalizing discourse and resurrected by the Pearl Harbor attack's unwritten treachery. On the contrary, the careful staging of the raids on Japanese Americans raised the specter of the shockingly calculated Pearl Harbor attack itself; moreover, an uninverted mirroring of the FBI's "fine young lawyers" in the media images of their Japanese American suspects exceeded the discourse of enemy difference necessary for wartime mobilization. David Palumbo-Liu has argued that the Yellow Peril's particular permutation in terms of white American anxiety over prewar Japanese invasion/immigration (seen as one and the same) "has to be seen as the mirror image of recently developed American neocolonialism in East Asia, a project deeply attached to the imagining of a modern state."[116] In order to manage white American anxiety about Japan's mimetic proximity, this mirror image had to be read as the opposite or inversion of Western modernity, as the theatricalizing discourse effectively repeated. In a prologue written in 1946, Edward Spicer et al. attributed the wartime suspicion of Japanese Americans to their economic success, particularly during the Depression: "Caucasians could not dismiss them with amused contempt as they did some minorities who survived only as cheap labor or tourist curiosities. They endowed Japanese success in the face of legal, social, and economic restrictions with the same aura of mysteriousness and sinisterness as their personalities."[117] Japan's (and Japanese America's) economic and military threat needed to be managed by framing this other as the West's (and white America's) mirror opposite rather than its mimetic double.

But certain unpredicted elements of the post–Pearl Harbor spectacles (ironic because of Hoover's emphasis on modernist aesthetics as the means to eliminate the unpredictable) created what Michael Taussig calls "mimetic excess" by showcasing an anxious fantasy of Japanese American over-assimilation.[118] Again and again, media images of the raids showed suspects clothed in dark suits, overcoats, and fedoras that suggested an unauthorized mimicry of the FBI agents' gentlemanly costume and appearance. Coupled with the uncanny similarity between the high modernist aesthetics of the FBI's routinely repeated, machine-like performance and the spectacularly calculated shock of the Japanese attack on Pearl Harbor, the FBI raids may have succeeded in rendering the public as spectators, but they failed to realize the reassuring exercise in marking difference and maintaining boundaries that Hoover had promised. Instead, the mimetic excess of the encounters reinscribed and spectacularized Japanese American difference and indicted the FBI's failure at fully containing it.

On a discursive level, politicians and journalists used the same terms to describe both events: the Japanese military "raiders" at Pearl Harbor paralleled the FBI "raids" on Japanese Americans. Both actions, despite their apparently opposing ends, used methods labeled by the press as "sudden," "swift," and "swooping," and both capitalized on the element of calculated surprise. The FBI's initial refusal to issue statements on the roundups of Japanese Americans seemed a secretive strategy, much as Japan's unannounced raid on Pearl Harbor, after weeks of diplomatic negotiations, was perceived as the culmination of the Japanese government's strategic secrecy about its true intentions for war—never mind that one secret was sold as gentlemanly and the other as barbaric. In Congress on the day after Pearl Harbor, U.S. representatives decided that Japan must have been undergoing secret preparations for "at least two weeks," thus surprising the U.S. military at Pearl Harbor with "an utterly inexplicable event" that also "stunned" and "amazed" Americans at large.[119] The raid on Pearl Harbor was seen as shattering the idyllic quiet of a Sunday morning in America—a narrative that was echoed in Japanese American recollections about the arrival of FBI agents later that afternoon and during the next few days. For instance, Nisei Kiku Hori Funabiki, living in San Francisco when the war broke out, recalled, "With Pearl Harbor, my father's world came crashing down. Soon after, the FBI, in one of their ruthless pre-dawn sweeps, rousted our family out of bed, searched our house recklessly, then handcuffed my father and led him away."[120] News accounts may not have demonstrated any awareness of the material violence against Japanese Americans underlying these "pre-dawn sweeps," but the suddenness and striking quality of the FBI's raids hardly escaped the reporters who covered the post–Pearl Harbor spectacles.

In addition, audiences to both the Pearl Harbor raid and the FBI raids commented on the highly constructed, orchestrated quality of the spectacles, a correlation that landed the FBI on the wrong side of the sincere-versus-theatrical binary established in the theatricalizing discourse about Japan. This discourse had been instantly activated in mainstream American characterizations of the Pearl Harbor bombing: immediately responding to the carnage, politicians in Congress and pundits in the newspapers characterized the Japanese attack as an outgrowth of deception that had been thoroughly rehearsed, as opposed to the American diplomatic position of good faith, sincerity, and improvisation (purportedly responding to every Japanese overture leading up to 7 December 1941 with honesty and integrity). However, it was difficult to fit Hoover and his agents into the heroic mold of artless American diplomacy because the qualities that were most remarkable about the FBI raids on Japanese American communities—their choreography, spectacularity, and secrecy—instead put them in bed with the enemy.

In addition to the structural similarities linking the FBI raids and the Pearl Harbor attack, the ideological underpinnings of both the FBI and Japanese society were understood as counter to Yankee individualism. As American filmmaker Frank Capra famously put it in his wartime propaganda film *Know Your Enemy—Japan,* Japanese soldiers were considered "photographic prints off the same negative" and the product of Japan's "Tanaka plan" to create a giant mass of apparent individuals "with but a single mind" in which the "humanitarian impurities are burned out." This American perception of Japanese people extended to immigrants from Japan, since most of white America perceived Japanese Americans as clannish, homogenous, and blindly loyal to their homeland.[121] But such affronts to the individual ethos of the United States were not confined to the Japanese; rather, Hoover's "army of essentially anonymous agents" presented a similar challenge to the ideology of the American individual. Despite the FBI's prewar popularity, Robert Gid Powers points out that only children completely accepted the anti-individualism of the Bureau: "Perhaps because American children had not yet been indoctrinated in the national myth of the self-reliant hero, what particularly fascinated kids about the FBI was the image it promoted of being one big team, a 'we' organization, even though that was precisely the aspect of the FBI's official image that put off their parents." [122]

Since taking over the FBI helm in 1924, Hoover had pursued an anti-individualist management structure that promoted science and valorized the elimination of human agency, both as preconditions of combatting human error and in vogue with the Progressive Era hegemony of scientific management. As noted above, Taylorism can be detected in much of Hoover's revolution at the Bureau but with an efficiency uniquely tailored to intelligence work. Significantly, this mission to rid the FBI of human error gained strength in response to the growing sophistication of transnational threats leading up to World War II, going against the current of mainstream public opinion, which increasingly questioned the dehumanization demanded by scientific management amid the human devastation of the Depression era. But Hoover believed that scientific methods like fingerprinting and magnification improved upon human sight and that machines like lie detectors subverted human deception and imperfect interpretative skills. One FBI writer claimed of Bureau investigations, "The chance of errors in judgment does not exist here. No one looks a man over and decides from his appearance, his actions or his story whether or not he has a record. It is a part of routine duty to learn the past of every person arrested." [123] FBI publicity thus trumpeted the organization's shift from referring to suspects by names or to crimes through narratives to categorizing them with objective numbers and statistical profiles. But this was no mere marketing ploy: even as late as the Pearl Harbor attack, Hoover's internal documents likewise insisted on a machine-like identity for the FBI, proclaiming in a 17 December 1941 memo, "The Bureau's function has been and is now that of merely being a transmission belt of information which its facilities obtain." [124]

In the 1930s FBI publicity had first espoused the compelling applications of science for crime fighting. Hoover and his other FBI writers heralded "crime-detective science" as able to upstage the "melodramatic stage devices" of crime, which included the staging of the tearful public confessions that were later withdrawn by defense attorneys. [125] Science gave the FBI a much needed edge over criminal melodrama because it could accomplish such illusion-breaking feats as reconstructing the remains of charred documents, determining the truthfulness of suspects' statements during interrogation, and positively identifying human beings and their traces at crime scenes. [126] It was of the last feat that the FBI seemed most proud. Positive identification could be attained,

Hoover thought, through fingerprinting, which the FBI director called "protection from impersonation" that makes "true identity" known.[127] Significantly, the origin of these "black smudges, spaced on white cards" can be traced in part to American attempts at controlling Chinese immigration. As FBI publicity indicated, it was in the late nineteenth century that "a San Francisco photographer had suggested the fingerprint method as a practical means for registering Chinese"; it foreshadowed the FBI's later dependence on fingerprinting to track "moral aliens" and its push to register "ethnic aliens" under the newly enacted 1940 Alien Registration Act.[128] FBI writers waxed rhapsodical about the potential of fingerprinting. Cooper, for instance, called the FBI fingerprint card "the patterned story of a life" and wrote of the fingerprint files, "Here daily parades the population of a thousand jails, each to be catalogued and studied, with the result that often a person's past is revealed, not as the life of honesty which had been assumed, but as one of vicious criminality."[129] Likewise, Turrou maintained the preemptive realism of fingerprinting, insisting, "Criminals can disguise themselves in many ways, but they can never change the lines on their finger tips."[130]

In addition to portraying the efficacy of fingerprinting and other methods of crime-detection science in fighting the melodramatics of criminals, in the 1930s (before the crackdown on public participation), FBI writers rendered Hoover's excitement about his brainchild contagious by encouraging amateur intelligence and by anthropomorphizing scientific equipment. Turrou invited public participation in a chapter of *How to Be a G-Man* called "Catching Crooks with Chemistry." After describing how the FBI tested a stain to see if it came from blood, Turrou encouraged the reader to reenact such experiments themselves: "Perhaps you would like to make such a test yourself now. You can get the supplies at almost any drug- or chemical-supply store for about $1.35, or maybe in your own chemical set if you have one." Turrou even went on to provide his readers with all the imaginative tools necessary to imitate the FBI as if they were themselves agents, offering in explicit detail "the directions for the test, step by step, exactly as you would make it if you were working on a case."[131] The popular public tour of FBI headquarters in Washington also gave its audience opportunities to engage with scientific methods and equipment and encouraged ambitions of mastery.[132] FBI discourse brought science closer to lay Americans by personifying items like microscopes and guns. Cooper, for instance, launched into one description of an FBI investigation by proclaiming, "Microscopes had gone into action. Then dusting powders had been brought forth. After that, the queer, elongated cameras with their self-contained batteries and shielded electric globes had clicked off their photostatic records." Later, he tellingly insisted, "The Division of Investigation questions a suspected gun as thoroughly as it investigates humans."[133]

By sublimely personifying its machines and depersonalizing its agents for an audience of FBI followers, Hoover went beyond merely embracing scientific management: the Bureau incorporated into its publicity program a particular strain of aesthetic modernism that Martin Puchner calls "modernist antitheatricalism." Motivated by high modernism's "fear of the masses and the public sphere," high modernist theatre reformers like Yeats and Craig sought to tightly control the aesthetics of theatre by ridding the medium of "the personal, the individual, the human, and the mimetic." This impulse rendered "living human actors . . . permissible only when they [were] utterly depersonalized"—at the extremes, by turning them into machines through rigorous training, as epitomized by Meyerhold's "biomechanics," or by replacing them with inanimate puppets, as Craig's infamous *Übermarionette* valorized. As chapter 1 revealed, the contemporaneous movement of Japonisme informed many of these depersonalizing methods because the theatricalizing discourse posed the foreign aesthetics of Japanese visual and performing arts as a powerful challenge to the Western fascination with naturalism and individualist psychology.[134]

Hoover's intelligence reform took up the antitheatrical modernist logic and its easterly inspiration in the FBI efforts to depersonalize the regretfully human agents needed to manage their superhuman machines. When Hoover took over the helm of the FBI at the age of twenty-nine, he set about removing the middle-aged and older special agents who populated the Bureau, believing them to be inefficient, unfit, and contaminated by decades of "rubbing elbows with the underworld." In their newly vacated places, the new director installed young men (none older than thirty-five) with law or accounting degrees. Above all, according to Cooper's foreword to Hoover's 1938 book, *Persons in Hiding,* "Physical fitness, he knew, would be a requisite. He fostered athletics, and, under his tutelage, the Bureau's teams soon began to win trophies."[135] One athletic activity in particular became an integral part of the FBI fitness protocol: the Japanese martial art jujitsu. As Turrou told his would-be FBI agents in *How to Be a G-Man,* "Along with exercise you will be taught the art of jujitsu, using simple tricks by which you can defend yourself in tight spots and handle crooks who may be much stronger and heavier than you." Turrou's book also featured a photograph of an agent getting "advanced instruction in the not too gentle art of jujitsu."[136] Turrou's repeated references to jujitsu as an "art" rather than a sport or exercise regimen signals its self-consciously foreign and avowedly aesthetic status in the FBI training program. In other words, Hoover's choice to instill a Japanese martial art in his new agents was based on his desire to make his G-men reflect a certain image.

In addition to being physically fit, Hoover's ideal G-men were, in Powers' words, to be positioned as "an army of essentially anonymous agents reporting back to the big brains in Washington. No gangbusting heroics to distract anyone from the big story, which was that Hoover's scientific crime detection machine had the ability to fit [a vast array of intelligence] reports together, to match them up against information in the files, until finally the answer to the 'Who dunnit?' question would pop magically out of one of the FBI's newfangled automatic card-sorters."[137] Devoid of human error or subjectivity and acting as extras to the star machines, FBI agents were interchangeable and indistinguishable and as a rule did not give individual statements about their heroics to the press. FBI writers also emphasized that crime fighting and counterespionage were not about individual creativity and autonomy but rather resembled a team sport or ensemble piece.[138]

While FBI protocol did not render them readily distinguishable from one another, FBI agents were at least easy to pick out of an ordinary crowd owing to their identifiable image as dark-suited gentlemen. They generally wore suits and, in the 1940s, fedoras, as one of their many concessions to Hoover's micromanagement of the Bureau's image; as one historian of the FBI put it, Hoover "wanted the Bureau's agents and employees to represent the best in middle-class values. They were to be neat, to be moral in their private relations, to be sober."[139] This attention to the manner and class image of FBI agents can be traced back to Hoover's first Justice Department boss, Attorney General Harlan Stone, who maintained that "the first essential in [the new recruit's] work as a Special Agent is that he conduct himself as a gentleman. . . . Officials of the Department of Justice can more effectively perform their duties by acting the part of gentlemen than by resorting to tactics of a different character." Under such influence, Hoover's first employee manual "devoted 131 pages to administration and comportment and only 38 to the actual conduct of investigations" and "struck many employees as a Bureau etiquette guide à la Emily Post."[140] In all these respects, Hoover's agents embodied a distinct fusion of two strains of self-conscious modernity: antitheatrical modernism's fetishization of depersonalized performance and economic modernity's Taylorist standardization of behavior, extended beyond the management of the factory worker to a casting of the FBI's white-collar company man as a mechanized "gentleman," popularly understood as white, Anglo-Saxon, and Protestant.

As noted, the gentlemanly performance projected by FBI agents was startlingly reflected back at them in the media portraits of the Japanese Americans seized during the raids, in a type of reversal Bhabha has described as the doubling of mimicry, which produces a "gaze of otherness" by subverting the hegemonic imperative to emulate the colonialist's civilized culture and instead mimicking metonymic characteristics of "the colonizer's presence." Bhabha suggests that this returned gaze shakes dominant power to its core because such unauthorized mimicry "necessarily raises the question of the *authorization* of colonial representations."[141] Japanese American accounts of the FBI raids record the suspects returning their captors' surveillance by scrutinizing the FBI agents' homogenous appearance as "gentlemen" in suits. Hosokawa remembers the scene as FBI agents descended on one Japanese neighborhood, writing that "strangers were to be seen almost everywhere—tall, well-built men in dark suits." Hosokawa testifies to the ubiquitous phenomenon of Japanese Americans watching for their suited captors, noting that as these raids unfolded, some Japanese Americans "lived in anxiety from day to day, waiting for the knock in the night, the hand on the shoulder, the appearance of the tall men in dark suits." [142] For the Japanese American communities under surveillance, a dark suit and its complementary accessory, the crisp fedora, became the metonym for FBI agents' recognizable omnipresence.

Of course most Japanese Americans had access to suits and fedoras of their own, the sumptuary weapons of mainstream American, middle-class respectability particularly crucial for the assimilative claims of racialized Americans. Owing to the prescripted nature of the FBI raids and the gentlemanly "watching and waiting" of the agents' performance, many Japanese American men had the occasion to change into suits before being arrested, so they appeared in the FBI spectacle (not to mention in the no less performative courts of judges and magistrates) wearing the markers of white bourgeois respectability.[143] As photographs of the raids played across the war news pages of the country's major newspapers, FBI agents were not alone in their dark suits and crisp fedoras: the Japanese Americans seized in the raids were dressed remarkably similarly to their captors' own infamous costumes. For example, a photograph from the 8 December 1941 *San Francisco Examiner* showed Aki Hotel owner Ichiro Kataoka wearing a dark suit and fedora, flanked by identically dressed FBI agents and local plainclothesmen.[144]

Such photographs broadcast a doubling mimicry because they brought together the criminal and honorific functions of photographic archives, as outlined by Allan Sekula. According to Sekuka in "The Body and the Archive," Western photographic portraiture first emerged as a more accessible (not to mention more realistic) alternative to the painted portraits usually available only to affluent, influential individuals. In the upwardly mobile United States, the resultant photographs yielded "a massive honorific archive of photographs of 'illustrious,' celebrated, and would-be celebrated American figures." The corollary to the celebratory photo archive, of course, became the criminal photo archive, which grew out of a repressive application of photographic methods to the disciplining and punishment of all sorts of behavioral deviants (the insane, the violent, and the racially other).[145] Although the post–Pearl Harbor FBI raids were staged for a veritable army of cameramen poised to capture still photographs and moving pictures for the criminal archive of mass media reportage, many Japanese Americans subverted this criminal spectacularization by instead donning the costume elements characteristic of honorific photographic portraiture. The two seemingly opposed registers of photographic meaning thus collided in the published images circulated about the FBI spectacles, and they assigned an anxious doubling and undecidable quality to the raids.

Sekula argues that the opposition between the two photographic registers in Western representation was desirable but not assured; the two opposed archives share an "essential unity" based upon the shared "belief that the surface of the body, and especially the face and head, bore the outward signs of inner character." After all, since the nineteenth century, the honorific photograph and the criminal photograph had accompanied one another in a dialectical fashion:

> The position assigned the criminal body was a relative one [because] the invention of the modern criminal cannot be dissociated from the construction of the law-abiding body—a body that was either bourgeois or subject to the dominion of the bourgeosie. The law-abiding body recognized its threatening other

FIRST S. F. JAPANESE PRISONER

Journalists recorded the apprehension of Japanese American suspects by similarly clothed FBI agents in the hours after Japan attacked Pearl Harbor. When FBI agents arrested Ichiro Kataoka, this photograph captured an anxious exchange of glances between spectacularized suspect and government police. Photograph from the 8 December 1941 *San Francisco Examiner.*

in the criminal body, recognized its own acquisitive and aggressive impulses unchecked, and sought to reassure itself in two contradictory ways. The first was the invention of an exceptional criminal who was indistinguishable from the bourgeois, save for a conspicuous lack of moral inhibition: herein lay the figure of the criminal genius. The second was the invention of a criminal who was organically distinct from the bourgeois: a *biotype*. The science of criminology emerged from this latter operation.[146]

Although the entire FBI mission culminating in a "modern version of counter-espionage" had sought to assure the American public of the visibility and distinctness of criminality enabled by scientific scrutinization, the photographic remains of the FBI raids on Japanese Americans instead raised the specter of the indistinguishable "criminal genius" in the midst of a Japan-U.S. conflict that required ideologically clear boundaries.

Moreover, as John Tagg reminds us, the 1920s and 1930s had exerted certain pressures upon the American concept of criminal visibility that drew from the era's "more developed capitalist democracies" and "new means of mass production"—namely, the public expected to be involved in the increasingly accessible evidence of social deviance and social problems. With the New Deal agency photos of Walker Evans and Dorothea Lange as instructive examples, documentary photographic practices "were addressed not only to experts but also to specific sectors of a broader lay audience, in a concerted effort to recruit them to the discourse of paternalistic, state-directed reform." Documentary photography also included investigative journalism, and both share in what Tagg refers to as a "mode of address" that "transformed the flat rhetoric of evidence into an emotionalised drama of experience that worked to effect an imaginary identification of viewer and image, reader and representation" and created "an ethnographic theatre in which the supposed authenticity and inter-relationships of gesture, behaviour and location were essential to the 'documentary' value of representation."[147] So despite the manner in which Hoover's live spectacles indeed passified Japanese American arrestees as well as public bystanders, the photographic representations of the FBI raids as published in the national mass media produced a differently coded "ethnographic theatre" that demanded public outcry for further repressive action.

The majority of the men on the FBI's prime list of Japanese suspects were fishermen, farmers, storekeepers, and priests—not the "Japanese businessmen" that would become stock figures of ridicule and alarm in later incarnations of the Yellow Peril anxiety about Japanese invasion/immigration. But the photographs printed in major U.S. newspapers pictured Japanese Americans as criminal geniuses mimicking the bourgeois respectability of FBI agents in a competition of overdetermined gazes—suspects watching themselves being watched—with the originator of the look anxiously unclear. In the 8 December *New York Times*, a photograph bearing the caption "Police Escort for Consul General" recorded such a moment, with the consular official (Morito Monishina) gazing at the camera's eye as his similarly dressed FBI captor looked at him. Comfortably estranged from this exchange of mimetic glances, the uniformed local police officer on Monishina's other side is facing forward with his eyes shut.[148]

Photographs that did not feature the mimetic encounter of captor and prisoner instead echoed the mass of unindividuated FBI agents through images of Japanese American groups taken into custody in the post–Pearl Harbor raids, the subjects often wearing suits, fedoras, and smiles directed at the camera's eye. As a photograph from the 10 December 1941 *New York Times* shows, German aliens arrested by the FBI were usually pictured in individual portraits that resembled the head shots featured on personal identification cards the FBI kept for its most wanted criminals: a frontal mode of criminal portraiture that used photography's "realism" to capture what Tagg called "the flat rhetoric

In much of the media coverage of the post–Pearl Harbor raids, groups of ethnic Japanese suspects were pictured in contrast to the individual head shots of most FBI suspects, such as the lone German American shown here. Photograph from the 10 December 1941 *San Francisco Examiner.*

of evidence." In contrast, Japanese aliens were presented in the large group-ings of environmental photos that characterized documentary photography's "emotionalised drama of experience" and "ethnographic theatre"—a very dif-ferent rhetoric that called for audience outcry. In a *San Francisco Examiner* photograph suite published on 10 December, all the suspects are suited (ethnic Japanese and ethnic German alike), but an individual German, Hans Bern-hard, is juxtaposed with three Japanese, G. K. Kawasha, Keyoshi Tsukada, and I. Hamano.[149] Also interesting is the fact that Bernhard's enemy ties are promi-nently signaled by a swastika that makes up the background of his photograph, while the Japanese suspects' guilt requires no visual cues beyond their ethnic markers. This strategy of presenting Japanese aliens in groups juxtaposed with German aliens in individual poses presented the fifth column problem in a very particular way: individual Germans living in the United States might be con-sidered suspicious, but Japanese Americans garnered suspicion en masse. Such a presentation also enlarged rather than contained the notion that Japanese Americans were dangerously group-minded, homogenous, and (in the FBI's own warning) "organized for every conceivable purpose."

If, as Miles Orvell argues, at this point in the history of mechanical repro-duction, in the wake of "the documentary culture of the [American] 1930s," photographs were believed to reveal hidden truths or essences and thus to inspire social action, then the similarity constructed in the photographs seemed to reveal several anxious facts.[150] First, Japanese Americans were spectacular-ized by these media images as criminal geniuses instinguishable from those of the white bourgeoisie, reinforcing the sumptuary anxiety of Japanese imita-tiveness and over-assimilation to Western modernity. Second, the FBI agents trusted to contain this threat were perhaps too similar to their Japanese targets to create the necessary ideological distance. Third, the "emotionalised drama" created by members of one unindividuated collective (the FBI) apprehend-ing members of another apparently unindividuated collective (the Japanese) clashed with the "national myth of the self-reliant hero" and thus presented an unsolved social problem to Americans who sought greater ideological distance from the enemy at this moment of national crisis.[151]

At the root of these media images was the FBI's desire to spectacularize modern counterespionage and criminalize Japanese American assimilative acts as "mere fronts" for anti-American espionage. The FBI sought to "make a spectacle" of Japanese American suspiciousness, which was constructed as the very precondition of their association as an ethnic group, whether they were ostensibly assimilating to white American culture or promoting cultural nationalism. Through this nationwide, simultaneously orchestrated spectacle, the FBI hoped to pacify its American audience, in the triple sense of control-ling public hysteria and vigilante activity, securing anew the public's consent

Slow Motion

The FBI successfully framed America's "Japanese problem" as a spectacle, but Bureau director J. Edgar Hoover did not expect the American audience to demand such an active role in dictating the pace and scale of the Japanese American mass evacuation that quickly followed the FBI's targeted raids. Editorial cartoon from the 31 March 1942 *San Francisco Examiner.*

for consolidation of the Bureau's power as a national police body, and eliciting an aesthetic reaction of passive awe toward the FBI's sublime mastery of human limitations through depersonalized methods. Yet the ultimate achievement of a modernist antitheatricalism that underwrote this new version of counter-espionage put FBI agents in uncomfortable and unauthorized proximity to the Japanese American "actor-criminals." FBI discourse had always understood the doubling of its publicity programs to occur at the level of simultaneously performing for the gullible American public and for criminals, in the latter case communicating the inevitability of their capture. But in the post–Pearl Harbor raids, the preparedness of Japanese Americans for the FBI's inevitable "suits and simultaneity" resulted only in a threatening doubling at the level of mimicry, as these suspects returned the "gaze of otherness" by dressing the part of suited gentlemen.

Hoover was confused and disappointed by the lack of solace Americans took in his Bureau's containment of the "Japanese espionage problem," as the media, politicians, and some laypeople, especially on the West Coast, increasingly rallied for the wholesale evacuation and internment of Japanese Americans regardless of their citizenship status or activities. In January and February 1942, Hoover even tried to satisfy the persistent U.S. lust for Japanese exclusion by changing the FBI's counterespionage strategy from highly orchestrated, simultaneous raids on Japanese American communities to impromptu "spot raids" on random Japanese American homes and businesses.[152] On 17 February 1942, Hoover's Justice Department boss, Attorney General Francis Biddle, tellingly wrote to the president that anti-Japanese journalists like syndicated columnist Walter Lippman were "acting as 'Armchair Strategists and Junior G-Men'" and that their editorializing "[came] close to shouting FIRE! in the theater."

But as one political cartoon from the 31 March 1942 editorial page of Hearst's *San Francisco Examiner* showcased, the presentation of the "Japanese problem" as spectacle had indeed become the dominant mode for addressing Japanese American evacuation. In the cartoon, entitled "Slow Motion," Lady Liberty (here symbolizing Californians) sits in a theatre holding a playbill labeled "Japanese Evacuation Program." With a look of concern on her face, she watches a projection of Japanese Americans (rendered in racist stereotypes) move inland with their suitcases. Cobwebs entangle the evacuees' legs to signify how slowly the evacuation has been progressing. The caption reads, "Japanese are on the move away from our coastal areas but the exodus cannot move fast enough to please the people of California. We will all breathe easier when this removal has been completed and the evacuation problem should be speeded up as much as possible."[153] The FBI had cultivated pacifying spectacles in which Japanese Americans were spirited away in speed and silence, but it had yet to wean its audience from participatory crime pageants in which public opinion affected the denouement.

CHAPTER 3

Performative Citizenship and Anti-Japanese Melodrama

The Mass Media Construction of Home Front Nationalism

> While citizens may envision the horizontal, fraternal community described by Benedict Anderson, identification is predicated on the internalization of a rigid hierarchy along the lines of gender, class, and race. Theatrical choreography situates members of the population in relation to each other. The visual arena allows a basis for identification, for in the public sphere "citizens" see themselves as somehow related to other citizens, most of whom (as Anderson notes) they will never meet.
>
> —Diana Taylor, *Disappearing Acts* [1]

> The typical features of melodramatic expression—exaggeration, emotionalism, Manichaeanism—can thus be redefined as the eruption of the machine in what is presumed to be spontaneous. . . . Being "automatized" means being subjected to social exploitation whose origins are beyond one's individual grasp, but it also means becoming a spectacle whose "aesthetic" power increases with one's increasing awkwardness and helplessness. The production of the "other" is in this sense both the production of class and aesthetic/cognitive difference.
>
> —Rey Chow, *Writing Diaspora* [2]

Fred Korematsu, the plaintiff in *Korematsu v. United States* (1944), singles out the disconcerting power of the American press when he looks back on the period during which he resisted the government's exclusion orders against Japanese Americans. When Korematsu, a Nisei, got word that he would be forcefully evacuated from his home, he decided to evade what he considered an unconstitutional policy. (In 1944 the Supreme Court instead sided with the government.)[3] A friend referred him to a plastic surgeon who transformed his face so he could pass as an American of Italian or Latino descent—anything but Japanese. Korematsu remembers that he almost never felt interpellated as ethnic Japanese; instead, he related many years later, "I felt like an American." Significantly, Korematsu said, "The only time that I felt uncomfortable was when I happened to glance at a newspaper, a newsstand, or somebody looking at it and it says 'Jap' this and 'Jap' that and all the bad things about the Japanese. I even refused to *buy* a paper because of that. That was it until the time I got caught."[4] As Diana Taylor argues, the media play a key role in controlling public attention by focusing it only upon the "given-to-be-seen"; in historic moments of national crisis especially, newspaper kiosks and other media presence on city streets have become microcosmic theatres where "people imbibed their national positionality, the us versus them" and spectators were "encouraged to enter the narrative."[5]

Scholars of the internment have echoed both Korematsu's testimony to the disconcerting power of the press and Taylor's articulation of the media's role in spectacularizing national belonging. Most internment scholars have indicted the wartime content of West Coast newspapers for arousing public opinion against Japanese Americans and influencing politicians to institute the policy of mass evacuation and internment. In his argument for the malevolent role played by the press, Roger Daniels, the most prolific scholar of the internment, assigns the lion's share of blame to the notoriously anti-Japanese newspaper chain of William Randolph Hearst—despite the fact that media scholars are skeptical of that outrageous newspaperman's power to influence opinion at all. However, the fact that the internment's leading historian characterizes Hearst's coverage as "spew[ing] forth racial venom against all Japanese" seems to demand serious consideration of the Hearst press as a particularly flagrant example of the influence the media held over internment policy.[6] But a close reading of the Hearst news coverage in the influential period between Pearl Harbor and the completion of Japanese American evacuation from the West Coast does not bear out the type of editorially racist stories that meet the evidentiary burden of "spew[ing] forth racial venom against all Japanese." Instead, a much more persuasive correlation can be found between the four-week period of calm coexistence that most Americans shared with their neighbors of Japanese descent—which extended from Pearl Harbor's attack to early January 1942— and the calm before Hearst's storm of patriotic spectacles was unleashed upon city streets and newspapers.[7] "Patriotic" campaigns like the "Buy a Bomber to Attack Japan" drive began in Hearst pages and at nationwide venues in January and continued at regular intervals through April 1942, by which point Japanese

American evacuation was very much under way.[8] So despite the fact that newspapers such as the *San Francisco Examiner* were saturated with every reportable incident of alleged Japanese "enemy alien disloyalty" from the moment the war broke out, public sentiment toward Japanese Americans en masse did not begin to truly sour until patriotic spectacles became a compellingly predictable feature of Hearst's newspaper coverage. While Japan's 7 December 1941 attack may have provided the opportunity for vengeance against the Japanese abroad, the nationalist self-righteousness that developed with the circulation of what I have been calling "the myth of performative citizenship" provided Americans the moral high ground that justified prejudice against their Japanese American neighbors, two-thirds of whom possessed U.S. citizenship.

As I argued in the introduction, the myth of performative citizenship acts as the public face of racial performativity, obscuring the extent to which national belonging has historically been withheld from various racialized groups based on visual scrutinization (measuring the object's distance from whiteness). The two-faced quality of racial performativity demands that scholars examine not only the public performances that seem to bolster the American myth—public enactments that Hearst himself staged in the form of patriotic pageantry and nationalist fundraising drives—but also the simultaneous spectacularization of excluded racial others.[9] As Debord contends, spectacle lulls its audience through surreal images that deny the social exploitation and material violations that undergird their production.[10] In this chapter I will briefly examine a few of the spectacles of performative citizenship staged by the Hearst press in order to demonstrate how they excluded Japanese Americans from the public sphere (coinciding exactly with their military exclusion from the West Coast). By denying Issei and Nisei access to the public sphere, Hearst's publicizing of the myth of performative citizenship (as well as such publicizing by other media) bolstered the illusion that the internment policy resulted from Japanese Americans' lack of patriotic demonstrativeness rather than from a historical ideology of biological racism that uncannily resembled European fascism—the other face of racial performativity. This other face emerged through the simultaneous spectacularization of Japanese Americans as melodramatic villains and impassive automatons. The spectacularization of Japanese Americans can be witnessed in the Hearst newspapers' framing of the evacuation and internment during the first six months after the United States entered the war (from Pearl Harbor's attack until the removal of these citizens and resident aliens from their West Coast homes was completed). These media spectacles not only blamed the internees themselves for their unprecedented mass exclusion but they also served to deny the historical magnitude and material disenfranchisement of what was taking place in plain view.

Melodramatic Media

In a fascinating analysis of the classic Charlie Chaplin film *Modern Times* (1936), Rey Chow posits the "modernist production of the space of the other" to be the spectacularization of human labor as unempathic automatons and melodramatic excess. She argues that modern technologies such as Taylorism's assembly lines and the cinema's enlargement allow for the "debased popular form, melodrama"—with its predictable characters and passifying polarization of good and evil—to be realized as "the eruption of the machine in what is presumed to be spontaneous." Imagining exploited human labor as physically ridiculous and mechanically insensate (much like the mustache-twirling melodramatic villain who possesses no motives for his inhuman evil and thus merits not even the most cursory empathy from the audience) allowed spectators to deny their own culpability and withhold fellow feeling from the other's suffering under capitalism's dehumanizing conditions. The production of modern human difference, according to Chow, has a distinctly aesthetic dimension that involves relegating the abjected other to an entirely different empathic realm or narrative structure from the one in which hegemonic society imagines itself—namely, segregating the other in the realm of melodrama while the spectator imagines him- or herself in the psychologically complex narrative of realism.[11]

When *Time* magazine called Hearst "the genius of a thousand melodramas," it was referring not only to his motion picture company's infamous production of serial melodramas such as the anti-Japanese silent film *Patria* (1917).[12] It also counted among these "thousand melodramas" the transferal of Hearst's melodramatic energy (which almost always picked Asians or Mexicans as the villains of his productions) from film serials to city politics and especially to yellow journalism, which framed complicated social issues as Manichaestic melodramas played out on his newspaper pages. A key wartime example of the latter was a series of six *Los Angeles Examiner* articles published in mid-April 1942 in which Hearst writer Joseph Timmons chronicled "the dramatic story of California's fight for a national law excluding the Nipponese," framing the incipient internment policy as a domestic battle waged against the "Japanese menace" and bravely undertaken "without support of other states" in the union. In the first article of the series, Timmons proclaimed, "No one can more than guess to what magnitude our Japanese population would have grown, had Californians been gentle, complacent souls, before the nation would have awakened to the menace."[13] In step with the New Deal era's resurrection of the plucky, androgynous heroine of sensational serial film melodrama (think Depression matriarchs like John Steinbeck's Ma Joad and World War II icons like Rosie the Riveter) in place of the pathetic heroine of turn-of-the-century melodrama, Timmons valorized the ungendered (but distinctly masculine) "California 'rough-necks'" over the rest of "the nation's tender solicitude for the lovely little cherry blossom people." As Timmons framed the story, the masculinized West fought against the feminized East (meaning both Japan and the eastern United States) to dispose of "the most incurable menace the nation ever faced from immigration"—namely, Japanese Americans.[14]

Each article in Timmons' series narrated the struggle between California "patriots" and the sneaky "Japs" (meaning both Japanese Americans and the Japanese government) over immigration and other legislation; each also culminated with coming attractions for the next day's installment. In addition to lurid descriptions of supposed Japanese treachery, Timmons, like other Hearst writers, shaped news events into a narrative rife with twists and turns, mimicking the patterns of traditional melodramatic suspense. For instance, describing one moment of California's legislative failure to squeeze Japanese farmers' livelihoods, he wrote, "AND THEN, BEFORE THE NEXT SEASON ARRIVED, THE CRACK OF DOOM SOUNDED." [15] Timmons' strategy of compelling sympathy for the anti-Japanese heroes relied upon the tropes of U.S. racial melodrama that Linda Williams has identified. "It is a peculiarly American form of melodrama in which virtue becomes inextricably linked to forms of racial victimization," Williams writes, illustrating her point through the popular American settlement myth, which disguises the genocide enacted upon Native Americans with the notion that white settlers were merely defending themselves against "savage" attack. Such inversion of the actual political economy governing U.S. race relations elevates the aggressors to the melodramatic status of "racially beset victims who acquire moral legitimacy through the public spectacle of their suffering." [16] This dynamic of obscuring real power through displays of "racially beset" suffering also played itself out in Timmons' anti-Japanese series.

Timmons' third article in the "Japanese problem" series professed that Japanese Americans had been brainwashed by the Japanese government into automatons who were mentally incapable of feeling loyalty to the United States. In addition to pathologizing their "mental attitude," Timmons accused the Japanese American "villains" of being "a Cocky Lot," taking advantage of Japan's diplomatic power to undermine the honest, humble folk of California.[17] The fourth article described how this diplomatic luck had finally run out at a "most dramatic climax, in a tense session of the Senate and final victory for the [anti-Japanese] exclusionists." But Timmons also narrates an alternate, "tragically evil" ending that would have transpired if "Congress [had] let them down": "There would have been banqueting in Tokyo as well as in Little Tokyo here and other Little Tokyos up in the Sacramento and San Joaquin Valleys and around San Francisco Bay." [18] The last two installments thus lingered self-righteously over the details of the final measures of the Japanese exclusion and told how the past forty years had made "the present crisis necessitating evacuation" inevitable. Timmons wrote that despite white Californians' endless patience with Japanese Americans, "too many of our Japanese disappointed us" by not performing ample displays of distress over Pearl Harbor and subsequent American defeats at the hands of Japan. Instead of offering the requisite patriotic demonstrativeness, Timmons claimed, "They were jollier than ever, faces wreathed in smiles as if the Japanese victories headlined in the papers gave them satisfaction."[19] Through Timmons' melodramatic serial journalism, the Hearst press instructed its readers to interpret the persecution of Japanese Americans occurring around them (and often through them, as white neighbors took economic advantage of evacuees and other Asian Americans distanced themselves from identity with the Japanese) as the inevitable and justified punishment of an unambiguous villainy: the mere possession of Japanese ancestry.[20]

Along with melodramatic news presentations like the Timmons series, Hearst newspapers devoted extensive coverage to non-Japanese Americans' patriotic demonstrations and bolstered the implied heroism of these displays by their juxtaposition with melodramatic villainy. The "Buy a Bomber to Attack Japan" fund-raising drive began in Hearst pages and at nationwide events in January 1942 and continued at regular intervals through April. The campaign featured daily news coverage showcasing an "Honor Roll" of notable participants, and Hearst often spatially juxtaposed the heavily illustrated feature on the page with stories of alleged Japanese treachery, establishing a dramatic conflict of good and evil through the reader's experience of navigating the newspaper. For instance, the 11 January 1942 *San Francisco Examiner* pictured a "YOUNG PATRIOT" by the name of "Bill Johnson, 13, who sells *Examiners* in San Mateo." The Honor Roll reporter explained that young Bill "has pledged to Defend America and Help Buy a Bomber and will donate profits [from his newspaper sales] to swell plane fund." Johnson's smiling portrait (showing an unmistakably white face) floats above a diametrically opposed article titled "Japs Hiss President in Movie; Set Free," which tells of two Japanese American youths who allegedly acted up while viewing a war newsreel in Los Angeles. According to the Hearst writer, the two boys laughed and hissed when President Roosevelt appeared on the movie screen. The story ends with the shocking anecdote that fellow audience member "Mrs. Winifred Stephens said one of them spit in her face when she protested their actions." The purported fact that these Japanese American hooligans escaped unpunished served to further arouse the reader's patriotic outrage. Hearst's spotlighting of this unabashedly public performance of disloyalty was also juxtaposed with another call to home front heroism in the article "Display Your Patriotism by Flying Flag at Home!"[21] Such contrasts created a repetitive series of newspaper melodramas hinging on the simple dichotomy of good and evil in which Japanese Americans appeared to cast themselves as the villains. In actuality, of course, Hearst and his like-minded editorial staffs controlled which stories to cover, how to shape their coverage, and where to place them in relation to the other morally pointed news they printed.

But the melodramatic vilification of Japanese Americans extended well beyond the pages of wartime newspapers through the highly publicized staging of patriotic spectacles that explicitly excluded Americans of Japanese descent.

The Theatre Is on Fire: The Anti-Japanese Spectacle of "I Am an American Day"

In February 1942, a Hearst editorial cartoon pictured the American people on the home front as audience members in the front row of a theatre on fire and declared, "The Comedy Is Finished." [22] The insipid dialogue bubbles from Mr. and Mrs. America in the proscenium theatre's front row (they are seated next to the snoring "Congress" and "Brass Hats") make it clear that the editorial staff advocated that Americans snap out of this spectatorial attitude toward the theatre of war. The stage, after all, was on fire, with smoke spelling out Japanese victories in the Pacific "theater" and dead American soldiers in the wings. In place of the depoliticized "comedy" that characterized the prewar public sphere—which left Americans expecting "always a happy ending of course," as Mrs. America puts it—the media roused the public to the moral stakes of the wartime melodrama necessitated by the threat of Japanese treachery at home and abroad. In place of the passive audience arrangement characteristic of proscenium-based theatrical display, American home front politics cast the wartime public in a continuous production of performative citizenship that rendered *theatrum mundi* ("all the world's a stage") the permanent condition of guaranteeing national belonging. For Hearst especially, it was not enough for patriotic Americans to simply be loyal to the United States, nor simply to express their nationalist feelings in private; Hearst turned his media empire's city streets into theatrical venues for the mandatory display of patriotic demonstrations that purportedly ensured each citizen's secure position as "hero" in the melodrama. The melodramatic imperative surrounding the myth of performative citizenship was particularly apparent in the 17 May 1942 celebration of "I Am an American Day," a Hearst-initiated annual celebration that had recently been conferred state-approved status by President Roosevelt and was staged just as the military was completing the last waves of Japanese American evacuation from the West Coast. [23] The 1942 spectacles staged around the country envisioned a diverse national body cleansed of Japanese Americans.

Scholars have noted how other Asian ethnicities were pitted against Japanese Americans in the frenzy of wartime hysteria by racist propaganda such as the oft-reprinted 1942 *Life* magazine feature "How to Tell Your Friends from the Japs" (which graphically displayed the supposed physiognomic differences between the ally China and the enemy Japan) and by self-defensive gestures such as Asian Americans' wearing of "I Am Not Japanese" buttons. Until the 1943 Magnuson Act and the 1946 Filipino Naturalization Act, no Asian immigrants were able to acquire naturalized citizenship, but this racist technicality did not prevent their performance "as if" they were American citizens. In fact, the particularly passionate war efforts and well-publicized patriotic displays of Asian Americans whose nations of origin were under siege by the Japanese Empire (especially Chinese and Filipino Americans) were influential in the eventual passage of these acts.

But these inter-ethnic dynamics also need to be understood as codified acts in the overarching myth of performative citizenship that serves to obscure the ongoing functioning of visual standards that racialize non-white Americans according to biological determinism rather than performative constructionism. Diana Taylor claims that "the hegemonic 'nation' tends to suppress or appropriate diversity; otherness either disappears or becomes absorbed as sameness."[24] I Am an American Day spectacles appropriated the diversity of Asian American and other ethnic groups and *appeared* to absorb visible differences into sameness while *disappearing* Japanese Americans from the public sphere all together. The interplay between the spectacularly visible difference and the invisibility of a persecuted minority yielded these patriotic events the power to interpellate the public into the myth of performative citizenship. I Am an American Day particularly appropriated signs of American diversity and absorbed them into spectacular tableaus of sameness that purportedly personified U.S. foreign policy (as cosmopolitan) and idealized domestic race relations (as tolerant). Take, for instance, the following newspaper description of the San Francisco launch of the 1942 celebration: "They turned out by the thousands—the Popadopuluses and the Yee Gat Sings, the Svensens and the O'Hoolihans, the DeVencezis and the Novaks, the Sanchez', MacGregors, and the rest of the races. They turned out in the native costumes of the countries from which they originally sprung and surged up Market Street yesterday afternoon. Not as individual nationalities, but as Americans all. Thus was American Citizenship Week opened here, and it wasn't just a parade; it was an eye-filling, pulse-pounding, heart-warming tableau, too."[25]

Compelling belief in this myth was particularly important to dispel the uncomfortable resemblance between the constant cycle of patriotic pageantry at home and the hallmarks of fascist aesthetics in Europe. As noted in the introduction, Henry Giroux defines the fascist spectacle as "embodied in the theater of giganticism with its precisely scripted pageantry around 'the mass of groups of people' . . . art glorifying racial purity and uniformed, white men." [26] So instead of foregrounding racial purity, American wartime pageantry leveraged the performative citizenship myth, which appeared to incorporate racially diverse groups based on their patriotic demonstrativeness and downplayed notions of racial purity—even as they were influencing the simultaneous enactment of the internment policy. But such an appropriation of diversity always already excluded Japanese Americans, creating a patriotic spectacle in which "even the nations with which the United States is at war will be represented, because marchers from all Axis nations *except Japan* will take part." [27]

Hearst and his fellow media magnates by no means invented the notion of performative citizenship; in fact, the racialized minorities celebrated in his wartime pages were often members of the "yellow hordes" he had poisonously slandered for decades. But Hearst's sudden about-face in now celebrating the patriotic performances of these same ethnic groups demonstrates how compelling the concept of performative citizenship becomes amid the imperatives of an America at war; moreover, it easily aligned with Hearst's nationalist philosophy, exalting what his papers called "expression and show"—an investment in the idea that public displays dictated national identity, not some psychologized, invisible sense of innate loyalty. But denying Japanese Americans public opportunities to perform their national identity instead relegated them to the melodramatic realm, in which they were vilified by the biological determinism epitomized in expressions like West Coast Military Zone Commander General John DeWitt's infamously circular statement, "A Jap's a Jap." In fact, patriotic gestures like the numerous petitions and proclamations presented by Japanese Americans as Japan's militarism escalated in 1940 and 1941—including the 21 October 1940 assembly of all Issei and Nisei from Imperial Valley, California, on the steps of the El Centro courthouse to formally proclaim their loyalty to the United States—were reappropriated by anti-Japanese advocates as evidence of a suspicious over-eagerness toward display. They interpreted such attempts to partake of patriotic citizenship as a ruse to hide actual sabotage and espionage plans. [28]

By contrast, Chinese, Korean, and Filipino American performances of citizenship were framed as symbols of U.S. tolerance and cosmopolitanism, rendering Japanese American exclusion all the more meaningful. Lili Kim notes that Korean Americans far surpassed white Americans' displays of patriotism. Demonstrating "more initiative than simply giving money, Koreans also organized American Red Cross fundraisers and benefit shows, featuring Korean dances and performances. These shows drew both Korean and [white] American spectators." [29] Ethnic and mainstream newspapers devoted significant coverage to such events, including a March 1942 mass meeting at the Korean Presbyterian Church in Los Angeles, at which was announced the formation of a California Korean Reserves of the State Guard as part of Koreans' "proclamation of independence from Japan." At the performance of this proclamation, Chinese American movie star Anna May Wong presented the U.S. flag, and the head of the Korean Women's Patriotic League presented the Korean flag, symbolically uniting the two nations (and a pan-ethnic Asian America) in a "colorful Flag presentation . . . with 200 Koreans marching in review." [30] Later that month, the Pershing Square Victory House held a "special South Pacific program" dedicated to General Douglas MacArthur and staged to stimulate Buy a Bomber sales through "a series of native songs and dances" performed by the United Korean Committee in America. Korean American actor Phillip Ahn served as master of ceremonies, and "Korean baritone" Frank Lee sang; Hawaiian and Filipino dancers also performed. [31] The constant intermingling of traditional markers of performative citizenship—oaths of loyalty, flag ceremonies—with displays of Asian performing arts evidenced the continued American fascination with, and scrutinization of, Asians as naturally aesthetic and exotic.

Ironically, the primary patriotic organization instrumental in planning Los Angeles' 1942 I Am an American Day was the infamously nativist American Legion, a veterans' organization that was perhaps the most vocal non-governmental group that campaigned for Japanese American removal from the West Coast. [32] The Los Angeles parade lasted for thirty minutes at midday and extended for nearly a mile through downtown city streets. Most of the parade route followed Spring Street south, from the starting point of Main Street and Olympic Boulevard, to the endpoint: ceremonies at the Victory House, located on Olive Street and Sixth Street's Pershing Square (named after the famed World War I general). Thus, for much of the parade, participants marched through and observed the spectacle from the heart of Little Tokyo, the rapidly vacating neighborhood where most Los Angeles Japanese Americans lived and worked. The sweeping evacuation of the Japanese ethnic enclave became the silently stark backdrop for a downtown parade that consisted of the usual militarist mix of color guards, bands, drill teams, and marching units from the California State Guard. But the march through a ghost-town-like Little Tokyo also showcased immigrant Americans through the debut of an unprecedented Foreign Legion, "an entire company of men who came to this country from other nations." The Foreign Legion's inclusion would have appeared as a remarkably liberal and tolerant concession by the notoriously nativist American Legion organizing the spectacle. [33] At this time, Japanese Americans were the only "foreign" group disallowed, regardless of citizenship status, from military service. (The "4-C" designation, delivered upon them by the U.S. government after Pearl Harbor, rendered them all "enemy aliens.") Declared ineligible for service and unceremoniously dismissed from their military positions, Japanese Americans were alone in experiencing stigmatization based on their hereditary links to an Axis enemy. (By and large, German and Italian Americans escaped their heredity unscathed.) As a result, Japanese Americans were being forced to evacuate their ethnic enclave while a patriotic spectacle, which pointedly included all ethnicities but their own, was being gloriously staged on its theatricalized streets. So as Southlanders throughout the county watched spectacles that were to be imagined in the context of "millions of other Americans" similarly congregating "in cities, towns and hamlets from coast to coast to rededicate themselves to Americanism and Victory," the exile of Japanese Americans served as the very precondition for the theatrical space in which Los Angeles' I Am an American Day parade was staged.[34] Much as the unremarked ghost town wrought by the internment policy served as the backdrop for a patriotic parade in Little Tokyo, these and many other wartime spectacles obliterated Japanese Americans from the national imagination and, as the next section will argue, relegated them to another aesthetic/cognitive realm derived (to riff on Chow) from another debased popular art form: farce.

Spectacular Segregation and Enforced Farce

While other ethnicities were glorified in spectacles asserting the solemn performative power of patriotic demonstrations, the media spectacularized interned Japanese Americans in a very different register. Stories about Japanese Americans in concentration camps were printed on the same Hearst newspaper pages as the unserious escapism offered by frivolously sensational celebrity "news" items, thus creating the 1940s equivalent of featuring the internment on a celebrity gossip television program like *Entertainment Tonight.*

In part, Japanese Americans found themselves displayed next to Hollywood entertainers because the internees' first stops following forced evacuation were the U.S. military-run "assembly centers," which had been erected at former entertainment venues like the Santa Anita Race Track, the Tanforan Race Track, and the Los Angeles County Fair Grounds in Pomona, California. The reinvention of peacetime playgrounds as wartime concentration camps provided endless opportunities for journalists to trivialize the injustice being enacted against Japanese Americans. Not only did the celebrity coverage of a profound racial injustice conjure up a very Debordian condition of spectacle; it also framed these events as grotesquely playful. In *Homo Ludens,* Johan Huizinga defined the essence of play as distanced from reality and entirely voluntary and argued that playgrounds existed for all ages and in all cultures, sharing the condition of containing playful behavior in a space apart from "real" life. This liminal space is innocuously suspended within a frame of "only play." Although Huizinga argues that play is an essential human activity, he also notes that players and observers alike understand such behavior as naturally "infe-

Actress Flies to Her Army Sweetheart

JEAN AMES

Yesterday was a b-i-i-g day in the life of Private Paul Ellis, stationed at Albuquerque, N. M.

His screen actress sweetheart, pretty Jean Ames, flew from Hollywood to Albuquerque to help him celebrate a six-day furlough.

His family came from his home town, Amarillo, Tex., to meet Miss Ames and to participate in the celebration.

And before she left Hollywood, Miss Ames hinted it was just possible that there might be a wedding before Private Ellis' furlough ends.

TWO NEW JAP OUSTER POSTS TO OPEN TODAY

Other Registration Stations Planned Here Next Week to Evacuate Remaining Aliens

Two new evacuation registration stations in areas heavily populated by Japanese will be opened today.

They are at 839 South Central avenue, Los Angeles, and 16522 South Western avenue, Gardena.

In the meantime preparations were being made by the United States Employment Service and the Wartime Civil Control Administration to open other stations next week, preparatory to evacuation of the 10,000 remaining Japanese in the Los Angeles area.

On Sunday, a registration point will be established in Los Angeles' "Little Tokyo," already somewhat a ghost town and destined soon to have only vacant buildings and homes and the Japanese signs on theaters, restaurants, hotels and stores, as reminders of the evacuees.

From Los Angeles processing stations yesterday, under Army escort, more than 1000 Japanese were taken by bus and automobile to the Santa Anita assembly center.

Similar motorcades will go to Santa Anita today and tomorrow, bringing the population of the center to more than 10,000 alien and Nisei Japanese, many of whom soon will be sent to relocation projects far removed from strategic military zones.

For the first time in many years, there were no Japanese yesterday in Santa Barbara, Ventura or San Luis Obispo Counties. The entire Japanese populations of those counties had been sent to the assembly center at Tulare.

POUND ARRIVES HOME

OTTAWA, Ont., April 29.—(AP) —Admiral of the Fleet Sir Dudley Pound, first sea lord, has arrived safely in England after flying the Atlantic from Canada, the Royal Canadian Navy announced today.

In a juxtaposition typical of the wartime media, Japanese American evacuation news found itself placed alongside celebrity human-interest stories in the 30 April 1942 *Los Angeles Examiner.*

rior" to the "seriousness" of consequential events.[35] The Hearst press and other media outlets relegated the U.S. government's violent disenfranchisement of Japanese Americans to Huizinga's inferior, unserious realm of "only play," thus erasing the coercion and painful reality taking place in the assembly centers and internment camps.

Hearst's staff writers repeatedly framed internment stories using literary allusions that implied the distancing of Japanese Americans from the seriousness of home front reality. "On the same turf where in the past the bangtails raced for fancy purses at Tanforan," opened a *San Francisco Examiner* story published on I Am an American Day, "another kind of race was run the other day by a Japanese lad who is one of 7,500 Jap evacuees assembled at the San Bruno track." Reporter Frank Raymond called such Japanese American sportsmanship "a symptom of the healthy spirit at the [assembly] center" and further remarked of the internment at Tanforan Race Track that he "couldn't help but feel that 'The Lemon Drop Kid,' one of Damon Runyon's horse players, would have turned a shade more yellow if he could have seen a Japanese nurse preparing a formula for a Japanese baby at one of the $5 pari-mutuel ticket windows."[36] Former Hearst baseball columnist and fiction writer Damon Runyon, perhaps most famous for his short stories drawn from the world of Broadway and for giving Broadway the storyline that became the musical *Guys and Dolls,* created the eponymous character of the Lemon Drop Kid as one of his literary band of lovable gamblers in trouble. Inserting the wartime internees into the fictional world of the Lemon Drop Kid shifted the internment camp's tone from one of inherent injustice to one of constructed hijinks. Although Raymond's reference to the Kid's turning "a shade more yellow" (amid the Japanese American internees) ostensibly hinged on the character's lemon yellow nickname and yellow-bellied cowardice, it also allowed for an unabashedly racist pun on the "Yellow Peril." As a result, Raymond simultaneously trivialized the internment at Tanforan and reinforced the racialized stigma of Japanese Americans.

Likewise, a March 1942 *Los Angeles Examiner* article, "Santa Anita Will Hold ONE Race," unabashedly punned on the meaning of "race" as both contest and ethnic group. The story opened by exclaiming of the as yet unopened internment camp, "When the sun lifted shadows off the foothills near the sleeping town of Arcadia today . . . a scene never witnessed before in Southern California was ready to unfold!" The reporter then continued by comparing Santa Anita's anticipation of the arrival of Japanese Americans to a film set waiting for "Action!" or a stage waiting for the curtain to rise: "All set to spring to life at the west end of the mammoth auto park at beautiful Santa Anita racetrack was the beginning of a 1,400-building wartime reception center for Japanese evacuees."[37] Two weeks later, an article published in the same Hearst paper opened as follows:.

On the broad acres where the late "Lucky" Baldwin lived his fabulous life and raced his blooded steeds, before there were many Japanese in California, and where in recent years great crowds gathered to wager vast sums on modern thoroughbreds, a new drama will be enacted today.

Santa Anita Park, storied site of the Baldwin rancho and since 1934 America's most lavish race course, has become a reception center for Japanese compelled by the exigencies of war to evacuate their coastal homes and farms.[38]

Amid the witticisms and flippant cultural references to Santa Anita's fame, the political economy and material violence of this "new drama" got lost.

Japanese Americans were treated to an extraordinary amount of media attention during the first six months of World War II, but—unlike the honorific archive of celebrity human-interest stories that accompanied internment articles—the scrutiny imposed upon Issei and Nisei rendered their humanity invisible to fellow Americans.[39] Such masking was especially important because the evacuation's ideological underpinnings plainly resembled Nazi tactics against Jews and other persecuted minorities in Europe, even if the violence was of an entirely different scale. But placing the spectacular scrutinization of Japanese Americans alongside frivolous celebrity-style spectacularization served to repress what Caroline Chung Simpson describes as an "uncanny effect" that otherwise threatened wartime national identity: "The unprecedented modern American trauma of massive Japanese American relocation and internment so clearly threatened the ideal of the American nation that it created an undeniable uncanny effect by seeming to dissolve the difference between America as a symbol of democratic freedom and the tyranny of a police state represented by the Axis powers."[40]

So despite the proximity of camp coverage to fawning celebrity coverage on the pages of the nation's newspapers, the fascination lavished upon the camps actually shortcircuited the usual human-interest cycle of sympathy and humanization to produce instead an overarching sense of alienation from Japanese American suffering. Instead of showing—as celebrity human-interest journalism generally does—Japanese Americans as "just like you and me" behind their spectacular public images (or masks), the intense scrutiny of the American press purportedly revealed internees as impassive automatons who were alternately comic and strange but always unsympathetic.[41] The extraordinary amount of media attention devoted to this unsympathetic spectacularization of Japanese Americans produced what I would like to call a "spectacle-archive." As I have argued in the introduction, the other face that haunts the public myth of performative citizenship is a disavowed performativity of the gaze that racializes the other through visual reading practices that bear much greater resemblance to the traumatic operation of the spectacle than to the self-determined constructions usually associated with performative identity. Allan Sekula is certainly correct that the nineteenth-century honorific archive of celebrity portraits and its opposite, a repressive archive of criminal portraits, "shared the belief that the surface of the body . . . bore the outward signs of inner character." [42] But after studies by Freud and other developments in psychological thinking of the twentieth century, the difference in belief systems between these two archival registers became increasingly apparent, as one was attributed with personalization and depth and the other was deprived such attributions. Celebrities and other honored subjects of spectacularization were studied for sympathetic signs of their personalization and depth beneath the visible surface, whereas criminals and other denigrated subjects were suspected for their lack of depth and unstable personalities. The wartime spectacle-archive showing Japanese Americans smiling through evacuation and impassively bearing their internment constructed them as depersonalized subjects who lacked psychological complexity and were thus pure, depthless surfaces.

The media's spectacle-archive produced around Japanese Americans' makeshift prisons has been particularly traumatic for former internees. Internee testimony poignantly counters the frivolous spectacularization of camp life by attesting to the dehumanizing effect of being housed in horse stalls, where the only slightly faded smell of manure and hay provided a constant reminder that the internees were thought to deserve little better than animals. "Those stables just reeked," Ernest Uno remembers. "There was nothing you could do. The amount of lye they threw on it to clear the odor and stuff, it didn't help. It still reeked of urine and horse manure. It was so degrading for people to live in those conditions. It's almost as if you're not talking about the way Americans treated Americans." [43] In her memoir, *Desert Exile*, Yoshiko Uchida summed up the cruelly farcical accommodations at the Tanforan Assembly Center: "That these stalls should have been called 'apartments' was a euphemism so ludicrous it was comical." [44]

Instead of these material violations, the *Los Angeles Examiner* internment coverage insisted on how "gayly" Japanese Americans had settled into their wartime house arrests. "Free from curfew restrictions in a new temporary 'home town' of their own," one Hearst writer maintained, "1000 Japanese from the Los Angeles Harbor district last night settled down gayly to life in row on row of barracks at Santa Anita race track." The reporter also described the "merry round of visits" undertaken by the evacuees, who "put a bright face upon their evacuation." [45] This gay tone and emphasis on artifice—putting on a "bright face"—certainly sought to alleviate reader guilt about the evacuation, referring to the assembly center as a "swank $2,500,000 race establishment" and implying that Santa Anita was neither depraved nor deprived like a Nazi concentration camp. An *Examiner* staff editorial said as much a week later: "The Japanese were not robbed, nor frightened, nor bullied; they were not thrown into concentration camps; they were neither starved nor beaten[;] there was no third degree, nor incommunicado dungeon. This is the American way, the Christian attitude. Decidedly NOT the way of the Gestapo. We can be glad and proud that justice and fair play prevailed." [46] But the Hearst coverage also suggested that the atmosphere of the Japanese American camps was patently surreal and that Japanese Americans had created this frivolity and unreality through their very natures—through their tendencies to be aesthetic or artificial and "put a face" or mask over their true motives. As a result, these articles relegated (while seeming to elevate) the internment at Santa Anita to a form of entertainment, different only in degree from horse racing. As one reporter put it, "The scene at the brand new reception center, with its long rows of frame buildings still redolent of fresh paint and lumber, was a sharp contrast to the usual 'opening day' of famed Santa Anita, and *yet it was scarcely less gay.*" [47]

Hearst writers repeatedly scrutinized the emotional reactions of internees and smugly remarked upon an apparent lack thereof. According to one article, a Japanese American family of five submitted to imprisonment at Santa Anita without signs of emotion: "Smiling blandly, they presented themselves for inspection." In what had by now become a trope in the Hearst press, much was made of the notorious dearth of tears from Japanese Americans as they evacuated their West Coast homes, and the reporter's commentary indicted this family's "presented" smiles, the implication being that these were fake expressions.[48] In a style typical of celebrity red-carpet reportage, another reporter recounted the details of internees' attire upon their disembarcation from a train at Santa Anita. But such human-interest formulation quickly gave way to yet another indictment of internees' failure to display their private feelings: "In the contingent arriving at Santa Anita from San Francisco yesterday were members of some of the bay area's wealthiest Japanese families. Women wearing expensive furs and adorned with costly jewelry mingled with servants, laundrymen and fishermen. Several babes in arms were carried by their mothers. The scores of children laughed excitedly but their elders stepped from the train as they had boarded it—impassively." [49] The writer holds in effective tension both meanings of "impassive": lacking emotion and hiding true feelings behind a mask.

Several articles boasted entire pages of accompanying photographs in the "Pictorial Review" section of Hearst papers. Under yet another headline exploiting the pun on "race," the 4 April 1942 *Los Angeles Examiner* photo essay "Uncle Sam Settles a Race Problem" provided five vivid images of the evacuees arriving, being inspected, eating, and observing the grounds at Santa Anita. One photograph, for instance, captures the Akasaki family "admiring" the racetrack's life-sized monument to famed racehorse Seabiscuit. Likewise, the 8 April 1942 *Los Angeles Examiner* article titled "Life in 'Japanita'" offered a full page of photos exposing the private lives of evacuees at the racetrack. This photo essay's top image resembles a panorama shot from a Hollywood movie, as laundry picturesquely hangs from a clothesline strung between two rows of barracks and people wander, miniaturized, in the middle of the long shot. "For some it is a vacation, filled with recreational pursuits and splashed with gay exchanges of visits to neighboring barracks," the caption explains. Other images showcase more private moments and closer shots of the Japanese American residents of Santa Anita. One shows a mother, Mrs. C. Hora, taking a break from her own dinner to feed her infant son a bottle; another shows "sober-faced" Sansei children playing marbles. The unabashed fascination with the manner in which Japanese Americans presented themselves in the camps far eclipsed any concern or sympathy for the injustice being suffered by these internees.

Furthermore, the extreme scrutiny of private details that pervades these articles upholds the agreed-upon excesses of human-interest journalism and replicates that genre's trademark of downplaying truly newsworthy concerns such as political economy. In 1940, sociologist Helen MacGill Hughes described human-interest stories as recording "touching but completely unimportant" events that could not carry the burden of newsworthiness in any other type of article. "The forms vary," she explained, "but the fundamentals are the same: they are marginal to news, being true stories of personal vicissitudes told with the exhaustive detail peculiar to gossip." [50] In the case of the internment of Japanese Americans, the United States was undertaking a monumentally historic transgression of civil liberties, and yet such newsworthiness receded into the background of stories reciting instead the gossipy and exhaustive detail of, for instance, internment camp eating habits. The *Los Angeles Examiner* reprinted the following menu from the Santa Anita assembly center on 4 April 1942, publishing such peripheral details not once, but twice: "The noonday meal, served cafeteria style in a huge mess hall, is a sample of what the Japanese will receive thrice daily. It included creamed tuna, beet and onion salad, mashed potatoes, steamed carrots, bread and butter, apple pie and tea." [51] The Easter Day menu at Santa Anita received similar attention in an article that described the holiday meal from its corned beef hash, tea ("milk in individual bottles for children"), and dessert of butterscotch pudding to the after-dinner "stroll" some evacuees took around the camp grounds. [52]

Another diversionary aspect of internee life eclipsed consideration of the larger implications of the internment camps: the all-American social dances held by Nisei youngsters. An 11 April 1942 Hearst story, "Jap Jitterbugs Amaze Elders at Santa Anita," opened with characteristic jokiness: "Japanese jitterbugs are cutting the rug at the Santa Anita evacuation assembly center as the radio gives out with the kind of jive that sends the hep cats out of this world. . . . Being translated, this swing lingo means that the entertainment program for the 4300 alien and Nisei Japanese sent to Santa Anita to await assignment to inland points is under way, with a nightly dance provided for the internees."[53] In similar fashion, journalists publicized the idiosyncrasies of internee weddings that took place in the camps, and these were written up like high society events. An article headlined "Santa Anita Camp Couple Will Wed" is worth quoting in full:

> Something extra special is slated to take place shortly among the 17,000-odd Japanese quarter at the Santa Anita Assembly Center.
>
> It is a wedding.
>
> Climaxing a camp romance, a Japanese couple appeared at the County Clerk's office for a marriage license. They were: Akira Ohno, 25, cook, and Sumako Takunado, 21. They had been granted a two-hour pass from the center.[54]

Likewise, "Japs Wed at Manzanar: No Honeymoon until after the War" related the details of another ceremony, performed for two hundred evacuees "in the flower-decked Manzanar mess hall." The reporter even detailed the attire worn by the bride, Kimiko Wakamura, and her attendant.[55]

Day after day, Hearst's *Examiner* insisted that Japanese Americans were "taking the evacuation as a lark," treating their exclusion from the West Coast as unserious because of their automatic, "smiling" nature.[56] One need not look far to find volumes of internee testimony attesting to the fact that Japanese American exclusion bore little resemblance to a "lark" for those who experienced it. Former internee Yuri Tateishi testified of the financial devastation wrought by evacuation: "You hurt. You give up everything you worked for that far, and I think everybody was at the point of just having gotten out of the Depression and was just getting on his feet. And then all that happens! You have to throw everything away. You just feel you were betrayed." According to Fred Fujikawa, many Americans took advantage of the incredibly vulnerable situation ethnic Japanese found themselves in after Pearl Harbor, and did so in a particularly gendered fashion. "Right away," Fujikawa remembers, "all of these junk dealers came into town, and oh, it was terrible." He goes on: "These poor women whose husbands were rounded up by the FBI; they were all fairly young and they had small children and no one to help them, and they had to somehow make ready to leave [Terminal] island in forty-eight hours. And here come these junk dealers, these opportunists. This was in December, so a lot of the families had already bought their Christmas presents, like new phonographs or radios, refrigerators—and they had no men around the house. These guys would come in and offer ten or fifteen dollars and because they had to leave, they'd sell." [57]

In *Desert Exile,* Yoshiko Uchida recorded the personal violation the U.S. government enacted by depriving internees of any semblance of privacy—a painful experience much remarked upon in Japanese American oral histories. Uchida speaks for many others when she writes: "The lack of privacy in the latrines and showers was an embarrassing hardship especially for the older women, and many would take newspapers to hold over their faces or squares of cloth to tack up for their own private curtain. The army, obviously ill-equipped to build living quarters for women and children, had made no attempt to introduce even the most common of life's civilities into these camps for us." [58]

Yet none of these violations appear in "investigative journalism" pieces such as *Los Angeles Examiner* staff writer James Lee's 22–24 March 1942 three-part illustrated series, which originated on the paper's front page. Lee had been part of the first caravan that delivered those Japanese Americans (mostly Nisei) who had "volunteered" to help set up the Manzanar camp in advance of their communities' mass evacuation. [59] Despite being privy to such an intimate view of the depravations of internment, Lee instead skates on the surface of Manzanar daily life, offering readers a grotesquely aestheticized frame to ideologically manage the evacuation. Following a panoramic description of the "lilac haze" of the surrounding Sierra Nevada range's "mountain twilight," Lee interpreted the swift erection of Manzanar's barracks and other infrastructure as having "arisen as if by Hollywood magic." [60] Lee repeatedly asserts the "thrilling" experience of being interned at Manzanar and imagines Japanese Americans as happily "flittering" around the camp's grounds, admiring the awesome views provided by the nearby mountain range. [61] Throughout the series, Lee makes clear his paper's investment in seeing the evacuation as "only play" by positing the friendliness of the soldiers stationed at the assembly center, the "voluntary" involvement of the first wave of evacuees, and the picturesque quality of the grounds. Lee quotes at length an unnamed Maryknoll priest visiting Manzanar who proclaims, "This is America! See—everyone's going willingly. There aren't any guns, there aren't any bayonets. This is the difference between democracy and the regime of Hitler." [62] If "Hitler," "guns," "bayonets," and "police" stand for harsh reality and the violence imposed on Jews in Germany and elsewhere in Europe, then "America" and "democracy" stand for the opposite: grinning and willing evacuees mark the events at Manzanar as harmless play, a spectacle outside of history and political economy in which impassive Japanese Americans perform.

Describing the first evacuees departing from their Owens Valley homes in the series' inaugural article, Lee writes, "There were no tears. Instead, there was laughter, and gay farewells." Under the subheading "Holiday Spirit Marks Start of Historic Movement," the *Examiner* printed a photograph of Lillian Ito, Miyo Kikuchi, and Richard Nishimura, all bespectacled, leaning out of a train window, and enthusiastically waving. The photo's caption classifies this as "Philosophic acceptance of Uncle Sam's edict." Lee remarks that internees carry on "without show of discontent," noting the supposed good spirits circulating within the play frame and reinforcing the sense of playacting by oblique reference to these Nisei's calculation to show or not show.[63]

Another news story, "Japs' Departure Like Excursion: 500 Off for Manzanar with No Tears, No Apparent Regret," referred in its very headline to the internment as a playful "excursion" and to the internees as remarkably impassive. "Except for the tall American soldiers," the reporter declared of the evacuation for Manzanar, "it might have been a scene on Shunki-Korei-Sai, the day of the Japanese spring festival, at the great Shimbashi railway station in Tokyo." Further down, the writer reasserts internees' lack of emotion, suspecting Japanese Americans of hiding their true feelings in a manner inconsistent with the imperatives of patriotic demonstration or the expectations of human-interest journalism: "If the Japanese who were sent on their way to Manzanar yesterday felt any deep regret at being severed from their homes and churches and businesses and jobs and schools here, *they did not show it.* . . . On the hundreds of bland, yellow faces were polite smiles, a beaming willingness to act exactly as directed by the military police who bustled helpfully about, relieving 120-pound Japanese of 200-pound bedding-and-baggage rolls. There was even a tinge of romance."[64]

As people of Japanese descent were absented from patriotic pageantry as the obscene (literally, "off-stage") exception to the promise of performative citizenship, spectacularizing news coverage relegated them to a surreal space apart from wartime America's idealized diversity. Whether framed in their representational exclusion as melodramatic villains, impassive aesthetes, or players in a racial farce, in the distorting glare of the mass media, which were determined to downplay the injustice of the government's internment policy, Japanese Americans found themselves denied the performative power to define their national identities.

CHAPTER 4

"Manzanar, the Eyes of the World Are upon You"

Internee Performance and Archival Ambivalence

> The Japanese people are known for their stoicism, and their characteristic of hiding their suffering or sadness with a smile or an emotionless face. It was disconcerting for the photographer [internee Toyo Miyatake] to make an appointment with a family in their barracks and find it neat and clean, and the family waiting in their Sunday best. We hope you will keep this in mind as you look at these photographs. Will we ever know the full story of this monumental tragedy in American history?
>
> —Sue Kunitomi Embrey, former internee at
> Manzanar Relocation Center [1]

Applause, distant but ongoing, is the first sound that greets today's visitors to the Interpretive Center at Manzanar National Park in Inyo County, California. In National Park Service (NPS) lingo, the operation of such interpretive centers facilitates "the process of helping each park visitor find an opportunity to personally connect with a place." [2] On the same grounds where the U.S. government interned Japanese Americans behind barbed wire manned by eight machine-gun-equipped guard towers during World War II, since 2004 the NPS has been welcoming tourists in the "adaptively restored" community auditorium, which was constructed by internees to serve as their theatre and sometimes gymnasium in 1944–1945. [3] These days, once visitors emerge from the air-conditioned Manzanar gift shop, which serves as welcome respite from California's arid Owens Valley (250 miles northeast of Los Angeles), a recorded loop of applause accosts their ears while numerous directional signs for different interpretive center "theaters"—as well as a prominent exhibition of the restored proscenium stage formerly used for internee performing arts—crowd the visual field otherwise reserved for displays of historical facts and figures. Other than the two guardhouses, past which tourists may drive in order to reenact the wartime experience of entering the concentration camp, the internee-constructed auditorium is the only original building that survives at Manzanar.[4] For the most part, only sagebrush interrupts the dust bowl landscape of what became a national historic site in 1992. In a real sense, then, a theatre is the only thing that remains of Japanese American internees' habitation at Manzanar, and, indeed, this structure helped Manzanar edge out the other nine former internment camp sites as the most viable grounds upon which to preserve and "interpret" the internment experience in the form of a national park.[5] The NPS's strategy of interpreting Manzanar through the spectatorial arrangements of an auditorium and through the camp's connections to the performing arts begs the question: what does such a spectacular lens tell us about the internment's place in U.S. history?

The recorded loop of applause emerges from the rear of the restored Manzanar community auditorium, where a display commemorating the 1988 passage of the Civil Liberties Act showcases a small television that endlessly replays archival footage of President Ronald Reagan signing the bill that provided redress and $20,000 in reparations to each surviving former internee. The "Great Communicator" Reagan's soft-spoken speech is not audible unless visitors stand a few feet from the exhibit, but every two and a half minutes or so the jubilant applause of former internees, Japanese American politicians, and other audience members present at the historic signing permeates most of the Manzanar museum, lasting for nearly a minute each time. Such a triumphal soundtrack should not surprise anyone familiar with what Robert Hayashi calls the NPS's "mission of retelling a progressive history." Many have been impressed by the U.S. government's willingness to memorialize a shameful, unconstitutional policy that flew in the face of all that America claims to stand for, but as Hayashi has noted, after redress was achieved in 1988, the Manzanar site "had lost much of its potentially controversial meaning. By 1991 [when redress checks had been distributed to surviving former internees] the nation had made amends to relocation survivors. That, too, was something that could be memorialized."[6] Moreover, the focal pointing of the former internees' theatre has allowed the NPS a proliferation of meanings in reference to the internees' "overcoming adversity"; most center on Japanese Americans' assimilative rituals and all-American recreational activities as performed at the community auditorium and elsewhere on the former camp's grounds. As the NPS puts it in "Remembering Manzanar," "Internees attempted to make the best of a bad situation. . . . They developed sports, music, dance, and other recreational programs; built gardens and ponds; and published a newspaper, the *Manzanar Free Press*."[7] In addition, NPS promotional materials, such as a postcard titled "Manzanar 2006 Calendar of Events," feature disturbingly triumphant images like an Ansel Adams photograph of "Florence Kuwata twirling batons, 1943," in which the wholesome internee majorette smiles down at the low-angle camera with the Sierras shining as her patriotic backdrop. By focusing on such performances of triumph, the NPS not only facilitates visitors' emotional connection by providing a shortcut around the unjust suffering and often insurmountable adversity imposed by the internment, but also perpetuates the theatricalizing discourse by framing Japanese American internees as inherently affected, natural-born actors. The poses created by these all-American performances of triumph render internees one-dimensionally available for public scrutiny, denying them psychological complexity while insidiously implying that the poses act merely as an assimilative mask.

As playwright-actor Cynthia Gates Fujikawa, whose late father was interned at Manzanar, incredulously put it when she spoke at the May 2005 "Manzanar Family Day" (hosted by the Los Angeles–based Asian American theatre company East West Players), a pronounced element of the Manzanar Interpretive Center suggests that "the question is still open" regarding the seriousness of the injustice that took place there during the war.[8] Manzanar National Park superintendent Frank Hays has expressed similar awareness of the ambivalence of this site and its commemorative politics. Hays has written that the NPS's "interpretive" mission was especially acute in this case because it had to immunize Manzanar from the frivolity of the surrounding area's recreational activities (this part of the Owens Valley is a popular vacation destination for Southern Californians on fishing, hiking, and skiing expeditions), as well as from the awesome natural wonders of the Sierra Nevada mountains (among them Mt. Whitney, the highest peak in the continental United States, which is nearby). While such recreational activities and spectacular sights draw tourists to the region, Hays asserts that such attention can detract from the historic site's integrity: "Some visitors [to Manzanar] have mentioned that given its location near such beautiful mountains, the camp experience couldn't have been so bad. For these visitors, the camp seems more like a summer camp in the mountains than an important site in the national history of the struggle for civil rights."[9]

The Ambivalence of "Manzanar Relocation Center"

Hays and others at the NPS seem to overlook the fact that well before the area became such a popular vacation destination, during World War II, when "the camp" was populated by more than ten thousand Japanese American inmates, recreational activities and aesthetic wonders had already threatened to overshadow and otherwise distort the injustice taking place at Manzanar. When the

U.S. government announced its plans to construct the Manzanar Relocation Center in early 1942, the people of the surrounding Owens Valley towns, in the words of one resident, "weren't just too sure what was the government's actual feeling in regard to this. We didn't know whether it was going to be a concentration camp, whether it was going to be a holiday on ice or what it was going to be." [10] Government propaganda and mass media accounts understandably advocated the "holiday on ice" interpretation of this ambivalence. Take, for instance, an April 1942 *San Francisco News* article, "Manzanar Nice Place—It Better Than Hollywood," in which United Press staff correspondent Harry Ferguson provided wartime readers "the first close-up report from a newspaperman who has visited one of the Japanese concentration centers in California." After painstakingly depicting the pleasant surprise that Manzanar presented for Japanese American internees who expected "a Nazi-style concentration camp," Ferguson goes on to profile Issei Emon Tatsui, whose words were culled as the headline for the article. According to Ferguson, Tatsui "was brought here from Los Angeles, looked around the camp a few days ago and decided to write a letter to his former employer, Murphy McHenry, Hollywood motion picture executive." Ferguson quotes from this letter, in which Tatsui wrote to his white correspondent, "I like to tell you about this camp. Nice place to live. It better than Hollywood. Snow on mountains. Fresh air. Snow is bright. Every day is 80 to 85. . . . Good ball ground. Baseball field. Swimming pool. School building. Danceroom is about start building then movie is next." [11] This article is remarkable for both its forced cheerfulness about the historic events taking place at Manzanar and its farcical implication that Manzanar is "Better Than Hollywood" because it rivals the motion picture capital of the world through its array of recreational and entertainment options, ranging from baseball and dancing to mountain viewing. Recently Japanese American National Museum (JANM) curator Karen Ishizuka explained such arrays of internment recreation as internees' "acceptance" of an unjust situation, and she thus interprets them as a form of "spiritual resistance": "When physically confined, you rely on your spirit. This spiritual stamina, in their words, was 'to make the best of things.'" Ishizuka goes on to define an internment-specific meaning for the Japanese American saying *shikata ga nai* (literally "nothing can be done"); she interprets it in the internment context as "smiling in the face of adversity, planting flowers in the desert, having a good time in a concentration camp." [12] Whether they pay tribute to "spiritual" resistance or not, such interpretations inevitably bolster the U.S. government's conscience-appeasing interpretation of Manzanar as the antithesis of a "Nazi-style concentration camp" that, in the end, "couldn't have been so bad." [13]

The ambivalent metonym of unnaturally cheerful, all-American performing arts has come to stand for the internment's place in official memory, effacing the question of whether other forms of resistance operated through other types of cultural performance in the internment camps, specifically in Manzanar.[14] The wartime rituals and shows performed at Manzanar were so prevalent that the internees built an auditorium for them that still stands in an unforgiving environment six decades later. Surely there is more to be said about these cultural performances than merely that they made "the best of a bad situation." In this chapter, I argue that many if not most of the cultural performances at Manzanar had sociopolitical implications that significantly undercut the hegemonic policy and the contemporary commemoration of these internee activities. The tendency to take these performances out of what were quite interculturally diverse festival contexts and turn them into triumphant metonyms for American assimilation has had the defeatist side effect of silencing Japanese American forms of resistance other than "acceptance."

The intercultural ambivalence of performing arts festivals at Manzanar countered the internment policy's ambivalence about "holiday on ice" concentration camps by resisting what Erica Harth has called the "moral vacuum" of the U.S. government's enforced "Americanization" of interned Japanese Americans. Harth is a white scholar who spent a year of her childhood at Manzanar while she attended school and her mother worked for the New Deal agency that administered the camps, the WRA. She is also one of the few writers on the internment to acknowledge that since the WRA's assimilationist policy of "educating for democracy in 1942 made no room for multiculturalism," internees took the initiative in offering extracurricular training in Japanese traditional arts, including tea ceremony and theatre. This unofficial course of instruction grew out of the WRA's single-minded course of Americanization, and it caused the practice of Japanese performing arts particularly to flourish among an internee population consisting of very few professional artists.[15]

Japanese traditional performing arts flourished in particular among the Issei as a corrective for WRA educational policy that often attempted to instill ethnic self-hatred in the second generation of Japanese American children interned at Manzanar and other camps. But the traces of these performances and their intercultural festive contexts can be found only in the cracks of official historical and community-based memorial accounts. That intercultural camp performance has fallen through the archive's cracks seems inconsistent with the institutionalization—indeed the archivization—of the performative remains of Manzanar in the form of the internee auditorium's "adaptive restoration" as an NPS interpretive center. Hermetically sealing Manzanar as a performance space that is legislated never to disappear would seem to suggest an official privileging of internee performing arts as the most compelling avenue for visitors to "personally connect" with the camp experience and to perpetuate a U.S. government agency's "retelling of a progressive history." But the NPS's selective institutionalization of Manzanar cultural performance only follows the path already well trod by the swollen archival record housed in the National Archives and other depositories across the United States. For the most part, the main performing arts that made their way into these archives at the end of the war and in the decades following were what *Farewell to Manzanar* authors Jeanne Wakatsuki Houston and James Houston characterized as "unmistakably American": Manzanar internees twirling batons and tap dancing, swaying to big band tunes and staging Christmas pageants, and even participating in beauty pageants that crowned "Miss Manzanar." [16] The selectivity of the archiving is evident not only in the administration's copious records but also in many Japanese Americans' own accounts, including the internee-run newspaper, the *Manzanar Free Press*.

The reason for this selectivity is not simply that internees censored themselves in order to comply with the government's policy of enforced assimilation—this sort of agency-robbing interpretation has been trotted out too many times either in support of the "model minority" stereotype of Japanese and other Asian Americans or else to blame the presumed passivity of internees for the birth of this stereotype in the first place.[17] On the contrary: internees entrusted to record camp performing arts did not fail to archive traditional Japanese cultural displays or their intercultural contexts in order to deny such performed resistance to enforced assimilation. Rather, the decision not to document such intercultural performances *fortified* the enactment of this resistance by allowing it to opt out of the vicious cycle of spectacularization imposed upon Japanese Americans during World War II.

Internees' Explication of the Spectacle-Archive

When Japanese troops bombed Pearl Harbor, U.S. public opinion considered this "sneak attack" to be in ideological opposition to Western codes of honor because Japan had reversed the textual hierarchy of war waging. International law and Western logocentrism dictated that war was to be declared through a performative signing and exchange of documents commencing a veritable battle of documents that cued bodily combat.[18] The Japanese Empire was seen as violating this textual ordering because it had acted first—attacking Pearl Harbor—and then declared war in writing. American newspaper headlines, such as the *New York Times'* front-page "TOKYO ACTS FIRST: Declaration Follows Air and Sea Attacks on U.S. and Britain," registered this shocking reversal. In response to official statements like U.S. secretary of state Cordell Hull's immediate characterization of the Japanese action as "infamously false and fraudulent," one senator announced to his colleagues, "The enemy is unmasked," and introduced editorials from newspapers across the nation describing the

Japanese attack as a premeditated act of surprise aggression that was disguised behind a mask of diplomacy and peace offerings that "were mere play acting" on the part of the Japanese government "to throw us off our guard."[19] In the House of Representatives, a strikingly similar discourse circulated, with the "false representations" and "deceptive dealing" of the Japanese government pitted against the "good faith," sincerity, and "grim, serious, and *undramatic* business" of the United States.[20]

Another editorial read on the floor of Congress declared the attack an "act of naked aggression" and reasoned, "Because Americans could not themselves take such action, it is difficult for them to conceive of the mind which instinctively acts without thought of law or honor."[21] As Diana Taylor has written of Western modernity, "The dominance of language and writing has come to stand for *meaning* itself. Live, embodied practices not based on linguistic or literary codes, we must assume, have no claims on meaning."[22] The unscripted militarism of the Japanese government (as represented by Japan's notorious aestheticism serving as disguise for its "treacherous" intentions) located those of Japanese descent beyond the pale of logocentric behavior and left Japanese American citizens and aliens alike characterized as unassimilable and inscrutable—and at the wrong end of the binary logic of patriotism deployed during wartime.[23] The resulting forced evacuation and internment of Japanese Americans near inland, rural communities that for the most part had never seen an "actual Jap" produced newly precarious race relations in which, as one senior U.S. government official in June 1942 remarked, in awed deference to the power of writing, "words alone can do immeasurable damage at this time."[24]

Such logic dictated that one of the U.S. government's first orders of business after it decided on the internment policy was to employ the services of public relations (PR) professionals to help "in planning the story and getting notices out through the Army to the Japanese people in the community." One of these PR professionals, Robert Brown, would become the "public information officer" at Manzanar. Watching "newspapermen by the droves" descend on the camp along with the first caravan of internees only bolstered Brown's faith in the published word as a way of "presenting Manzanar to the nation." "It's a publicity man's dream," he would say of Manzanar. "All the elements of drama, color, and human interest are here."[25] The notion of forging relationships among diverse groups of people and facilitating their intercultural encounters through written notices in their public spaces led Brown to propose an internee newspaper, rather farcically named the *Manzanar Free Press,* before most Japanese Americans had even been evacuated from their West Coast homes. Two of the first Japanese Americans to arrive at Manzanar in March 1942 were journalists by trade, Chiye Mori and Roy Takeno; together with several other Nisei, on 11 April 1942 the nascent internee staff launched

In the wake of Pearl Harbor, politicians and media pundits characterized the Japanese attack as the unmasking of uncivilized treachery that had been hidden by Japan's notorious aestheticism. The fact that Japan had "acted first"—attacking the United States without declaring war in writing beforehand—appeared in diametric opposition to Western logocentrism and civility, epitomized in the oft-printed photographs of President Roosevelt signing the U.S. declaration of war. Editorial cartoon from the 10 December 1941 *Chicago Tribune*.

the camp newspaper, which would eventually grow to a triweekly bulletin (mimeographed and printed editions). From the start, the newspaper's mission was twofold: to facilitate communication among the Japanese American constituents within the camp and to improve public relations with the outside world.[26] The Nisei on the newspaper staff wrote with balanced awareness of their divergent readerships, appealing both to their immigrant parents through a translated Japanese section and to the outside world through subscriptions and other PR distribution methods. The newspaper staff publicized and documented what the WRA would later admit were events "shaped . . . with the entertainment of the people of the Owens Valley in mind" in order to "better public relations." Although at the time camp administrators claimed that the purpose of allowing—indeed encouraging—their Japanese American prisoners to playact, dance, make music, and enact other performing arts was "to make life as pleasant as possible for the people of Manzanar," performing arts festivals open to the public, in which primarily white outsiders were invited to judge the "creative talents" of the internees, were clearly understood by all involved as publicity stunts, if not part of the legacy of ethnological museum displays constructed around colonized others since the nineteenth century.[27] Instead of "exotic" displays of an enemy culture, though, retrospective accounts by local Owens Valley residents in attendance suggest that these ethnographic exhibits showcased the spectacle of what many would have called, in offensive wartime parlance, "Japs who think they're American."[28]

Although the *Manzanar Free Press* certainly complied with such spectacles "shaped" for outside consumption, it is important to point out that these Japanese American journalists added another self-conscious aspect to the newspaper's mission, one that subtly indicted the PR mindset of their white overseers. Through theatrical metaphors, the *Free Press* staff explicated the spectacle-archive being made of the internment experience by the outside media as well as by the WRA's publicity agenda. One staff writer commented: "Manzanar, the eyes of the world are upon you. Though seemingly isolated, Manzanar is a cynosure of all eyes. We are principals in a social drama unparalleled in history. Already our scrap book runs into five huge volumes filled with thousands of clippings from every large and obscure publication in the country."[29]

A good deal of this "scrap book" was reprinted in the *Free Press,* under recurring headlines like "What the World Is Saying," thus creating a critical archive of Japanese Americans' spectacularization by the U.S. government, mass media, and laypeople. Sometimes the explication of this spectacle-archive reproduced the dominant terms constructed around Japanese American representation, such as one WRA photograph, taken on 2 April 1942, that documented an unnamed, smiling young female *Free Press* staffer who was, according to the official caption, "clipping stories on their migration at this War Relocation Authority center for evacuees of Japanese ancestry."[30]

The potentially complicit and compromising position created for internees by the public relations mission of the *Manzanar Free Press* can be illuminated by the convergence between Homi Bhabha's notion of colonial ambivalence and Diana Taylor's opposition of the operations of the archive and the repertoire. The ambivalence of the dominant discourse around the evacuation and internment lay in the repeated assertions that Japanese Americans were being treated to a "holiday on ice"—courtesy of "military necessity" and for their own safety—antithetical to "Nazi-style concentration camps" but not quite separable from these European counterparts. Bhabha writes that the "civilizing mission" of colonial discourse demands mimicry of the colonial subjects, but "the excess or slippage produced by the *ambivalence* of mimicry (almost the same, *but not quite*) does not merely 'rupture' the discourse, but becomes transformed into an uncertainty which fixes the colonial subject as a 'partial' presence . . . both 'incomplete' and 'virtual.'" [31] The portrayal of Manzanar internees as festive players that circulates at the Manzanar Interpretive Center grows

Although the *Manzanar Free Press* staff was charged with officially compiling news clippings that featured the internment camps, many internees intently read world news headlines about the latest war developments at the Manzanar newsstand. They were cognizant of the impact that the progress of the American war with Japan had on their lives as internees. Photograph by Francis Stewart for the War Relocation Authority.

out of the ambivalence of internment policy, whereby the government and mass media rendered Japanese Americans as spectacularly available for public scrutiny to underscore the benevolent nature of U.S. racial containment and the unnaturally performative disposition of the domestic enemy. The resultant spectacularization of Japanese Americans projected the benign transparency of the United States to an international audience and projected the seemingly inhuman stoicism of these "enemy aliens" (two-thirds of whom were American citizens) to a home front audience. In other words, internment discourse asserted, these were not Nazi-style concentration camps, and these inscrutable people actually enjoyed their abjection from mainstream America.[32] As Bhabha points out, the ambivalence of colonial thought can be assuaged (though never resolved) only through constant repetition asserting the correct interpretation of such uncertainty. The U.S. government and mass media's constant scrutiny of Japanese Americans—even and *especially* once they were interned—repeated the guiltlessness of U.S. policy and made the camps spectacularly available in a fashion absolutely opposed to Hitler's secrecy about the Nazi genocidal camps.

Caught in the ambivalence of such spectacularization, internees such as the Nisei staff of the *Manzanar Free Press* operated within a similarly ambivalent space between what Diana Taylor calls "the *archive* of supposedly enduring materials (i.e., texts, documents, buildings, bones) and the so-called ephemeral *repertoire* of embodied practice/knowledge (i.e., spoken language, dance, sports, ritual)."[33] In the oppressive web of complicity and resistance in which Manzanar internees found themselves entangled, such operations—of the archive, of the repertoire, and of spectacle itself—became likewise entangled. Through their newspaper, internees archived in meticulous detail their coercively choreographed, embodied repertoire (consisting of performances "smiling into the camera," as Cynthia Gates Fujikawa puts it) of mostly anti-Japanese government and media scrutinizers.[34] *Free Press* staffers used their newspaper (editions of which are now held in the U.S. National Archives) to explicate and thus resist the spectacle-archive imposed upon them by this glaringly ambivalent attention.[35]

As they resisted this spectacle-archive, *Free Press* staffers realized they needed to perform the images they instead wanted disseminated about them and their fellow internees to the outside world, so in their words they "shook hands and exchanged quips" with every journalist who visited camp and acted as tour guides for local residents curious to visit the camp during proposed weekly "open houses," "Reciprocity Days," and novelty fairs, thus casting themselves—in word and deed—as consummate performers.[36] In escorting and entertaining these white visitors, *Free Press* staffers performed gestures culled from an embodied repertoire compiled over nearly a decade of hosting the annual "Nisei Week" festival in Los Angeles' Little Tokyo, the ethnic enclave from which most Manzanar internees had been evacuated.[37] In 1934, Los Angeles Issei had initiated the idea of staging an annual performance festival that deployed the talents of their Nisei children as a marketing tool to celebrate the business achievements of Little Tokyo and entertain outsiders (particularly white businesspeople) with parades, beauty pageants, traditional Japanese folk dance, and fashion and talent shows. One of the highlights of Nisei Week was the crowning of the Nisei Queen, a Japanese American beauty selected at the beginning of the festival by a panel consisting of ethnic Japanese and Caucasian judges.[38] The Nisei Queen would lead processions of the Japanese American elite who ventured out to visit downtown Los Angeles businesses and extend formal invitations for non-Japanese to visit the ethnic enclave during Nisei Week. Manzanar internees, persuaded by the white administration and the *Free Press* staff, reenacted Nisei Week in a fragmented and irregular fashion, with rural Owens Valley neighbors standing in for cosmopolitan Los Angeles businesspeople and financial agency replaced by enforced interracial outreach.

While internees also drew from the Nisei Week repertoire to resist the spectacle-archive by somehow controlling the image they projected to the outside world, these touristic performances for outside audiences mostly presented what scholar Elena Tajima Creef called "a visual rhetoric of 'good cheer'" that helped appease the internment policy's ambivalence.[39] But these performances also betrayed the artificial arrangements of an internment camp pretending to be a tourist destination—what one audience member recognized as merely putting "a good face on their internment."[40] Still, such a "good face" insidiously endorsed the internment policy as internees played gracious hosts and hostesses to white neighbors who, for the most part, would not dream of returning the invitation.[41]

Manzanar's 1943 Fall Fair epitomizes the type of "shaped" camp events that have come to metonymically stand in for all camp performing arts, in both scholarly and popular accounts. Historian Lon Kurashige excludes the Fall Fair by name, and all other cultural performances staged at Manzanar by association, from the lineage he constructs in his *Japanese American Celebration and Conflict,* concluding that Manzanar performances held no political significance, demonstrating instead a desire to entertain white authorities that was a "faint imitation of the original [Nisei Week]."[42] However, even before Pearl Harbor, the intercultural operation of Nisei Week had clearly become a double bind, with Los Angeles mayor Fletcher Bowron visiting the 1941 Nisei Week opening ceremonies to deliver a speech in which he told Japanese Americans, with impossibly circular logic, "We are going to rely on you to show your loyalty, because we know you are loyal."[43] On the eve of internment, with hostilities mounting between Japan and the United States, Nisei Week had already been compromised by a coerced imperative that Japanese Americans, presumed innocent yet commanded to perform demonstrations proving lack of guilt, dance for their citizenship and freedom. The last pre-internment Nisei Week festival thus bore insidious traces from both faces of racial performativity in the United States.

Moreover, Kurashige rightly argues that in its transplantation from Los Angeles to Manzanar, the fragmented and dispersed Japanese American community fell prey to the often illegitimate leadership of the JACL, who infamously denied membership to Issei because they were not U.S. citizens, in callous disregard of the U.S. prohibition on naturalization for Issei and all other Asian immigrants. The opportunistic leadership of the JACL spread among "Manzanites" (as Manzanar internees came to be called) a reactionary brand of what Kurashige calls "mono-Americanism" and what Arthur Hansen and David Hacker call "superpatriotism," which patricidally dispensed with Japanese culture.[44] With all that being true, how did these "faint imitation[s]" staged at Manzanar also *intervene* in a sociopolitical arrangement in which Japanese elders were deprived of authority and a few aggressively opportunistic Nisei disenfranchised their emasculated Issei parents?[45]

A closer look at the range of cultural performances in the camps that departs somewhat from Kurashige's method reveals much more complex sociopolitical negotiations and hybrid identity construction, even in events "shaped" for an outside audience like the 1943 Fall Fair. As the *Manzanar Free Press* staff openly discussed in various editorials, they found it advisable to open the "first official Manzanar Fall Fair," held 18–19 September 1943, by performing as tour guides for Owens Valley residents who were curious to inspect the internment camp in their midst. *Free Press* staffers explained this self-exoticizing move as an attempt to "bring about a better understanding of our problems" and make the outsiders' visit to Manzanar "a memorable one."[46] But if we read between the lines of *Free Press* coverage and reconstruct this tour within the spatial experience of the original camp layout, its embodiment and choreography vividly emerge, illustrating how its performers invoked the carnivalesque so as to muddy the terms of internment policy. Internee tour guides employed the subversive potential of embodied performance to comment upon the irony of playing hosts in the coerced domestic arrangement of an internment camp and to cast white audience members themselves in the alienating if temporary role of inmates.

The arrival of white visitors physically reenacted the Japanese American internees' much publicized arrival at the camp more than a year before—only with three crucial staging differences. Curious visitors were first introduced to the internment camp by embodying the experience through which Japanese

Americans actually became internees, restaging the first traumatic moments of confinement as they arrived at Manzanar's two guardhouses. And while Owens Valley residents stood in for internees, the Japanese American staff members of the *Free Press* swapped their original role in this social drama for a more empowered (if complicit) position as journalists-cum-guides, scrutinizing and guiding the mass movement of people into Manzanar as "close to 400 outsiders" attended the Fall Fair.[47] This was also a rescripting of recent history. The initial military-escorted caravans of Japanese Americans to arrive at Manzanar in March 1942 were accompanied by journalists: along with the first three busloads that arrived on 21 March came a writer from the notoriously anti-Japanese *Los Angeles Examiner*, and he was followed on 23 March by a caravan of 140 automobiles carrying "about twenty newsmen and newsreel people."[48] The first Manzanites (almost entirely Nisei) were thus intimately displayed for massive media scrutiny as they passed the two guardhouses that marked the breach between their former lives as free citizens and their indeterminate future as incarcerated threats to national security. In the tour reenactment more than a year later, non-Japanese from the Owens Valley were the ones who rode past military inspection and guard towers in a caravan of "car after car," scrutinized in their uncomfortable passage by journalists who were interned Nisei.[49] This role reversal was made possible by the proximity of the *Free Press* office to the camp entrance in the spatial arrangement of Manzanar; the internee newspaper staff worked just steps away from the guards, in the closest structure to the entrance.

Owens Valley residents vividly remember visiting Manzanar for the 1943 Fall Fair (or "Reciprocity Days" and "novelty fairs," as these public festivals were variously called).[50] Katherine Krater's testimony is typical; when asked, "Did you walk in as a group or did you just come to the gate?" Krater answers, "Oh, we went in individually, but you had to be interviewed. . . . You couldn't get in without an interview. I don't remember whether they gave us some kind of admission card or what. [Her husband interjects:] 'They gave us that after we got down in there, but they interviewed us pretty carefully.' But anyway, you couldn't just walk in, you had to pass both those guardhouses before you could get in." Through this entrance, internees' embodiments of their roles as tour guides carnivalized their first introduction to the camp, inverting the subject and object of the gaze.[51] In spring 1942, the U.S. military forced Japanese Americans to don identification tags, imprinted with dehumanizing government identification numbers, from the very first moment of their evacuation until their confinement in a camp. In the carnivalesque revision performed for the September 1943 fair, Nisei again wore dehumanizing identification tags, this time bearing not ID numbers but "the word 'Guide'" to distinguish them as the internees who had volunteered to shepherd the outsiders through Manzanar. Once the visitors were through the gates, however, all surviving accounts insist that they were treated with the utmost in hospitality and ingratiating displays. The "close to 400 outsiders" in this caravan later judged exhibits prepared especially for the visitors' discriminating attention and showcasing the "creative talents" and agricultural feats of the internees. Approximately 150 of them took part in a two-and-a-half-hour tour led by *Free Press* staffers; hundreds of the visitors also ate dinner at the camp that weekend and were entertained in the evening on one of the camp's outdoor stages by internees performing *odori,* European concert music, swing band numbers, Hawaiian tunes, and a beauty pageant culminating in the crowning of Nisei Diane Tani as "Miss Manzanar." The pageant was emceed and judged by non-Japanese Owens Valley residents. Just in time for the Fall Fair, artist-internee Masasuke Henry Kumano had completed his Japonisme painting, "Cherry Blossoms of Springtime," as the backdrop of the outdoor stage where these performances occurred.[52] Adapted from the prewar repertoire of Nisei Week festivities, the crowd-pleasing mix of U.S.-grown Orientalia and assimilated talent contests that sought outsider approval were also archived in meticulous detail through a half dozen articles published in the camp newspaper. The fair's part in the spectacle-archive loudly broadcasts internees' spectacularization by white observers, but the internee performances themselves (in their admittedly reconstructed and partial form as presented here) quietly speak of the carnivalizing performance choices made by the Nisei tour guides in their furtive agency *as* scrutinized performers.

Whereas the performance festivals "shaped" by Manzanar publicists were intercultural only insofar as they established contact between Japanese American internees and their white neighbors from the outside through a rigid spectacle-spectator relationship—albeit shot through with instances of surreptitiously seized agency—internee festivals that included traditional Japanese performing arts such as Kabuki and Noh theatre were radically intercultural, bringing together immigrant Issei and assimilated Nisei, Japanese speakers and English speakers, "Asian" and "American" acts, either on the same bill or in flexible performer-audience relationships that were decidedly for internee eyes only. I will now turn to four historical examples of such cultural performance that illustrate these different intercultural approaches and show how internees' repertoires were deployed differently for the spectacle-archive than for events closed to the (potentially) hostile public. These examples will be the September 1942 Hospital Open House; the Fourth of July 1943 Manzanar Carnival; the May 1944 Evening for Issei; and the June 1944 inaugural performance, at the new Manzanar community auditorium, of WRA teacher Louis Frizzell's operetta, *Loud and Clear.*

Internee Resistance and Social Change through the Prism of Manzanar Performance

The complex intergenerational, intercultural, and interracial political negotiations that Kurashige finds through a synchronic and diachronic approach to six decades of Nisei Week celebrations also can be uncovered in Manzanar cultural performances by correlating these internee festivals to the dynamic camp politics of their particular historical moments between Manzanar's 1942 opening and its 1945 closure. The most overt political conflict at Manzanar was the 6 December 1942 camp "riot," precipitated by a mysterious and seemingly deliberate food shortage that one group of internees accused another of perpetrating. The bitter exchange of accusations escalated until the WRA jailed one internee for beating another, which led to a widening and violent rift between collaborators and internees who refused to cooperate with the WRA. This rift generally cracked along generational lines, with assimilationist Nisei accused of being WRA "stooges" and Japan-educated Nisei (called Kibei; they represented more than six hundred of Manzanar's internees) seen as undermining the WRA's policy of disenfranchising the Issei elders (who were considered obstacles to the ethnic group's overall Americanization). The uprising had a deadly outcome, killing two protestors and wounding at least ten others. Significantly, Kurashige, while deliberately ignoring internee cultural performances, examines the Manzanar riot. But by seriously examining two internee performance festivals that bookend the infamous riot—the September 1942 Hospital Open House and the Fourth of July 1943 Manzanar Carnival—we can detect the political pulse before and after this camp collapse. In other words, these events were not merely "faint imitation[s] of the original" prewar performance negotiations (as Kurashige would have it) but were themselves performative indicators of the dynamic political climate at Manzanar, as well as performative events that in turn influenced the intercultural, intergenerational relations governing everyday camp life. These cultural performances showcased and also shaped camp politics.

In the late summer and fall of 1942, sociopolitical conditions at Manzanar were ripening for the violence that would explode that December. The growing rift between the assimilationist and cultural nationalist factions of internees threatened to absorb even neutral bystanders into partisanship, in part because the division found infectious expression through participatory displays of culture that performatively communicated each participant's place in the debate. While Nisei sympathetic to the WRA's assimilationist policy enthusiastically participated in festive U.S. war bond drives and other patriotic displays of Americanization, internees who passionately disagreed with the camp administration broadcast a deepening affinity for their Japanese roots, as their growing commitment to ethnic retention in opposition to enforced Americanization, by unabashedly performing Japanese cultural practices such as *odori* and singing pro-Japan anthems.[53]

So at this early point of settling into camp life the debates over cultural practices and political ideologies became increasingly intertwined. As a result, the September 1942 "gala two-day Hospital Open House Celebration," occasioned by the opening of a 250-bed hospital at Manzanar, ostensibly segregated the two nights of live entertainment along these same lines so as to minimize conflict. Both evenings' programs were performed on an outdoor stage facing the new hospital, with Saturday's offerings devoted to Japanese-language performances and Sunday's to English-language performances. But the scheduling of the twenty-seven entertainment numbers rendered the division between assimilationist displays and cultural nationalism quite permeable. On Saturday night's "Japanese" program, *odori* numbers intermingled with Kabuki theatre scenes and *utai* (Noh-theatre chanting) as well as with tap-dance numbers, a hypnotism display, and even a Nisei interpretation of a Mexican dance. Likewise, the Sunday program included the obligatory speeches by WRA officials congratulating the internees on the hospital construction, along with typical demonstrations of American youth culture, such as band performances (including "The Star-Spangled Banner"), internee magic tricks, popular music vocal solos, and more tap dancing. But again, these presumed performances of assimilation were often preceded or followed by Japanese cultural performances such as *Nihon buyo* (classical Japanese dancing), *shakuhachi* (Japanese flute) music, and more *odori*.[54] This festival was certainly performed with full awareness of the white administrators in the audience, but the most salient strategy for selection and scheduling seemed to be the presentation of a public rhetoric to appease both factions of the divided camp population through ostensibly segregated programs while simultaneously satisfying the lived complexity of the majority caught in the middle by intermingling "Japanese" and "American" performances.[55] The sociopolitical rift required tact in the official publicity presented in the spectacle-archive of the *Free Press* program, but the repertoire performed both nights had the more prosaic imperative of entertaining all the internee constituents involved with a camp institution as universally vital as an adequate hospital.

Nine months later, after the national publicity about the December 1942 "Jap uprising" at Manzanar had died down, the most polarizing figureheads from both factions had been ousted from the camp. The WRA removed the most alienating superpatriots of the JACL for their own safety after the protesters had threatened these individuals' lives. Likewise, fifteen Japanese Americans accused of being the most incendiary protesters were arrested and transferred to high-security isolation camps.[56] In the dust that settled after this chaos, Manzanar internees produced a Fourth of July (1943) carnival with a two-day entertainment program that was thoroughly intercultural and intergenerational, this time for the ostensible reasons of competing with other Japanese American camps' carnival offerings as well as helping internees "forget their cares." But the safety valve explanation cheerfully proffered in the *Free Press* spectacle-archive camouflages the complex sociopolitical negotiations taking place through the carnival's performances. Nowhere in the publicity for this "gay festival"—billed as "breaking the monotony of camp life"—do the Nisei writers frame the carnival as an "Independence Day" event, despite the fact that it took place July 4–5; this missed opportunity to "show your loyalty" (in Los Angeles Mayor Bowron's words, as noted above) points to a delicate negotiation among the internees coexisting after the most recent rounds of chaos.[57]

According to the *Manzanar Free Press,* the July 1943 carnival's mixed programs of Japanese-language skits and *odori* along with the camp's "Hill-Billy Band" (white folk culture of the American South), mandolin performances, and the high school chorus were so thoroughly entertaining and accessible that "the isseis enjoyed it as much as we niseis did."[58] This despite the fact that the carnival was offered through the WRA's Community Activities Department, with proposed performances and other carnival attractions vetted by an "entertainment committee" consisting of two white female administrators and three internees. In fact, the entertainment committee established the carnival's petition process in an official, bureaucratic fashion, insisting that only presenters "affiliated" with approved organizations, such as the YMCA and *Free Press,* would be considered and then allowed to "register" for inclusion in the program.[59] Such bureaucratic protocol presented little obstacle for Japanese cultural performances such as "Y. Tanaka's Japanese skits and dances" because even activities that the WRA would consider anti-assimilationist (and thus hostile to its administration) had achieved the trappings of club status by this point in Manzanar's sociopolitical existence.[60] This was in part because the Manzanar administration's single-minded attention to public relations and its belief that such intercultural encounters were primarily driven by the printed word and by literate presentations (such as speeches) meant that as long as performances were embodied only in the repertoire, they were not patrolled. This blind spot allowed internees a certain degree of freedom to construct private performances for internee (and administration) eyes only—many of which undercut the assimilationist message the WRA attempted to publicize about internment life. At the same time, the crackdown following the 1942 riot inevitably instilled a degree of self-policing among the internees who remained at Manzanar, newly aware now of the systematic surveillance that had made possible the WRA's speedy removal of the radical political elements and "disloyals" among them. In other words, Japanese cultural practitioners participating in the July 1943 carnival likely would have downplayed the cultural nationalism of their practices to avoid attracting the potentially punitive surveillance of the administration.

Planned since the 1920s and constantly implemented since Japan had attacked Pearl Harbor, government offensives like the FBI's raids on influential Issei—labeled dangerous because they led their communities in Buddhist ceremonies, judo training, and other Japanese cultural practices—had criminalized Japanese ancestral culture to the extent that Japanese Americans anticipating FBI inspections intuited that they must destroy objects connected to the Japanese cultural repertoire such as kimonos, martial arts paraphernalia, and traditional music recordings in order to avoid being associated with enemy practices. Mass media constructions such as editorial cartoons broadcast this assumptive correlation between Japanese cultural practices and anti-American treachery to the American public. But the U.S. government's anti-Japanese campaign of "cultural extermination," as historian Bob Kumamoto characterized it, did not extend to Manzanar, where performances of Japanese traditional culture could be staged right under the administration's logocentric nose.[61] Whereas the Japanese-language section of the *Free Press* had to be translated prior to

Internee photographer Jack Iwata took this portrait of Nisei teenagers from Eddie Tanaka's Sierra Stars performing "all-American" music at Manzanar. Gift of Jack and Peggy Iwata, Japanese American National Museum (98.102.138).

publication each week, Japanese-language performances were presented in all their foreignness with the tacit blessing of white administrators. This meant that these practices found fertile breeding ground to grow from surreptitious activities to events legitimated by club status in Manzanar and at many of the other Japanese American camps.[62] However, the extent to which Manzanites took advantage of the WRA's blind spots remained nervously contingent upon the fluctuations of political tensions and social chaos during the internment.

The internees' institutionalization of cultural difference within the Fourth of July carnival's tight supervision, then, probably did not openly resist the WRA's limited tolerance of Japanese displays, which were deemed allowable only insofar as they were an unpublicized and useful safety valve for the administration's policy of Americanization. Nonetheless, the organizational status extended to "Japanesey" and American activities alike signaled that cultural differences were being respected in a cooperative rather than combative relationship in the wake of the riot. Without irony, carnival framers planned for a performance of contemporary Japanese folk dancing (ondo) to coexist on a program with its American counterpart, performed by the Manzanar Folk Dancing Club. Likewise, in the same breath the *Free Press* boasted that "both string and wax Japanese concerts" were offered at the carnival, a significant dichotomy because string music would likely be performed by the Nisei Concert and Swing Orchestra while "wax Japanese" music referred to cylinder recordings from turn-of-the-century Japan.[63] The July 1943 carnival paid no heed to the mono-Americanist patriotic imperatives of the U.S. Independence Day, choosing instead to turn this official national holiday over to the legitimization of both sides of us-them dichotomies and to the institutionalization of harmonious intercultural displays.

Despite such harmonious coexistence through cultural performance, the internee performers still adhered to their WRA-expected roles in the Fourth of July carnival: Nisei musicians played Southern "hillbilly" tunes while Issei performed Japanese skits and listened to Japanese music recordings. Nisei girls and young women likely danced *odori*, but this was not a radical casting choice because they had been the medium for transmitting this Japanese performing art in public ever since Nisei Week had debuted in 1934. Such expected role assignments radically shifted in May 1944, when Project Director Ralph Merritt green-lighted the production of an "Evening for Issei" (also called the "Consultation Night for Issei") that disrupted the predictability of internee casting choices along generational lines. A cast of "nisei volunteers" performed the Evening for Issei talent show to honor the "half a century of hardship" endured by the first generation of Japanese immigrants to the United States, culminating in the violent wrenching of the social positions and material wealth they had struggled to achieve as they were "called enemy aliens and evacuated to centers." As the Nisei framers of the event also put it, "Finally, [the Issei's] posses-sions became only their sons and daughters." For this reason, "Nobody except the Nisei can comfort these Issei, and this is a duty that we must carry out from our heart." In order to comfort their disenfranchised parents, the Nisei perform-ers of the Evening for Issei presented the "gift" of Japanese cultural practices through their own bodies. The only Nisei allowed at the event were the per-formers; the audience consisted entirely of Issei. For this reason and to sidestep the spectacle-archive of the *Free Press* English-language section, the notices advertising and commemorating the Evening for Issei were published only in the Japanese-language section of the newspaper. Therein Nisei Takashi Kubota wrote that he hoped this "excellent talent shown by the nisei" would help "the issei and nisei . . . get together and go through center life in peace." [64]

The diachronic trajectory of Manzanar cultural performance suggests a progressive history, though not the one of American exceptionalism and "over-coming adversity" that the U.S. government wants to tell about the intern-ment experience. Rather, the progress from the September 1942 Hospital Open House through the 6 December 1942 "riot" and the (non–)Fourth of July 1943 Carnival (which was closely followed by the fall 1943 "surgical separation" of those deemed disloyal and sent to Tule Lake Segregation Center) culminated in significant performance festivals in 1944 that deconstructed the assumptive binary of assimilation versus pro-Japan loyalty.[65] Through the Evening for Issei and other performances that year, the distinctiveness of Japanese culture and American culture was respected, but these cultural practices were de-essen-tialized.[66] By criminalizing Japanese culture in the roundups following Pearl Harbor and then tolerating Japanese displays at Manzanar only because they evaded the administration's logocentric public relations mindset, the U.S. gov-ernment had attempted to establish the essentialist argument that performing Japanese culture was a telltale sign of a Japanese heart—therefore a duty to enact disloyalty against America. But the "duty that we must carry out from our heart," the Nisei performers of the Evening for Issei proclaimed, did not bear any relation to national loyalty, despite their embodiment of Japanese cul-ture for an exclusively Japanese-speaking audience. The event, and its tacit approval by Manzanar's WRA director, asserted that Nisei could showcase Japanese performing arts for a discerning Issei audience as a way of thanking their unassimilated elders for establishing the precondition of their own (albeit precarious) U.S. citizenship, thus de-essentializing Japanese culture as well as emphasizing the constructedness of national loyalty.

Moreover, the increasingly mixed audience composition at Manzanar per-formance festivals—Issei and Nisei together enjoying mixed bills of Kabuki and big band music, *odori* and tap dancing—further undermined the admin-istration's privileging of American culture above Japanese culture in a high-low cultural divide that was predicated on a logic equating spectatorship and national incorporation. The internees' resistance of this binary was especially apparent in the Nisei high school drama production that inaugurated the internee-constructed auditorium in June 1944. After years of discussion and months of construction by internee builders, the WRA invited public fanfare as a means of inaugurating the completed auditorium in June 1944. Manzanar High School drama and music teacher Louis Frizzell (a white man whom many former Manzanar internees remember fondly) had composed an operetta called *Loud and Clear* before the war, when he was a student at UCLA. Since the auditorium was to provide much needed infrastructure for Frizzell and the students of Manzanar High School, he dusted off the unproduced *Loud and Clear* for a dedicatory performance. The operetta was about fictional college students struggling to save a campus faced with a funding crisis; a chorus of thirty-six internee singers, backed by the Manzanar orchestra, would sing of young love and adolescent yearning. *Loud and Clear* was to premiere after a speech by Merritt. "The camp administration had advertised [the event] far and wide," such that it brought in "people from all over the Owens Valley." More outsiders turned out than expected, sparking a social drama among the internee performers and the administration before the house opened. The student cast and musicians had reserved a section of the community auditorium for their Issei parents, but "faced with an influx of valley residents," camp administrators prioritized public relations over internee relations by announcing that the white visitors would take the seats promised to Issei spectators.[67]

Learning of their parents' displacement, the performers of *Loud and Clear* "staged an instant strike," saying "they were not going to perform unless those seats were used for their parents." Frizzell negotiated with the student strikers and convinced them to put on a good face and perform for the sake of public relations and as a personal favor to him and his hard work on the show, thereby ending a behind-the-scenes performance of resistance that never found its way into the *Free Press* account of the auditorium's inauguration.[68] The newspaper instead proffered this reticent remark on its front page: "The first activity in the Manzanar community auditorium was applauded enthusiastically by a *capacity crowd* last night."[69] After observing the media circuses created around the Japanese American "riots" staged at Manzanar in December 1942 and at other camps in 1943, internees knew that the students' performance of resistance might be twisted by the outside media and Owens Valley community members. Nevertheless, the *Loud and Clear* strike quietly communicated the students' opposition to the administration's patricidal spectacularization in the name of PR. The operetta controversy also demonstrated the resistance of young Nisei to the WRA's ideological directive mandating the audience composition for such performing arts.

Closing the Curtain on Manzanar

Six months after the inauguration of the auditorium, in the wake of military losses throughout the Pacific theatre and particularly in the Philippines, the inevitability of Japan's defeat had become clear. After the Supreme Court unanimously sided with Nisei plaintiff Mitsuye Endo on 18 December 1944, agreeing that the internment policy was unconstitutionally detaining loyal citizens, the WRA announced the camps' imminent closures, and the U.S. Army's Western Defense Command finally reopened the Pacific Coast for Japanese Americans to return to their prewar homes, and some began to do so. Not only had two Manzanar Nisei recently moved back to Los Angeles (both to attend university) but the camp was also abuzz with news that the apparent promise of performative citizenship would be restored as well. This hopeful news came in the form of a nationwide backlash against the Hood River, Oregon, branch of the American Legion, which had brazenly attempted the performative erasure of Japanese American U.S. military service by removing the names of sixteen Issei and Nisei veterans from its local memorial plaque. While the erasure of Japanese Americans from militaristic spectacles since the early months of 1942—even when such pageantry was enacted in their own neighborhoods—had provided the melodramatic agon that helped "patriots" bolster the myth of performative citizenship, by 1945 similar symbolic exclusion was deemed "inconsistent with the doctrines of democracy" and dangerous to "the preservation of our Constitution."[70] The *Manzanar Free Press* staff devoted itself to these 1945 developments, with a regular Saturday front-page feature tallying the number of Manzanites who had departed that week for "indefinite," "seasonal," and "short-term" leaves.[71]

While the vast majority of the WRA's assimilative efforts had been aimed at reforming Issei through the indirect influence of their Nisei children,[72] the imminent closure of Manzanar and most of the other internment camps necessitated a suddenly earnest cultural campaign to directly inculcate "American" values and customs in the presumably un-American Issei who had yet to relocate. The 27 January 1945 front page of the *Free Press* announced the decision of the "Adult English Activity Hall" staff (the "activity" being a euphemism for the WRA Americanization program aimed at Issei) to hold "the 'loveliest room' in Manzanar" open for daily inspection by Issei the following week—the implication clearly being that Manzanites who held a suspicious distance from Americanization activities were now being benevolently granted the power to "inspect" the WRA's own activities. The ostensible role reversal performed by these daily open houses emerges from the *Free Press* staff writer's account: "On Wednesday afternoon at 2 Miss Dee Murray, friendly resident of Manzanar, will give a demonstration on how to make those 'delicious' cream puffs; on

Thursday and Friday evenings Mrs. Ruby Beale of the elementary school and Miss Lucile Smith of the high school will go into the mysteries of glazing and scalloping vegetables; and on Saturday morning from 8 to 10, Mrs. Helen Hill of the elementary school will disclose the secrets of her success with a white birthday cake." The scare quotes that offset descriptions of the Adult English Hall as Manzanar's "loveliest room" and the "deliciousness" of Miss Murray's cream puffs, in tandem with the almost parodic tone of the article overall, construct an alienated performance of American domesticity within which Issei are positioned as passive spectators absorbing the "mysteries" of assimilated practices. The article closes with the WRA's invitation for "Issei men and women with problems in English . . . to bring their problems to the hall and get help." [73] At this point in the internment, the dominant public relations program of the WRA—dubbed "Education for Relocation"—thus feminized and infantilized Issei by focusing on their supposed handicaps in American domestic practices and their relative ignorance of the English language. [74]

The dominant scholarly interpretation of the Issei and their families who remained in the camps until they were forced once again by the U.S. government to uproot is that they represented "the spoilage," to use Dorothy Swaine Thomas and Richard Nishimoto's famous phrase. [75] The traditional Japanese practices enacted by this population have been read as deludedly chauvinistic (insofar as these lingering internees apparently believed Japan would emerge triumphant) and as defiant performative statements of disloyalty against a nation that had pushed them too far. On the contrary, the elaborate Japanese performing arts festivals staged by Manzanar internees at this late point in the war demonstrate both a resistance to the U.S. myth of performative citizenship—now being dangled in front of Japanese Americans as a promise to restore their place in society if no questions were asked—and a deeply empathetic understanding of the futility of Japan's militarism and their fatal association with that enemy. Moreover, in the face of the U.S. government's criminalization of Japanese culture and the WRA's enforced assimilation and disqualification of Issei from most community leadership roles, traditional Japanese performing arts stood as one of the very few arenas in which Issei could present themselves with dignity (insofar as these practices were embodied and thus did not depend upon Western textualism or the English language) and with cultural authority.

Within this context, a group of Manzanites presented "the best New Year's present for everyone" on 20–21 January 1945, in the form of a live entertainment program that was, in a *Free Press* writer's Japanese words, "the product of the arts that Manzanar is proud of, and might even be too good to watch and listen to surrounded by barbed wire." Produced on the community auditorium stage, the New Year's show started at 6 p.m. each night, with a program of acts repeated on both Saturday and Sunday. The program opened with an informal

Noh dance *(shimai)* performed by a female internee, followed by *Chigo zakura* (Baby Cherry Blossom), a Meiji-era piece of music composed for *shakuhachi* flute and *koto* drum. Third on the bill was the performance of a song welcoming the year of the rooster (Toridoshi), which was the zodiac for 1945 in the Chinese astrological calendar.[76]

The heretofore rather nondescript New Year's program takes form with the fourth number, a *buyo* piece performed by Manzanar's beloved Ueda sisters; the piece inaugurated the theme of Hōrai that would be reprised later each evening. Hōrai exists in Japanese mythology as a mountain village that was derived from the Chinese mythological imagination; an idyllic but ambivalent place, Hōrai balances an unforgiving climate—created by an atmosphere thick with one's ancestral ghosts—with a utopian community of open-hearted inhabitants who practice "the simple beauty of unselfish lives."[77] In devoting a beloved classical dance performance (*buyo* was extremely popular at Manzanar) and a *chikuzen biwa* (lute and *shamisen* guitar) musical number (in tenth position on the program) to the theme of *Hōrai-san,* the producers and performers of the New Year's show acknowledged their liminal stations as a people cruelly interned because of their ancestry but drawn together, if for this evening only, in a utopian community of like-minded artists and spectators. Hōrai is a bittersweet imaginary place that inspires believers to imbibe an atmosphere of old souls and treat one's neighbors with respect and kindness—a message of tolerance and a recognition of shared hardship at this celebratory event in an internment camp.

In between the two performances about Hōrai, internee-performers gave their audience a series of *shigin* (traditional songs) about war, more *biwa,* another *buyo* number danced by a girls' troupe, a *jōruri* puppet drama, and a display of Kyoto dolls presented by the Association of Eight Thousand Generations (Yachiyo-Kai).[78] Following a *rōkyoku* solo storytelling act by a male internee, the program closed with two remarkable theatrical performances: one chanter-*shamisen* team performed a *jōruri* rendition of *Taikōki jūdanme,* or the tenth day of *The Picture Book of the Taikō,* also known as "The Amagasaki Cottage" or "Taijū" act; the other group performed the Kabuki play *San'nin Kichisas* (The Three Kichisas). Both climactic dramas depict the dark sides of Japanese feudalism, recognizing through their anti-heroes the roguish international position of Japan at this point in the war with the United States and its allies, as well as the remaining internees' precarious position as socially and politically outcast Americans.

The penultimate act of the New Year's program, "The Amagasaki Cottage" or "Taijū" act, was from Chikamatsu Yanagi, Chikamatsu Kosuiken, and Chikamatsu Chiyōken's 1799 puppet play *The Picture Book of the Taikō.* As James Brandon and Samuel Leiter argue, *Picture Book* and other plays of the "golden age" of Kabuki "clearly reflect, if unconsciously, contradictions that were becoming evident in feudal society." Feudal Japan demanded unquestioned obedience to one's master, a system difficult to accept when that master proved undeserving of such subordination. The lead character in *Picture Book* is a middle-aged *samurai*, Takechi Mitsuhide, a villainous anti-hero based on a figure Brandon and Leiter call "one of the greatest traitors to feudal honor in Japanese history." [79] In "Taijū," Mitsuhide causes both his mother's and his son's painful deaths as the result of his dishonorable, bloodthirsty ambition to become shogun. As the play's chanter says at one point, in the voice of Mitsuhide's mother Satsuki—dying from a spear wound accidentally inflicted upon her by her son—"Ill-gotten power is ephemeral, like floating clouds." [80] Yet Mitsuhide continues to pursue his ambitions in a desperate and merciless manner that more than resembled the Japanese Empire's military aspirations, especially at the end of World War II, as Japanese commoners made unbearable sacrifices to follow the orders of increasingly undeserving leaders.

At the same time, Mitsuhide operates not purely as a villain but also as the protagonist, with whom audience members are compelled to identify: his stoic displays mask his emotional agony as his dishonorable actions bear poisonous fruit in the form of his son and mother's slow deaths before his very eyes. Although it is difficult to know how the internee-performer presented Mitsuhide at Manzanar in 1945, the sustained focus on the the character's familial losses necessitated the camp audience's identification with his situation. As a personification of Japanese feudalism gone terribly wrong, Mitsuhide represented the legacy of Japan with which internees found themselves inextricably linked in the Western imagination. Japanese Americans could not (and some did not want to) disown their transnational connection to their nation of ancestry, just as Manzanar audiences could not refuse all sympathy to the anti-hero Mitsuhide on the community auditorium's stage.

Quite contrary to Ruth Benedict's prediction that the feudal glory of the *Chūshingura* drama would resonate most strongly among interned Issei (and conflict most strikingly with the assimilationist hopes of the Nisei), neither of the long performances that climaxed the Manzanar New Year's show of 1945 valorized feudalism or upheld what Benedict had described as a distinctly Japanese sense of sincerity. Instead, "Taijū" questioned feudal obedience by depicting its potentially disastrous outcomes, and Mitsuhide's murderous ambitions elicited the audience's horror through a culturally universal sense of sincerity and drew on a commonly American (if also commonly Japanese) ethos of melodrama in demonstrating the dark side of Japanese life.

Kawatake Mokuami's 1860 bandit play, *The Three Kichisas and the New Year's Visit to the Pleasure Quarters (San'nin Kichisa kuruwa no hatsugai)*, was a Kabuki piece that also dwelled in the underbelly of feudal society but compelled audiences to at least partly identify with the unapologetic criminal anti-heroes whose intertwined fates generated the dramatic plot. It is significant that the Manzanar cast for *The Three Kichisas*—particularly the internee-actors who played the bandits Ojō Kichisa, Oshō Kichisa, and Obō Kichisa—remained anonymous in the published program for the 20–21 January 1945 shows. Brandon and Leiter characterize *The Three Kichisas* as a *kizewamono*, or raw, domestic drama characteristic of the late Tokugawa era; these Kabuki plays are often "set in grim surroundings [on the] margins of human society," with major characters, like the Kichisas, depicting "social outcasts" such as callous murderers, pimps, and thieves. In the world of Kabuki, these social outcasts emerged not as one-dimensional villains but as "romantic outlaws" produced by the decay of feudalism's waning years.[81] Such romanticism, which presented a palpable parallel through the outcast status of internees existing on the margins of U.S. society, invited the Manzanar performers' and audience members' identification.

Each of the three bandit-heroes has a metatheatrical layer to his performed identity in *The Three Kichisas*: Oshō Kichisa is a temple acolyte who has fallen into a life of criminality; Obō Kichisa is the heir Yasumori Kichisaburō but has found himself a masterless samurai (or *rōnin*) and thus thinks nothing of indulging in brazen acts of thievery; and Ojō Kichisa is an itinerant actor who uses his skills at female impersonation to pose as the "well-brought-up young woman" Oshichi, an effective lure for victims of his thievery. The most celebrated act in the play takes place on the Ryōgoku Bridge over the Sumida River, an apt border space that represents a stage within a stage and creates one of the play's many opportunities for metatheatrical reflexivity on the role playing and transience inherent in modern life.[82] Parallel to the manner in which Japanese Americans found themselves spectacularly lumped together in their suspect status because of the assumed association of their shared heredity, Ojō, Oshō, and Obō are yoked in public notoriety by their shared surnames—a non-biological affiliation that does little to prevent them from coming to blows early in the play. But the priest, Oshō, intervenes to inspire a blood brotherhood among the three outlaws through which they eventually kill on behalf of one another (with the slogan "All for one, . . . and one for all!") and finally kill themselves in the inescapable suicide pact that ends the play.[83] By remaining nameless in the publicity circulated in the camp, the actors who embodied the three Kichisa bandits avoided the taint of being identified with callous criminals, but at the same time this anonymity suggested a universal identification of all remaining Manzanites with the brotherhood of outcasts dramatized by Mokuami.

The Kichisa bandits' blood brotherhood also had a metatheatrical analog for the performers and audience members of the 20–21 January 1945 entertainment program. Much as the three Kichisas banded together in their shared exile from law-abiding society in order to provide themselves safety in numbers, the Community Activities Cooperative Association (CACA), a grassroots organization lately formed to oversee internee cultural production at Manzanar, had banded together the various Japanese performing arts organizations who shared an exilic relationship to the forced assimilation of the camp's mainstream, English-language activities. Explaining the CACA's "new project" in a December 1944 article in the Japanese-language section, a *Manzanar Free Press* writer noted, "So far a variety of events and performances have been held. But these were enjoyed only among those interested or within small groups, and these people were split into many factions." The characterization of groups variously practicing *buyo, utai, biwa, shakuhachi, jōruri,* and other Japanese arts as "factions" underscores the article's stated ideal "that all residents in Manzanar should enjoy these events and performances" on a shared bill and in a large communal audience, an ideal toward which the CACA had resolved "to play the role of connecting all the experts" of Japanese performing arts in the cultural battleground of Manzanar.[84] Aware that the practice of Japanese culture rendered them un-American in the performative logic of U.S. citizenship—as the surname "Kichisa" enveloped the three bandits in their shared notoriety—the remaining factions of performers at Manzanar yoked their fates together, not in resigned acceptance of the dominant policies that enforced their exile, but in reasoned resistance to them.[85]

CHAPTER 5

Transnational Theatre at the Tule Lake Segregation Center

> Looking at performance as a retainer of social memory engages history without necessarily being a "symptom of history"; that is, the performances enter into dialogue with a history of trauma without themselves being traumatic.
>
> —Diana Taylor, *The Archive and the Repertoire* [1]

> The spectacle's cultural sector gives overt expression to what the spectacle is implicitly in its totality—*the communication of the incommunicable.*
>
> —Guy Debord, *The Society of the Spectacle* [2]

> Culture is the meaning of an insufficiently meaningful world.
>
> —Guy Debord, *The Society of the Spectacle* [3]

While "Japanesey" performances like the Manzanar New Year's production of *The Three Kichisas* easily fit the theatricalizing discourse that affixed the feudal soul of Noh and Kabuki to all those of Japanese descent, the "peculiar hodgepodge and medley of things Japanese and things American" that characterized most internee performance festivals was uncategorizable to outside observers of the camps. Despite their bafflement, the resident white anthropologists of the WRA Community Analysis Section had to admit that this "mixture of new and old, of Japanese, of regional West Coast, and of general American traditions was fairly typical of relocation center entertainment interests." Indeed, the routine mixing of national performance traditions proved so typical that—at all ten camps—such transnational performance became "a characteristic feature of center life." [4] However, at the Tule Lake Relocation Center, where Japanese Americans designated "disloyal" were segregated in 1943, the administration attempted to forcefully segregate internee performing arts in order to cleanse the camp of this characteristic transnationalism and bring what it considered the "salvageable" internees back into the fold of U.S. performative citizenship. These administrative attempts at performative segregation would prove disastrous, resulting in 42 percent of "Tuleans" (as Tule Lake internees came to be called) refusing to pledge unqualified allegiance to the United States, in stark contrast to the overall camps' average of 11 percent. By examining the performance festivals produced at Tule Lake during the year between its opening and its designation as a segregation site, I will show how Tuleans negotiated the polarizing terms of American nationalism using transnational theatre as their medium.

Tule Lake remained in operation the longest of any internment camp; it held Japanese Americans in Newell, California, until 20 March 1946, with a peak population of 18,789 internees. Until its conversion to a "segregation center" in July 1943, Tule Lake Relocation Center mainly incarcerated former residents of Northern California, Oregon, and Washington. (After July 1943, the camp was flooded with more than twelve thousand Japanese American "segregees" from around the country who had been interned at the other nine camps.) From the camp's opening on 27 May 1942, the demographic diversity of Tuleans resulted in factional conflicts beyond the generational (Issei, Nisei, Kibei) and class-based stratification that characterized all the WRA camps. The original Tule Lake population of 15,279 internees had been forcibly removed from a wide swath of the West Coast, producing an immediate factional divide between those from the northern states of Oregon and Washington and those who had lived in California. Likewise, Tuleans had widely divergent prewar occupations and lifestyles in their rural and urban communities. But the most divisive factionalization was manufactured (by internee accounts) by a series of incompetent WRA camp directors, starting with Elmer L. Shirrell, who systematically pitted internees against one another to deflect criticism away from the white administration.[5] One of the principal vehicles through which Shirrell and his successors sought to factionalize Japanese Americans was internee performing arts, which the WRA regulated in a highly prejudicial fashion. In resisting the administration's performative "divide-and-conquer policy," internees negotiated their own sociopolitical arrangements by means of performance festivals that enacted transnational combinations, poached upon U.S. nationalist spaces and rituals, and theatricalized race in order to dispute the American myth of performative citizenship.[6]

As a result of its demographic and manufactured divisions, Tule Lake saw a great deal of violence and protest during its four-year history as an internment camp. One of the consequences of this unrest was that it had the highest percentage of internees who opted to be labeled "disloyal" rather than comply with the U.S. government's latest promise of performative citizenship. The government decided in February 1943 to require that all adult Japanese Americans in the camps register their national loyalty through completion of either Selective Service Form 304A, titled "Statement of United States Citizenship of Japanese Ancestry," or (for Nisei women and for Issei) the "Application for Leave Clearance." Together these two documents came to be called "registration" or the "loyalty questionnaire," with two of their questions taking on the most importance. "As an ultimate proof of loyalty" to the United States, former internee Michi Nishiura Weglyn wrote in her landmark internment history, *Years of Infamy*, "all male and female internees aged seventeen and older were expected to give 'yes' answers to two crucial questions at the end of a long questionnaire." One of these asked internees whether they would serve in the U.S. armed forces or, if ineligible owing to age or gender, to promise not to aid America's enemies in wartime; the other asked internees whether they would "forswear any form of allegiance or obedience to the Japanese emperor"— wording that assumed American-born Nisei had until then harbored allegiance to Japan and a vow that would leave Issei without a country.[7] Both questions demanded that internees promptly answer with an unequivocal "yes" or "no" in order to establish their undivided loyalty or disloyalty to the United States, and any attempts by an internee to moderate his or her responses resulted in an automatic designation as "disloyal."

This mass sorting of "loyal" Japanese Americans (those who answered "yes" on both counts) from "disloyals" (all the rest) aided the U.S. government's bureaucratic handling of the internment camps and sought to appease public opinion by showcasing the WRA's follow-through in cracking down on ideologically dangerous elements in the camps. Yet the administration peddled the loyalty questionnaire to internees as an opportunity to "prove" their patriotism. Thus the government repackaged what amounted to "the wartime inquisition of Japanese Americans" (to use Weglyn's apt phrase) into a more marketable form: the deferred promise of performative citizenship finally delivered.[8] Whereas General John DeWitt had rationalized Japanese American exclusion under the logic that "it was impossible to establish the identity of the loyal and the disloyal with any degree of safety" and had thus rejected as illegitimate the performative assertions of patriotism acceptable from every other ethnic group at the dawn of World War II, the United States now offered a most logocentric enactment of American citizenship's magic through the deceptively simple writing of "yes" in two places on the questionnaire.[9] WRA national director Dillon Myer recognized the performativity of this registration in his 11 March 1943 letter to U.S. secretary of war Henry Stimson, promising "this would constitute an assurance to the American public that the *bad actors* have been effectively dealt with."[10] Since "the official interpretation of 'disloyalty' bore more heavily upon *sentiment* than upon behavioral attitudes," administrators overlooked the bitterly coercive situation created by internment and instead asserted the transparency of Japanese Americans' agency to freely perform either U.S. or Japanese citizenship through a set of simple "yes" or "no" answers that professed invisible, unverifiable inner feelings.[11]

In reality, of course, the other face of racial performativity exposed the lie of such simplistic promises of performative citizenship. Compliant "actors" who assented to the loyalty questionnaire found that they were expected to continue such good acting according to an extensive script and submit to constant surveillance once they "resettled" in inland cities such as Chicago and Detroit. Richard Drinnon has sharply but accurately described the resettling Japanese Americans' encounter with the underbelly of the myth, writing of them in the second person: "After you have said yes, you will pledge allegiance, will stay away from concentrations of 'Japanese,' and will become an informer, you wait and hope another inmate has not already performed a like service for the administration by saying something real or imaginary about you. . . . Though a citizen who has been 'cleared,' you have been told where to live, with whom to associate, how to dress and act, and what to do for a livelihood. You have been and will continue to be spied upon."[12] Nisei who left the internment camps while World War II still raged found that their resettlement in U.S. society was constantly interrupted by FBI agents who insisted on paying "visits to five or ten neighbors to inquire about [their] loyalty" (Issei were eligible for resettlement only later).[13]

Moreover, the loyalty questionnaire coincided with President Roosevelt's chipper announcement that Japanese Americans were again eligible for military service and the draft, although they were to be segregated in an all-Nisei unit, the 442nd Regimental Combat Team of the 100th Infantry Battalion. As a result, government officials deployed to the camps to explain the loyalty questionnaire shared a bill with the U.S. Army's recruitment drive in the camps; thrown together on a double bill, registration and military recruitment were marketed together as exercises allowing internees "to prove their patriotism in a dramatic manner" and finally put to rest the biological racism and circular logic of "a Jap is a Jap." Both sets of officials performed these exercises with constant awareness of the American public as their audience, seeking to "dramatically reawaken" these powerful spectators to Japanese Americans' worthiness to live among them. Taken together, Myer called these two exercises "the most massive and effective public relations job of the century, Madison Avenue notwithstanding"—unintentionally pointing out the spectacularization imposed upon Japanese Americans in order to charm the society of the spectacle.[14]

The Japanese Americans who were deemed "bad actors" through the performative tests given in early 1943 would come to be called "no-no boys" and "segregees," the former for citizen men and the latter for women and aliens, with the largest concentration of such internees living at Tule Lake. Of the 78,000 internees mandated to register, 75,000 filled out the questionnaires; of these, 65,000 answered "yes" to both key questions.[15] This response rate yielded a mean ratio of about 11 percent "disloyals" across all ten camps. But Tule Lake fared far above this average, with 42 percent of Tuleans ending up as "disloyals" because they either refused to complete the questionnaires or else answered "no" to at least one of the two key questions. The disastrous experiment in forced "Americanization" at Tule Lake resulted in "the amazement of all," in large part because "more U.S. citizens ended up as disloyals than aliens (43 percent to 17 percent)."[16] Armed with such "proof," the government selected Tule Lake as the camp that would serve as the "segregation center" where the uncompliant internees from the other nine camps would be thrown together in isolation, apart from the performatively loyal elements of the internee population. In the fall of 1943, the latest mass movement of Japanese Americans took place as 6,538 "loyal" Tuleans left the segregation center and 12,173 "disloyal" internees arrived there. The camp's appearance as a prison underwent a spectacular transformation: "A double 'man proof' fence, eight feet high, was constructed around the whole area; the external guard was increased from a couple of hundred soldiers to full battalion strength; and a half dozen tanks, obsolete but impressive, were lined up in full view of the residents."[17] Having rejected the U.S. government's belated offer of performative citizenship, these "bad actors" at Tule Lake would bear the brunt of intense military scrutinization and sensational media spectacularization for the remainder of the war.

The Intergenerational Politics of Tule Lake Performance Culture

Cultural performance actually prospered in the oppressive conditions that marked Tule Lake from its opening, in part because the spatial planning of the camp converted one barrack in each of the seventy-two blocks into a "recreation building" under the oversight of the WRA's Community Services Division. While these recreation buildings were not always devoted to recreational activities per se, they often served as the sites of a wide range of instructional offerings, from sewing to tea ceremony. In addition, each block's mess hall often doubled as a theatre, with regular performances of Kabuki and other internee performing arts. As Issei Noboru Shirai, who was interned at Tule Lake from 1942 until 1945, put it, "The administration knew the importance of keeping us occupied. It established a recreation department to plan activities for us."[18] And because the WRA needed to keep its prisoners busy, such infrastructure allowed cultural performance to quickly take root at the camp. The first social dance took place only five days after the first internees arrived at Tule Lake, and within a month of its opening, internees had been allowed to organize their own Recreation Department "to plan and sponsor a full program of recreational activities [which] included, besides frequent dances, a monthly variety show . . . which brought out and showcased the rich range of talent present among the evacuees."[19] The WRA administration at Tule Lake turned over the reins of "recreation" management to internees so quickly and willingly because such decentralized power served the pedagogical model of educating Japanese Americans in democracy through the practice of "self-government"—a policy of internee governance that excluded Issei from community leadership because they were not U.S. citizens and excluded women because they were not deemed suitable for paternalistic roles overseeing their fellow inmates. Therefore, Nisei men ironically found themselves in charge of the Issei recreation staff when it was "reorganized" in July 1942 in order "to better serve the elder residents of the Colony." In the internee-run camp newspaper, the *Tulean Dispatch,* the newly reorganized Issei recreation staff's Nisei leaders "asked that arrangements for any entertainment program be given notice to the staff so that they may be able to give aid."[20] The careful wording of this announcement spoke of the awkward sociopolitical situation created by Nisei leading their Issei parents in the planning of Japanese-language entertainment programs; the recreation staff members balanced their administrative power as designated puppet leaders with their inherited status as generational subordinates as they demanded to "be given notice" of planned, potentially subversive (pro-Japan) performances while at the same time they offered to "give aid" to their respected elders. The Recreation Department's Nisei staff members were the only internees (besides one dance instructor) who were paid by the WRA for providing live entertainment;[21] their paid status created yet another administrative privilege that divided the generations at Tule Lake by instituting a stratification between professionalized and amateur producers.

No such paternalistic system of "notice" and "aid" oversaw Nisei performances of potentially pro-American culture; this disparity both served the WRA's assimilationist agenda and pitted internee factions against one another. The white patronage and administrative freedom accorded to Nisei performance at Tule Lake meant that English-language performers could cast themselves in a diverse array of identities, with a variety of audience arrangements that allowed for sociopolitically subversive moments in performance. This identificatory mobility was matched by the freedom with which Nisei performers toured the camp's numerous theatrical venues, in stark contrast to the enforced fixity of most Issei cultural performances. Perhaps the most illustrative instance of Nisei performative mobility is the late October 1942 debut and November 1942 tour of the Café International Cabaret (alternately called the Cabaret International). The front page of the 12 October 1942 *Tulean Dispatch* stated that the new Nisei vaudeville troupe "promise[d] to bring to the City [that is, Tule Lake] one of the most colorful and entertaining programs of its kind." Announcing an initial tour of sixteen sites throughout the camp's eight wards, starting on Friday, 30 October 1942, the "colorful," "international" qualities boasted in the promotional materials and the internee troupe's name turned out to be more than just sloganeering.[22] Throughout the cabaret evening, Nisei performers enacted dance and comedy routines associated with a wide range of other races and ethnicities—decisively transcending the racist limitations of "a Jap is a Jap" military logic—including a Siamese (present-day Thai) dance number, an "Italian dialect" monologue, a Ziegfeld-inspired rendition of "A Pretty Girl Is Like a Melody," and a "voodoo" routine (how the troupe imagined this Caribbean-derived religious practice in performance remains unclear).

The unapologetic ambition of the Tulean Cabaret International's diverse lineup shared the bill with the unapologetic campy humor of a transvestite performance of "Mama Yo Quiero," a musical number made famous by Brazilian diva Carmen Miranda in the 1940 Hollywood film *Down Argentine Way.* Already oft-parodied for her oversized fruit hats and flamboyant "Latinness," during World War II Carmen Miranda also symbolized President Roosevelt's

Nisei perform a "Siamese dance number" at the Cabaret International Café premiere for a mostly WRA audience at Tule Lake on 30 October 1942. Photograph by Francis Stewart for the War Relocation Authority.

presumptions of international diplomacy; FDR had imported her musical talents (and bombshell good looks) as part of his administration's Good Neighbor Policy to forge better relations with Latin America. On opening night, before a mostly WRA audience, Nisei Yukio Shimoda took every advantage of the trickster license that came from flamboyantly cross-dressing as Miranda.[23]

To approximate a nightclub, the Cabaret International troupe had arranged the barrack venue with individual tables complete with tablecloths and beverage service (in paper cups); Tulean high school students escorted audience members to their seats.[24] It was at one of these assigned seats that Tule Lake's "Carmen Miranda" sat on WRA housing staff director Frank Smith's lap "for a brief rest during her act."[25] Another *Tulean Dispatch* account had Smith seated with his wife and another white couple; according to this internee reporter, Smith "display[ed] a beautiful deep blush when 'Carmen Miranda' came to his table and tickled his chin, almost sitting on his lap." Whatever degree of con-

Nisei Yukio Shimoda impersonates Carmen Miranda at the Cabaret International Café premiere for a mostly WRA audience on 30 October 1942. Photograph by Francis Stewart for the War Relocation Authority.

tact Shimoda made with one of his jailers, Smith's post-show comment made it clear that the Miranda impersonator got away with this brazen performance of transgression: after the show the administrator stated, "'Carmen Miranda' was more like Miss Miranda than herself."[26]

The transgressive virtuosity of Shimoda's "Carmen Miranda" had its precedent in the fall 1942 Tule Lake tour of a Nisei vaudeville troupe called the Nuthouse Gang, which, according to the *Tulean Dispatch,* "presents impressions in professional style." Reviews of the Gang's October performances prepared the ground for the social mobility and ethnic diversity of the Cabaret International, as well as the appraisals of professional virtuosity that undergirded such representational freedom. The camp newspaper summed up the Nuthouse Gang program as "rollicking sketches, with the color of true international flavor." It also called the troupe "Tule Lake's 'Hellzapoppin' crew," referring to the 1941 Hollywood film *Hellzapoppin',* which was based on the "backstage" musical of the same name that ran on Broadway for more than 1,400 performances in 1938–1940. But the hand-drawn illustration that accompanied a 16 September 1942 *Tulean Dispatch* article on the Nuthouse Gang demonstrated that "color" and "international" may have been simply euphemisms for the caricaturing of racial difference: the drawing shows two Nuthouse actors, one wearing whiteface, a clown cap, and ruff, and the other wearing blackface, a chef's hat, and bow tie.[27] An official WRA photograph showing members of the Nuthouse Gang participating in the October 1942 Harvest Festival corroborates the use of blackface for the troupe's personas: this street performance of the Gang featured a male actor wearing blackface, a top hat, and tails (or their internment camp costuming approximations) and a female actor wearing blackface and a kerchief headscarf—standard markers of the African American stereotypes "Zip Coon" and "Mammy" respectively.[28]

Eric Lott has noted the "slippery political valences" of blackface masking, which was often used in nineteenth-century America as a tool of oppressed segments of the population to protest their treatment using "a derisive celebration of the power of blackness." It is precisely this *derisive* quality of black cultural appropriation that prompts Lott's skepticism of critical interpretations that herald whites' blackface minstrelsy as an anti-racist elevation of African American culture that might have grown out of a cross-racial acknowledgment of shared suffering. Lott seizes upon the ambivalence of blackface performance in the United States, an ambivalence pithily captured in his book's title, *Love and Theft.* "Acting black," he writes, "a whole social world of irony, violence, negotiation, and learning is contained in that phrase."[29] Likewise, as a *Hellzapoppin'*-tribute troupe, the Nuthouse Gang took as its inspiration a film that glorified white humor (the comedy duo of Ole Olsen and Chic Johnson) but held at its center a virtuosic eight-minute swing dance scene starring

African American performers from the Harlem Congaroo Dancers, also known as Whitey's Lindy Hoppers. The famous Lindy Hop scene takes place "backstage," instigated by two African American men in overalls delivering a package; they happen upon a piano and other instruments and improvise a swing jam that draws uniformed workers and maids from the wings to demonstrate their amazing dance routines (choreographed by Frankie Manning).[30] On the screen, the hidden talents of the theatre's African American behind-the-scenes work crew are approvingly espied by the white performers who are putting together their own musical. Likewise, the Tulean Nuthouse Gang aimed for an offscreen parallel, to be found in the camp's white administrators' approval of these displays of hidden internee talent. This parallel combined with the Gang's donning of blackface to suggest an ambivalent identification with the oppression and spectacularization delivered upon African Americans but also a theft of racist black tropes in order to elevate the internees' own hidden talents.

Snippets of dialogue reprinted in the *Tulean Dispatch* show that Nuthouse Gang performers also caricatured foreign Chinese—rendered in stereotypical dialect as "Dithe Shong-hai . . . stashon! [This is Shanghai station]" (followed in the article by the presumably black dialect "Why yazza boze!").[31] Such racial caricaturing suggests that the Nisei vaudeville troupes at Tule Lake attempted transgression of the sociopolitically oppressive conditions of their internment by trading their own racial typecasting for others'. At the same time, these racial caricatures played to an approving audience of WRA staff members, unthreatened by the trickster potential of such performances both because they were in many ways the intended audience and because they saw such Nisei theatrics as rehearsals for American assimilation (racist acting being typically American and pitched to an Anglo-American ideal). Consequently, embodying different racial and national identities through vaudevillian caricature also allowed the Nuthouse Gang to enjoy unlikely mobility (for an internment camp) through extensive unscripted "ad-libbing" and an uncharted performance tour throughout Tule Lake, armed "with loud speakers to bring the highlights of the coming attractions."[32]

By contrast, the Issei at Tule Lake found that the creative license and mobility of their performing arts were increasingly regulated by the Nisei puppet leaders of the Recreation Department. In late September 1942, the Japanese-language section of the *Tulean Dispatch,* under the curt headline "From the Recreation Department," announced that a 30 September Issei entertainment program had been forcibly postponed until October. The article also announced a set of strict rules censoring Issei cultural performance: "If you are planning to have an entertainment event in your block, you must report to the recreation department, present the program, and ask permission to use a loudspeaker. Otherwise, you will not be allowed to hold any event."[33] A week later, the

Japanese section listed the expanded regulations patrolling Issei entertainment, including the requirements that programs be approved by two overseers at the Recreation Department; that the programs' "titles, contents, performers, and performers' addresses" be submitted two days ahead of the proposed event; and that all publicity be first presented in English and then translated verbatim into Japanese. Item five of the expanded list of regulations unequivocally stated—in stark contrast to the informal relationship between the white administration and Nisei performers—that "Unreported programs or improvised programs cannot be performed."[34] Shirai describes the approval process forced upon Japanese entertainment as "humiliating" for Issei, who struck back at such subordination through an impromptu performance: "One evening [September 1942] when the Issei knew that the Caucasian in charge of entertainment [Ted Waller] was away on business, the Issei seized their chance-in-a-lifetime opportunity to stage an extremely pro-Japanese show called 'Call to Duty.' This was a cathartic victory for the Issei, who relished every minute of it, but the next day word got back to the administration. Needless to say, the Issei entertainers were reprimanded. Who could have informed the authorities? It must have been a Nisei *inu* [literally "dog"; an informer]."[35]

The inverted social arrangements governing internee cultural performance, in which Nisei patrolled their Issei elders, were compounded by the inverted aesthetic estimations that privileged the amateur performances of interned youth—celebrated as virtuosic and billed under the misnomer of "professional"—instead of the dignified tradition of native Japanese performing arts embodied by Issei Tuleans, some of whom were actually professional actors. Whereas Nisei troupes mimicked vaudeville routines and dance moves culled from mainstream American movies like *The Great Ziegfeld* and *Hellzapoppin'*, Issei performers drew from a deep prewar repertoire of Kabuki evenings performed in West Coast Japantowns, from which they brought professional-grade costumes and props with them to camp. Moreover, visiting Kabuki artists from Japan had been trapped on tour in the United States when war broke out, so these highly respected professional actors found themselves interned at Tule Lake, where they performed "on a grand scale" for appreciative audiences and taught Kabuki performance techniques to other internees.[36]

Perhaps the most often performed of Kabuki plays at Tule Lake was *Chūshingura* (The Treasury of Loyal Retainers), although Tuleans (like Manzanites) often enacted these feudal plotlines according to sympathetic politics quite different than those surmised by Ruth Benedict in *The Chrysanthemum and the Sword*. On the evening of 29 August 1942, an Issei "adult program" on the camp's outdoor stage featured a Kabuki performance from this most famous Japanese drama of the forty-seven *rōnin*, preceded by various group and individual performances of *odori*, vocal solos, and monologues.[37] That day, in the English section, the *Tulean Dispatch* printed the entire program (a list of sixteen acts), complete with performers' full names—thus exposing for a primarily English-speaking readership of Nisei the "Japanesey" personas to be donned by their Issei elders. This program had already been postponed from its original performance date (21 August), presumably owing to administrative restrictions.[38]

The Internee Theatre Referendum

The undisguised disparity between the oversight imposed upon "American" and "Japanese" performance at Tule Lake created the conditions for a camp-wide referendum on the use of theatre spaces in an internment camp. In October 1942, Elmer Shirrell brought to the all-Nisei Community Council, which officially but unpopularly represented the camp, the idea that the internee Construction Department build an eight-hundred-seat theatre using profits from the camp's co-op store ($8,200 in internee investments, which were to be repaid from theatre ticket sales). The council members unanimously approved Shirrell's proposal for the theatre building, in part because it would give seemingly democratic billing to live performances, American movies, newsreels, and Japanese pictures (once the latter had passed censorship).[39] But when the *Tulean Dispatch* announced the Community Council's acceptance of the theatre construction on its 8 October 1942 front page, many Issei internees immediately resisted the plan and called for a referendum to override this behind-closed-doors decision on the future direction of Tuleans' entertainment and the use of co-op funds. A week later, the *Tulean Dispatch* again used its front page to announce a special election on the theatre issue, to be held 19 October 1942; all internees (over the age of sixteen) would be asked to express their opinion using a secret ballot. The newspaper also promised to outline "the arguments for and against the construction of a theatre" in its pages in advance of the election.[40]

Thirty-two blocks that had joined together to form an Issei-led committee in opposition to the theatre building published their opinion alongside that of the Nisei Community Council. Unsanctioned by the WRA's assimilationist system of self-government, this large group of internees had been activated by the theatre controversy. The Issei committee strongly questioned "the necessity of building a theater" during wartime, especially considering the precarious economic situation of the disenfranchised internees. The cost of the building (borrowed against internee co-op capital) and the cost of attending paid productions (15-cent tickets were proposed, the "equivalent of 1/3 our daily pay") led to opinions "unalterably opposed to this theater construction." On the other side, the Community Council warned internees that "this is your last and only opportunity to have a theater" because the WRA "has definitely stated that due to wartime restrictions they will not build a theater" using government funds. By distancing the proposed theatre from WRA oversight, the Nisei supporters framed the building as an internee-governed institution that would, in fact, pay particular attention and respect to Japanese culture. The council insisted that "no picture offensive to the Japanese or [anti-Japanese] propaganda will be shown." Instead, the council's argument emphasized the large seating capacity of the proposed theatre, appropriate to the widely popular "production of Japanese plays and dramas"; in addition, the theatre's productions supposedly would be "managed by Japanese directors . . . for the best interest of the colonists at all times."[41]

Rejecting this sales pitch, an improvised political coalition activated by the WRA's attempts to install Nisei as Tule Lake's de facto theatre producers was able to broadcast its opposition and mobilize 8,938 voters—the biggest turnout to date for a Tulean election over camp governance. According to the *Dispatch*'s 20 October 1942 front page, "The results of the election indicated almost all eligible voters, more than sixteen years of age, cast their ballots."[42] In a passionate enactment of democratic "self-government," every ward voted down the theatre construction, yielding a 2.5 to 1 margin against the Community Council's proposal.[43] In other words, using the presumably exceptional American tradition of democracy, the presumably undemocratic (because traditionally Japanese) Issei at Tule Lake made their wisdom into law. The privileging of "Americanized" Nisei performance presented the most immediate cause of opposition to the theatre building. For instance, Noboru Shirai relates the polarizing impact of a mess hall variety show (staged about a month before the theatre proposal) in which "the emcee spoke only English." The cumulative effect of the tightening administrative control over Japanese-language performance also created a deep skepticism about the Community Council's promise that Japanese culture would be respected and that its representatives would be given directorial control, particularly since everyone knew that Shirrell had initiated the theatre idea.

But all these "entertainment"-related developments also took place in the shadow of an aborted propaganda performance in which the U.S. Office of War Information (OWI) attempted to cast internees, with Issei in pivotal roles.[44] In September 1942, the Nisei Community Council unanimously adopted OWI's proposal to have Tuleans perform in short-wave radio broadcasts to counteract the Japanese government's international allegations that the United States was mistreating Japanese American internees. Aware of the dangerous diplomatic implications of such statements about racist U.S. policy, OWI figured that interned Japanese Americans themselves would be the most compelling actors to rebut imperial Japan's propaganda by attesting to the benign conditions of their captivity. The Nisei leaders at Tule Lake agreed and enthusiastically brought to their internee constituents this long-awaited opportunity to perform their loyalty to America and their rejection of Japan, all for an international audience. Yet most Issei instead recognized that internees were again being spectacularized by the U.S. government and anti-Japanese agitators who now wished to dramatize the "holiday on ice" ambivalence of Japanese American internment camps for an audience in the Pacific theatre. Such a command performance would not prove internees' loyalty nor guarantee them performative citizenship; instead it would simply deny the injustice of their internment and aid Japan's defeat, which was not a universally desirable outcome among Tuleans. Led by an unauthorized Issei-dominated assembly, all seventy-two Tule Lake blocks roundly refused the Community Council's proposed production of the OWI propaganda performance.[45]

Gary Okihiro has maintained that Tuleans deployed the "dignified weapons of Japanese culture" as tools of "cultural resistance" rather than means of "open rebellion." [46] Nonetheless, these instances of Issei-led internee resistance against the WRA's attempts to deputize Nisei as Tule Lake cultural leaders produced a very public and self-consciously democratic rebellion—all in the name of live entertainment. The WRA sought to keep its prisoners benignly busy by making them pay for the construction of their own community theatre. By winning the referendum against this policy and thus defeating the WRA's Nisei-proffered theatre, the Issei began to wrest away control of cultural performance along a steady slope that culminated in the open rebellion against the February 1943 loyalty questionnaire. In other words, the cultural resistance evident in the theatre referendum and its precipitating events (including the OWI propaganda incident and the covert performance of a pro-Japanese program) were modest instances of open rebellion that escalated into the much publicized open rebellion of February 1943. But even months before that, the outcome of the 31 October 1942 Harvest Festival illustrated how the theatre referendum had already turned the cultural tide at Tule Lake.

The festival had been in the making since early October as a work holiday declared by Shirrell. The Nisei planners of the Halloween- and Mardi Gras–inspired parade at the center of the Harvest Festival wanted to "stress the humorous and colorful side of the day with clowns, hula dancers, negro minstrels, samurais, etc." With this diverse cast of caricatures announced, the Harvest Festival Planning Committee sought entries and asked that they be pre-registered at block 18, barrack 8; these costumed entries were to emphasize embodied performance, with budgets limited to ten dollars per entry and truck-based floats prohibited (to conserve wartime resources of gasoline and rubber tires). The planning committee announced it would segregate the entries into five divisions for judging purposes:

1. Issei (Japanese style)
2. General (commercial service organizations and clubs)
3. Senior (14 years and up)
4. Junior (13 years and under)
5. Nurseries (2–5 yrs).[47]

Segregated prizes were to be awarded in each division by a panel of judges mainly consisting of white administrators.[48]

Now called the International Nuthouse Gang, this Nisei troupe had traveled widely throughout the camp's wards in advance of the Harvest Festival to advertise its "free stage shows" at the festival and to encourage entries in the Mardi Gras parade. But in the aftermath of the theatre referendum's Issei-led victory, the Harvest Festival outdoor stage hosted a forty-five-minute cycle of alternating repertoire between the International Nuthouse Gang and the Issei Engei (Entertainment) Club, yielding a dialectical display oscillating between Hawaiian hula dances, *odori* and magic displays, and Chinese and African American minstrel performances.[49] Issei cultural performance secured a victory beyond such parity in programming. Popular vote awarded the "sweepstakes" prize for overall best entry *regardless of division* in the five-hundred-participant, mile-long costume parade to the Engei Club. Ten male performers from the Engei Club, costumed in *hanten* (emblazoned work jackets traditionally worn in Japanese festivals), carried aloft a portable Shinto shrine called *mikoshi*, preceded by what the *Tulean Dispatch* described as "an eery [sic] looking lion head."[50] In addition to popular support for these traditional Japanese *matsuri* (festival) paraders and their offering of a religious emblem associated with what American popular opinion deemed to be Shinto "emperor worship" and Japanese militarist indoctrination, the mostly white judges awarded top prize in the Issei division to another potentially subversive pro-Japan float. The winning farmers' float was carried by farmworkers and decorated with fresh produce grown at Tule Lake. The white administration's sanctioning of the farmers' float was significant because this entry held aloft another symbol of Japanese "indoctrination": on top of the float rode two very young Japanese American children costumed in Kabuki wigs and kimono, thus making an important point that Japanese performing arts pertained not only to the Issei elders but were also being passed on to internee youth. In the aftermath of the overwhelming theatre referendum results favoring improvised community leadership instead of the WRA's top-down approach to management, the panel of mainly white judges made a powerful concession to popular opinion and Japanese culture in awarding top prize to the farmers' transgenerational display.

Despite signs that the administration recognized the intercultural dynamics that created a delicate balance among the inmates, official WRA policy continued to patrol "Issei entertainment" to a far greater degree than Americanized Nisei performances, although performers of Japanese traditional culture found themselves increasingly empowered to circumvent and poach upon dominant camp institutions.[51] The front page of the 30 November 1942 *Tulean Dispatch* reiterated the system of regulation exercised upon Japanese performing arts alone, this time publishing such humiliating rules in English: "Any Japanese entertainment program, whether given by an individual or by a group in any block, must be filed with the Community Adult Recreation department not less than two days previous to the day of performance, it was announced. The program will be subject to approval of the Adult Recreation Advisory Board and the supervisor of Community Activities." [52]

Although Issei performance now posed a force to be feared, it was not yet a cultural movement to be universally respected. For instance, in the first *Dispatch* article since the Harvest Festival to give side-by-side coverage to Americanized Nisei and Japanese-language Issei entertainment, the camp newspaper compared how "two of the Colony's traveling entertainment shows had their share of confusion" during a campwide blackout the preceding Saturday evening. In block 6's mess hall, "the scene of the issei entertainment" witnessed the Japanese-speaking crowd "patiently waiting" for the light service to resume and then getting lost in adjacent blocks when they attempted to head back to their home barracks in the dark. After relating the stereotypically polite

Taken on 31 October 1942, this Tule Lake administration photograph captures two very young Nisei children riding atop an Issei-directed float, garbed in Japanese theatrical costumes signifying a samurai and noble lady. This float won first prize in the 1942 Harvest Festival. Photograph by Francis Stewart for the War Relocation Authority.

resignation of the Japanese elders, the *Dispatch* reporter snidely notes, "Call was finally made to the wardens' office and the people were guided back to the mess hall. Trucks were then borrowed from the motor pool and the lost [Issei] chauffered [sic] back to their barracks." Meanwhile, in the mess hall at block 58, the English-speaking internee audience for the performance of Cabaret International (now called Café Internationale) refused to politely wait during the blackout, instead inventively borrowing lanterns from adjacent blocks and spontaneously singing along with "a vocal solo by Martha Fukami, a member of the audience," until the borrowed lanterns were in place to go on with the cabaret show.[53]

The Ascendance of Transnational Performance

While the Nisei *Dispatch* reporter characterized the Issei audience's reliance on borrowed trucks during the blackout as a sign of culturally infantilized weakness, the unauthorized adoption of camp resources to piece together some sort of infrastructure for Issei performance can also be interpreted as symptomatic of the ascendance of anti-assimilationist cultural politics at Tule Lake. The 5 December 1942 Construction Show produced by Issei Tuleans demonstrates how assimilationist culture was losing its foothold in favor of transnational performance festivals, often produced by poaching upon U.S. government resources. On the two days preceding the first anniversary of Japan's 7 December 1941 attack on Pearl Harbor, four-and-a-half-hour evening programs planned by Issei entertainment chairmen took place at the newly completed factory building, which, at 60-by-300 feet (the size of a city block), easily qualified as the largest structure at Tule Lake. While Issei (and many Nisei) had rejected the WRA and Community Council's proposed eight-hundred-seat theatre building, this "gigantic issei drama and talent show" inaugurated a makeshift performance space because the new three-story factory doubled as a four-thousand-seat venue when equipped with "improvised benches and a four foot [tall] stage platform." The English-language preview of the Construction Show published in the 28 November 1942 *Dispatch* arrived only ten days after the mocking account given of the floundering Issei audience in the Tule Lake blackout.[54] The English article emits a begrudging respect for the "mammoth occasion," later described as occurring on a huge stage extending the sixty-foot width of the factory space and showcasing "a galaxy of the Colony's outstanding *issei and nisei* talents."[55] The overwhelming scale and transnational inclusivity of the Issei-planned Construction Show commanded Nisei respect and participation in a manner that upended the WRA's attempts to factionalize internees and privilege assimilationist performance.

While Issei and Nisei talents—"Japanese" and "American" acts—indeed shared the bill on both days of the Construction Show, it is clear that Anglo-American customs and U.S. government resources served merely as opening acts and opportune vehicles, respectively, for the empowerment of a more transnationally subversive celebration of Japanese culture *alongside* other cultures, including that of mainstream America. Significantly, the newly built structure that served as improvised performance space had been planned by the WRA as a tent factory in which internees would produce tenting materials for the U.S. military. In addition to poaching upon the nationalist intentions of the tent factory, the Issei entertainment chairmen mobilized Nisei to institute a bussing system whereby women and children (and presumably elderly internees) would be shuttled by cars from their barracks to the factory venue and back again. Since the vast majority of Tuleans did not have automobiles of their own, this shuttle system involved poaching upon the transportation resources provided by the WRA, and the Issei planners wisely tapped their WRA-connected juniors for this endeavor.[56] The 5 December 1942 program started at 1 p.m., with the Tulean Brass Band's performance of the U.S. National Anthem, followed by an equitable interchange of Americanized numbers (like English-language popular songs) with Japanese traditional cultural displays (like *buyo*) interspersed with "international" acts such as a Mexican dance and a Hawaiian

Internee photographer Jack Iwata recorded this 1942 *Nihon buyo* performance by a Tulean youth. The dance was accompanied by female *shamisen* players, seated at stage left. Such diverse generational and gender-based casting characterized many internee performances of traditional Japanese culture at Tule Lake. Gift of Jack and Peggy Iwata, Japanese American National Museum (98.102.57).

hula. These musical acts served mostly as interludes to several plays that stood as the main attractions of the Construction Show. On Saturday, 5 December, the English-language domestic drama *Husband* was performed as the twenty-sixth (!) act in the four-and-a-half-hour program; on Sunday, 6 December, its counterpart, the English-language "comical play" *Advice to a Wife* was the twenty-second act.[57] The undeniable culmination of both days' Construction Show came in the climactic Kabuki performances of *Chūshingura* acts, both performed by the Gōdō troupe.

The sixth and seventh acts of *Chūshingura* provided the climactic spectacles for the Saturday and Sunday shows respectively. Staged for an audience of up to four thousand internees, the production values for both acts dwarfed the mess-hall Kabuki performances that regularly took place at Tule Lake. One of the most pivotal and oft-performed chapters of *Chūshingura*, Act 6 concerns the "forty-sixth" *rōnin*, Hayano Kampei, who had been dishonored by failing in his service to Lord Enya Hangan on the fateful night that set the infamous vendetta in motion. At his superior Lord Ashikaga's estate on a formal occasion, Lord Hangan bucked rank and, acting upon his passionate devotion to his wife Kaoyo instead of the samurai code of honor and obedience, lost his temper and struck the maliciously lascivious Lord Kō no Moronao after he discovered Moronao's attempts to seduce Kaoyo. While Kampei should have been at Hangan's side as his lone attendant, Kampei instead snuck away with his lover Okaru, thus abandoning his lord at the moment in which his service was most needed to encourage noble restraint in his master. Without the support of any of his loyal retainers, Hangan fails to perform his noble role and lashes out, wounding but not killing Moronao—an act that offends Ashikaga and necessitates that Hangan commit *seppuku* (ritual suicide) and relinquish all his property. In retribution for the slight that forced Hangan's hand and caused them to become masterless samurai, forty-five *rōnin* loyal to Hangan, headed by the incredibly heroic Ōboshi Yuranosuke, band together to avenge their master's death by carrying out the murder of Moronao. However, they exclude Kampei from this noble vendetta because of his careless service at Ashikaga's house; Kampei thus becomes the forty-sixth *rōnin,* excluded from the pact. In the meantime, Kampei has married Okaru and spends his days desperately planning how to raise enough money to atone for his offense and give an honorable offering at Hangan's monument. Okaru's farmer parents decide to sell their daughter into a five-year contract as a prostitute in Gion in order to raise the money for their beloved son-in-law, thus allowing him to serve the celebrated vendetta against Moronao. Okaru willingly resigns herself to this fate to save her husband's dignity. However, returning from the brothel with Okaru's contract money, her father is killed by a highwayman. Moments later, unaware of his father-in-law's murder, Kampei shoots at a nearby boar but hits the highwayman instead, killing him. Kampei searches the dead man for identification and pockets the ill-gotten but much needed money.

Act 6 picks up at this point and takes place at Okaru's home, where the brothel keeper has arrived to collect Okaru. Moments later, Kampei returns to announce his serendipitously discovered fortune. The highly melodramatic scene contains Okaru's humble self-sacrifice in submitting to prostitution in exchange for her husband's return to grace, as well as her mother's realization that her husband has been brutally murdered for the brothel fee—and her mistaken accusation that Kampei killed his own father-in-law for the money. Most important, Act 6 ends with Kampei's own *seppuku* as he realizes that everything he does "goes at cross purposes, like the cross-bill's beak." Suspecting that his "luck as a samurai seems to have run out," Kampei suddenly stabs himself in the abdomen, just moments before two of the *rōnin* reveal that the body of Okaru's father acquits Kampei of his murder.[58] But Kampei has already mortally wounded himself, and the only consolation for this second unjust suicide comes in the decision of the two *rōnin* to add Kampei's name to the scroll listing the samurai who have committed to killing Moronao and then killing themselves at Lord Hangan's monument. After pressing his protruding entrails to the document to seal it with his blood, Kampei dies a painful death, and the scene closes with his mother-in-law weeping over both his body and her husband's.

The Tulean Gōdō troupe's presentation of this hour-long Kabuki melodrama, jammed with unbelievable acts of self-sacrifice and pathos from men and women, samurai and commoners alike, would have ended the Saturday program of the Construction Show with an emotionally exhausting spectacle. While Ruth Benedict assumed that *Chūshingura* played out in the daily lives of the Japanese American internment camps through the generational conflict between Americanized Nisei and the Issei loyal to Japan, the performance of this drama at Tule Lake, on the occasion of the first anniversary of Pearl Harbor, proved quite different. In actuality Tuleans—a most factionalized internee population—staged *Chūshingura* not to attest their loyalty to either the United States or Japan, nor even to underline the "sincere" conflict between the two extremes, but as part of an intercultural program that united the two positions in a transnational alliance based on their shared suffering as internees. In the closing words of Act 6, Okaru's mother speaks not of feudal loyalty but of universal familial loss: "Is there in all the world another person as unlucky as myself? My husband is dead, and the son-in-law who was my support has gone before me. My beloved daughter is still alive, but we have been torn apart. How can I, an old woman left alone in the world, go on living?" As she collapses, the two *rōnin* approve her unrestrained sobbing, saying, "You have every cause to weep, old lady." And the narrator closes the scene by describing the "world of sadness" that joins all these characters' suffering.[59]

On the following evening (6 December 1942), the Gōdō troupe presented Act 7 of *Chūshingura*. This act represents perhaps the most celebrated part of the play, in which the valiant samurai Yuranosuke conceals his ardent plans for retribution by posing as "a slave to physical pleasure" at Okaru's brothel in Gion. As Yuranosuke is visited by various representatives of Moronao who try to ascertain his part in the vendetta, Yuranosuke "assumed many guises, but his every motion has been governed by his sense of loyalty and his awareness of the importance of the mission." In order to convince these spies that he has no intention of attacking Moronao, Yuranosuke must pretend great disrespect toward his late master and toward the samurai code itself, telling his former colleague Kudayū (who now treasonously serves Moronao) that he is liberated to do so by the grudge he holds against Hangan owing to his late lord's "reck-lessness." Kudayū seeks further proof of Yuranosuke's "grudge" against Hangan and thus entices him to eat a piece of octopus on the night before the first anniversary of Hangan's death. Defying his culture's deep repugnance against consuming meat during the one-year mourning period following a loved one's death, Yuranosuke puts on a calm demeanor and artfully passes Kudayū's test, as "with the greatest aplomb he gulps down the fish in a single mouthful, a sight that stuns even the crafty Kudayū into silence." [60] For such displays, in Donald Keene's assessment, "Yuranosuke is probably the greatest role in all of Japanese drama." [61] Consequently, Act 7 poses perhaps the most complex meta-theatrical action of the play because the audience's experience of this scene emerges from its awareness of the various attitudes or "guises" that the hero must balance in order to protect the integrity of his vendetta.

It is true, as Keene puts it, that "Yuranosuke's loyalty is absolute. There is nothing to suggest that he would have been a particle less loyal to Hangan even if the latter had been a cruel or contemptible master." [62] But the audience's interpretation of this loyalty in the context of the intercultural program of the Construction Show cannot be called absolute in the sense that Benedict characterized Issei as unswerving devotees to the Japanese nation and impotent adherents to their positions in some ancient feudal order. Rather, as Tuleans of all ages, classes, and genders participated in a performance of *Chūshingura's* seventh act on the stage of an internment camp factory built to aid the U.S. war effort *against* Japan, the opposing attitudes balanced by Yuranosuke could be compellingly translated to describe the compromising and conflicted position in which all internees found themselves on the first anniversary of Japan's world-shattering attack on the United States. The coincidence of enacting this seventh act, which stages the night before the first anniversary of Lord Hangan's death, on the self-same evening before 7 December 1942, is no coincidence at all.

However, the U.S. government demanded much less ambivalent statements of national loyalty from Japanese American internees and offered no sympathy for the complexly layered "behavioral attitudes" of transnational identity. This simplemindedness was evident when the government commanded perversely simplistic written statements of performative citizenship either for or against the United States in the form of the February 1943 loyalty questionnaire or "registration." Destroying the delicate balance of intercultural performances achieved by the December 1942 Construction Show, the WRA Community Activities Department initiated a cultural performance initiative that coincided with and reinforced the perverse performative citizenship of the government's registration drive. On its 6 February 1943 front page, the *Tulean Dispatch* announced "'Hidden Talent' Search On," proclaiming that Community Activities' music and dance division representatives would be canvassing "every block and ward in the Project" in order to search for entertainment acts to take part in a cycle of competitive talent shows at Tule Lake. The reporter described the competition cycle in detail: "According to the plans of the special committee, miniature shows will be held in each ward to select candidates for the semi-finals. After the ward competition, a gigantic Talent Show at the factory building will bring together the winner and runner-up of each ward to compete in the finals for valuable prizes. Special talent scouts, made up of members of the Youth Social Activities and ward recreation leaders, will begin booking talents for auditions. Each ward will then hold a contest of its own to pick the winners." [63]

Although this rigorous search for "hidden talent" among internees envisioned a finale on the factory stage only two months after the "mammoth" Construction Show programs, the February 1943 performance differed markedly in its planners' explicit requirement that all "numbers must be Occidental." Therefore, as the cultural auxiliary to the instrumentalized performative citizenship spun by the loyalty questionnaire, the "hidden talent" search (usually referred to in these scare quotes) explicitly excluded Japanese cultural performance and implicitly excluded the "Japanesey" Issei since most of them could not speak the English requisite for "Occidental" acts. Now deemed "bad actors" according to the cultural logic of performative citizenship, practitioners of Japanese performance were ineligible for entry. Much of this competition took on the air of a talent inquisition, with its own registration ("sign-up") deadline for the submission of talent set for 28 February 1943. [64]

Two days before this deadline, however, all public performing arts activities at Tule Lake were halted by the psychological chaos and potential for violence erupting throughout the camp in response to the loyalty questionnaire. Once the wrenching but trivialized decisions had been made in response to the two key questions, recreation clubs and cultural classes regrouped in the second week of March 1943, "picking up where they left off as though nothing had happened," in one Nisei *Dispatch* reporter's self-consciously flippant words.[65] Of course, something monumental had shifted in the WRA's attitude toward Tulean internees, who had outpaced all other camps' inmates in turning back the U.S. government's cynical offer of performative citizenship through compulsory registration of one's "loyalty" status. The administration had already begun to look at Tuleans with new eyes, no longer planning for enforced Americanization and democratization of all internees equally, but now liberated to sort the "good" from the "bad" actors and concentrate its efforts on those who had passably performed U.S. identity in the loyalty questionnaire. These people, the WRA felt, could be salvaged, and the others should be left to spoil. The resumed search (as of 16 April 1943) for hidden talent thus took on an overdetermined sense of rehearsing for American reentry, as "Occidental" acts competed for the top prize awarded by a panel of white judges. Harking back to the International Nuthouse Gang's blackface revelation of hidden Nisei comedy talents through performance arrangements appropriated from *Hellzapoppin'* and its borrowing of African American virtuosity, the eventual winner of the spring 1943 "hidden talents" competition won the white judges' approval by "acting black." Two days before he left Tule Lake to join his parents at the Minidoka WRA camp in Idaho, Nisei Yukio Ozaki easily won first prize in the "untrained" division of the final talent show (8 May 1943) with his highly emotional rendition of "that negro folk song, Old Man River"; meanwhile, in the "trained" division, two young girls split the votes for first and second prize with their song-and-tap-dance routine and baton-twirling act respectively.[66]

Despite the fact that Ozaki was only one of three winners, it was his award for singing a white-manufactured "Negro spiritual" (Oscar Hammerstein's "Ol' Man River," from the 1927 Broadway musical *Show Boat*) that received top billing in several articles in the *Dispatch*, in part because Ozaki wrote an occasional column for the camp newspaper, "Daybreak by Yukio Ozaki." In a 20 April 1943 installment, Ozaki had announced that the Tule Lake Little Theatre—a relatively new performance troupe, of which he was a part and which had been spawned from the mold of the Cabaret International's successful tours—planned on "presenting in the next series of plays an all-colored drama entitled 'White Dresses' performed solely by the Caucasians of the Colony." Ozaki named two white teachers from the camp's secondary school, Tri-City High, as likely to be cast in the leading roles.[67] The fact that Ozaki was involved in the Little Theatre's plan to stage an African American folk play—Paul Green's 1926 one-act *White Dresses* (subtitled *A Tragedy in White and Black*)[68]—with the conscious artistic decision that white actors embody black Southern characters originally created by a black playwright, sheds some light on his contemporaneous motivation for performing a "negro folk song" in his bid to impress the white panel judging the hidden talents competition. Neither "Ol' Man River" nor *White Dresses* lends itself to blackface ridicule; rather, both pieces showcase the racist injustice and racialized suffering of their black characters. Green's "attractive mulatto," Mary McLean, whose tragic attempt to pass as white through a fantasized relationship with the white landlord's son, challenges the derisive tropes of blackface performance since her racial difference emanates not from visual or aural markers but from her audience's (including Green's other characters') preconceived knowledge of her biologically determined race. Likewise, although "Ol' Man River" counts as exploitative racial impersonation insofar as Oscar Hammerstein concocted it to benefit his hit musical theatre piece, the unabashed indictment of white racism that constitutes much of the pathos of the song has fooled many listeners into thinking that "Ol' Man River" is an authentic black spiritual. In other words, in both cases Ozaki's motivation for racial impersonation derived not only from racist mockery but also—paradoxically perhaps—from an identification with black suffering and a performative assertion of the permeability of such cross-racial empathy. Of course, Ozaki also selected a white-manufactured "negro spiritual" (and an "all-colored drama" for his Little Theatre) in order to win the white administration's praise by showcasing his hidden talents through a virtuosic performance of "acting black."

While cross-racial performance impressed the white insiders who sponsored the spring 1943 talent search, the posse of nineteen American journalists and photographers who accepted the WRA's invitation and visited Tule Lake in mid-May 1943 to inspect the conditions at the "disloyal" camp were not privy to this type of cultural performance. Instead, in order to impress these representatives of the nation's press—which had almost universally vilified Tuleans in the wake of the registration crisis and its attendant violence—the camp administration pushed to the foreground a display of Americanized cultural performance that sought to showcase the salvageable "loyals" amid the internee population.[69] According to the *Dispatch*, the 19 May 1943 performance program to "honor" the visiting journalists and photographers was "well received by the press," who "took pictures of various members" of the cast.[70] Extant photographs showing these visiting cameramen taking pictures of actors applying realist stage makeup suggest that the visiting press also checked in on the Little Theatre, which was simultaneously presenting one of its usual repertory evenings of Western realist dramas and light comedies.

As if purposely cultivated by the spring 1943 "hidden talent" competition, two of the Nisei representing the "various outstanding talents of the Tule Lake Center" ("various" being a misnomer, since neither Issei nor Japanese culture appeared on the program) were the first- and second-place winners from the "trained" division: baton twirler Myrtle Yamanishi and tap dancer Reiko Kumasaka. Along with tap dancing and baton twirling, all-American band music and

Western instrumental numbers shared the bill.[71] The reporting team from the *San Francisco News* seemed impressed by the naturalness of these encounters with Tuleans; in an article on their visit, the newspaper testified, "There was no 'tour,' no speech of explanation. Questions were answered, records opened, and no ostensible effort made to hide any phase of the project."[72] The months of cultivating Tule Lake's "hidden talents" for "Occidental" acts proved highly successful in presenting an unthreatening picture of assimilated internees to the visiting investigators.

Despite the visiting reporters' lack of skepticism, strategically hidden from their view and kept offstage to promote the WRA's assimilationist public relations agenda were Issei performers and transnational displays of Japanese culture. These finally achieved some semblance of their pre-questionnaire scale when Japanese performing arts returned to the outdoor stage on Saturday evening, 26 June 1943—the first time these were allowed to be performed

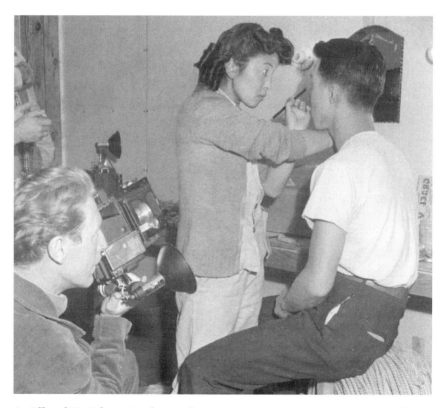

An Office of War Information photographer captures internee actors putting on stage makeup before what was likely the Tulean Little Theatre's May 1943 performance program. Photograph by Francis Stewart for the War Relocation Authority.

outdoors since 1942.[73] Until then, "adult entertainment" (as the elders' performance was usually called by Nisei) remained circumscribed on mess-hall stages and recreation barracks—in other words, venues that precluded large intercultural gatherings of internees on a par with the thousands who took part in the December 1942 Construction Show.

The restoration of Issei performance to large-scale audiences coincided with the inauguration of nightly instructional programs in *ondo* (Japanese folk dancing) on the outdoor stage, to which all internees were "invited to come out and participate."[74] The mass effort to teach every internee the *ondo* choreography (numbers including Tokyo-ondo, Sakura-ondo, Kagoshima-ondo, and Mizuho-ondo) emerged from Issei and Nisei leaders' joint plans to include participatory Japanese folk dancing as an all-inclusive activity for the 1943 Fourth of July celebration at Tule Lake.[75] The two-day "gala program" ambivalently observed both the one-year anniversary of many Tuleans' arrival at the camp

A *San Francisco News* photographer captures internee actors putting on stage makeup before what was likely the Tulean Little Theatre's May 1943 performance bill. Photograph by Francis Stewart for the War Relocation Authority.

and the U.S. Independence Day. With an Issei as "general chairman" and "Wild West" as the program's theme, the 1943 Fourth of July observances demonstrated a concerted effort to goodheartedly ridicule and respectfully include all constituents of the fractured Tule Lake internee community. An example of this levity was the assignment of Mrs. Sada Murayama as the chair of the celebration's "whiskerino and bald head contests," in which Issei and Nisei alike competed for prizes based on staged presentations of their facial hair (or lack thereof). Murayama's chairwomanship of this intergenerational and unserious contest constituted a significant departure from her usual role as an assimilationist cultural leader at Tule Lake; she had been mainly associated with the Nisei Little Theatre, where she served as artistic director over high-minded productions of Western realist dramas (including Chekhov) and highly civilized English-language comedies. The bald head and whiskerino presentations took place on the outdoor stage on 3 July 1943, after that evening's first round of participatory *ondo*; the humorous contest was judged by Murayama and two Nisei.[76] The 3 July program also included one hour of "Nisei performance" on the outdoor stage and another round of participatory *ondo*. Also illustrative of the intercultural festiveness of the event was the fact that the program began with a Japanese sumo tournament from 2 to 7 p.m. (Tule Lake had its own sumo pit), followed by all-American softball games between the camp's "All-Stars."[77]

The second day of the Wild West Fourth gala at Tule Lake continued these efforts to pay tribute to both Japanese and American cultures and to include all constituents at camp. The one-hour daytime ceremony on 4 July 1943 enacted the traditional routines of a mainstream American Independence Day pageant, including the Boy Scouts' U.S. flag dedication, a participatory singing of the National Anthem, and young people's marching bands. But the evening program on the Fourth, sponsored by the Issei, featured another consciously transnational mix on the outdoor stage. Starting at 6:30 p.m., a slew of opening acts alternated Nisei singing popular music solos with *buyo* performances from the camp's various schools (the Tachibana school and Bandō school), dance troupes (the Takeda sisters, Suekawa sisters, and Chikuyū troupe), and individual dancers. These acts warmed the crowd for the climactic performance of the evening: a *shibai* (Japanese play) performed by Tule Lake's Tomita troupe.

The apparent blasphemy of performing Japanese theatre on the occasion of a prominent U.S. national holiday while the United States was at war with Japan is easy to misread. But the performance of Japanese theatre at the culmination of a Fourth of July celebration at a government internment camp pointedly refuted the dominant U.S. discourse that suggested that Japanese Americans' unassimilability as U.S. citizens emanated from the dangerous foreignness of Japanese theatricality and its supposed permeation of everyday Japanese behavior. So the Tulean celebration's syncretism neither asserted "disloyalty" to America nor admitted an overriding allegiance to Japan and its culture. Rather, the suturing together of national pastimes and cultural performances from both nations asserted the transnational community of these Japanese Americans and their performative statement that this intercultural identity entitled them to partake in U.S. Independence Day.[78] This most popularly nationalist of all U.S. holidays could *not* be celebrated at Tule Lake by strategically hiding the complicating or mitigating aspects of these Americans of Japanese descent in order to render an unambiguous image of "loyal" internees (as had been so convincingly done for the nineteen visiting reporters several weeks earlier). Only through performing transnational ambivalence could Tuleans come together in honor of their diasporic status as Americans—however circumscribed that status had become behind barbed wire.[79]

Two days after the Fourth of July celebration, however, the U.S. government would forcibly end this peaceable intercultural equilibrium at Tule Lake. On 6 July 1943, the U.S. Senate activated the perverted promise of performative citizenship through the passage of a resolution implementing a segregation policy that would wrench nearly nineteen thousand Japanese American internees through yet another forced relocation and end in the imposition of martial law in November 1943. Refusing to recognize the transnational complexity of the inmates over whom it had presided for more than a year, the WRA rejected notions of hybrid identity by calling the implementation of the segregation policy "the inevitable result of a public reaction to the indiscriminate intermingling of evacuees who are loyal to Japan and those who are loyal to the United States."[80] When the dust settled, 11,227 American citizens had decided to give their citizenship back, and they demanded that the U.S. government deport them to Japan, a homeland in which the majority of these "renunciants" had never even set foot.[81]

Michi Weglyn has exposed the process whereby Tuleans renounced their U.S. citizenship out of a highly contagious sense of fear—fear of being separated from their Issei elders, fear of being forced to leave camp to "resettle" in violently racist communities—combined with bitterness at a nation that had severely mistreated them. Weglyn notes how absurdly theatrical this renunciation period became: "thousands, out of terror and hopelessness, play-acted the part of fanatic" in order to convince authorities of their intentions to move to Japan, thus qualifying for the now desirable "instant alien" status. The WRA and its government overseers accepted what they disingenuously considered performative displays of active "disloyalty," which continued in the "spectacular transfers" that took a total of 1,016 American citizens out of Tule Lake in early 1945 to begin the deportation process. The performative efficacy of this fanatical playacting was truly perverse, as these U.S.-born Japanese Americans were "turned into 'instant aliens' and hauled away amidst wildly patriotic demonstrations which accompanied the send-offs," staged by massive crowds of sympathetic internees left behind at the camp.[82] These mass deportations would not be the last alienating demonstrations of performative citizenship to be staged across the barbed wire fence surrounding Tule Lake Segregation Center. As former internee Noboru Shirai testified, on the night of Japan's 15 August 1945 surrender, the WRA staff living at Tule Lake "set off fireworks outside the fence around our camp and held a boisterous victory celebration," as if to performatively enact for the remaining internees ("the spoilage") their caged alienation apart from U.S. nationalism.[83]

Meanwhile, on the interior side of the fence, "it was as if somebody had turned our lights off. With painful expressions on their faces, people in camp wondered what was going to happen to them."[84] Unlike the spectacular manner in which Japanese Americans were first contained in the weeks and months following Pearl Harbor—ranging from the FBI's reenactment of Perry's founding scenario through its spectacular raids to the media's unsympathetic spectacularization of the suffering experienced by Issei and Nisei forced to leave their West Coast homes—the government prohibited any fanfare surrounding the 1945–1946 closures of the ten WRA camps. As a result of the unspectacular release of this spectacularized minority, Japanese Americans were left with little sense of how they would be treated upon their "resettlement," knowing as they did that no official statements had been announced to persuade the American public that these much maligned people were benign. Despite internal pressure by government officials like Under Secretary Abe Fortas, who urged the War Department to make a public declaration of Japanese American loyalty, no such announcement was ever made. Fortas rightly worried that in the absence of such a performative statement, "the War Relocation Authority is going to be accused—much more widely and vehemently than at present—of engaging in an underhanded and backstage attempt to return evacuees to the coastal areas in disregard and defiance of the military orders."[85]

President Roosevelt also remained silent, refusing to release one of his highly persuasive statements telling the public to trust returning Japanese Americans. Instead, FDR put political strategizing ahead of the internees' interests on more than one occasion. The president wrote an internal memo on 12 June 1944 that postponed any advancement of the slow resettlement process until *after* the November 1944 election in order to avoid upsetting voters by waiting and "seeing, with great discretion, how many Japanese families will be acceptable to public opinion in definite localities on the west coast."[86] Once the election was over, FDR again refused any dramatic announcement of the internment policy's demise by delaying release of the December 1944 Supreme Court decision on *Ex parte Mitsuye Endo* (323 U.S. 283) in order to make a more politically expedient announcement of the camps' imminent closures. In essence, he stalled the announcement by one day in order to upstage the unanimous court decision—which found that the government was unconstitutionally detaining demonstrably loyal U.S. citizens—by instead creating a veil of further euphemistic language around the internment camps, calling interned Japanese Americans "guests of the government."[87] Allan Bosworth may have put Japanese Americans' suddenly unspectacular plight best when he suggested, "If Roosevelt had gone on the air with his masterful stage presence and charming diction to say, 'These people are Americans, innocent of any traitorous or treasonable conduct and important to our economy and the successful prosecution of the war . . .' it seems certain that the evacuees could have been reestablished on the West Coast with less difficulty than was finally encountered. The trouble was that nobody in high authority ever spoke up on their behalf."[88] Or to reappropriate a line from the poet T. S. Eliot, despite its spectacular history, this was the way the internment ended: "Not with a bang but a whimper."[89] Spectacularized in their traumatic expulsion from American society but rendered all but invisible in their release from the camps, former internees had little choice but to face the next chapters of their lives with stoic silence—a reaction mistaken by many as evidence that Japanese Americans had emerged from the persecutions of racial performativity entirely unscathed.

Notes

Introduction

1. Philip Kan Gotanda, *Fish Head Soup and Other Plays* (Seattle: University of Washington Press, 1991), 37.

2. Cathy Caruth, ed., *Trauma: Explorations in Memory* (Baltimore: Johns Hopkins University Press, 1995), 10.

3. This characterization came from within and without the ethnic group. Nisei journalist Bill Hosokawa famously called Japanese Americans "the quiet Americans" in describing their history of settling (and resettling) in the United States. Bill Hosokawa, *Nisei: The Quiet Americans* (New York: William Morrow, 1969). While the designation "model minority" was first applied to Japanese Americans (in a series of American popular press articles starting in the mid-1960s), it was soon extended to other Asian minorities. Its domestic rationale certainly came from the post-internment "rebounding," but I also agree with David Palumbo-Liu that "the particular attention given to Japanese Americans was filtered through the optics of an international remapping of the United States' relation to the 'Pacific Rim,' in which Japan emerged as a newly hegemonic economic power." David Palumbo-Liu, *Asian/American: Historical Crossings of a Racial Frontier* (Palo Alto: Stanford University Press, 1999), 171. I explore the impact of Japan's economic modernity on diasporic perception of "the Japanese" in chapter 1.

4. Shoshana Felman, *The Juridical Unconscious: Trials and Traumas in the Twentieth Century* (Cambridge, MA: Harvard University Press, 2002), 13.

5. Caruth, *Trauma*, 4.

6. Although early books on the internment used the term "concentration camps" as a rallying point to protest U.S. hypocrisy in failing to acknowledge the injustice exacted upon Japanese Americans as well as Jews during World War II—see, for instance, Allan R. Bosworth, *America's Concentration Camps* (New York: W. W. Norton, 1967), and Roger Daniels, *Concentration Camps USA: Japanese Americans and World War II* (New York: Holt, Reinhart, and Winston, 1971)—such linguistic analogization to the Holocaust remains controversial to the present day. Despite the fact that President Franklin Roosevelt himself used the term to describe the Japanese American camps and the fact that these camps fit the dictionary definition of a concentration center (versus an extermination or death camp), the implied comparison to the Holocaust has always ended up belittling the suffering of Japanese American internees. Karen Ishizuka eloquently

summarizes this debate in her recent book, which recounts the process of mounting the controversially titled exhibit "America's Concentration Camp: Remembering the Japanese American Experience" at the Japanese American National Museum (JANM) in Los Angeles. Ironically, Ishizuka's original book title included the term "concentration camp," but she and her publisher removed the term prior to printing. Karen L. Ishizuka, *Lost and Found: Reclaiming the Japanese American Incarceration* (Urbana: University of Illinois Press, 2006), 155–156.

7. Raymond Y. Okamura, "The American Concentration Camps: A Cover-Up through Euphemistic Terminology," *Journal of Ethnic Studies* 10, no. 3 (Fall 1982): 95.

8. The U.S. Commission on Wartime Relocation and Internment of Civilians (CWRIC) estimated internee income losses of $108–164 million and property losses of $11–206 million. The Federal Reserve Bank of San Francisco estimated that Japanese Americans lost $400 million in property in 1942 alone. Yasuko Takezawa, *Breaking the Silence: Redress and Japanese American Ethnicity* (Ithaca, NY: Cornell University Press, 1995), 32–33.

9. Chalsa M. Loo, "An Integrative-Sequential Treatment Model for Posttraumatic Stress Disorder: A Case Study of the Japanese American Internment and Redress," *Clinical Psychological Review* 13 (1993): 89–117; Takezawa, *Breaking the Silence*, 120.

10. Ishii quoted in Arthur A. Hansen, "Oral History and the Japanese American Evacuation," *Journal of American History* (September 1995): 625–639.

11. I take instruction from Karen Shimakawa's characterizations of the Vietnam War and Asian American difference as embodying Julia Kristeva's notion of the abject. Karen Shimakawa, *National Abjection: The Asian American Body Onstage* (Durham, NC: Duke University Press, 2002).

12. The classic account of the "pretended threat to national security," arguably still the best demystification of the internment policy, is Michi Nishiura Weglyn, *Years of Infamy: The Untold Story of America's Concentration Camps* (Seattle: University of Washington Press, 1976), 52.

13. In particular, Malkin defends the internment policy by dismantling "The Myth of the American 'Concentration Camp'" in a point-by-point fashion that includes a cryptic reference to the performance of Kabuki by internees as proof of the camps' benign playfulness. Michelle Malkin, *In Defense of Internment: The Case for Racial Profiling in World War II and the War on Terror* (Washington, DC: Regnery Publishing, 2004), 105.

14. I am using "alienation" in the classic Marxist sense that suggests a profound estrangement from the material conditions underpinning one's position in a capitalist society.

15. Felman, *The Juridical Unconscious*, 174.

16. Guy Debord, *The Society of the Spectacle*, trans. Donald Nicholson-Smith (New York: Zone Books, 1995 [1967]), 23, 14.

17. Diana Taylor, *Disappearing Acts: Spectacles of Gender and Nationalism in Argentina's "Dirty War"* (Durham, NC: Duke University Press, 1997), 125, 27.

18. Dori Laub, "Truth and Testimony: The Process and the Struggle," in Caruth, *Trauma*, 65. See also Shoshana Felman and Dori Laub, *Testimony: Crises of Witnessing in Literature, Psychoanalysis, and History* (New York: Routledge, 1992). Caruth points

out that the prevailing scholarly characterization of trauma as a "crisis of witnessing" needs to be remembered in its original context, even if it is also elsewhere applicable: "While Dr. Laub's remarks define a specific quality of the Holocaust in particular which we would not wish too quickly to generalize, he touches on something nonetheless that seems oddly to inhabit all traumatic experience: the inability to fully witness the event as it occurs." Caruth, *Trauma*, 7.

19. Cathy Caruth, *Unclaimed Experience: Trauma, Narrative, and History* (Baltimore: Johns Hopkins University Press, 1996), 24.

20. In describing the structure of the Holocaust experience, Laub states that the German public was unable to "step outside of the coercively totalitarian and dehumanizing frame of reference in which the event was taking place" in order to "provide an independent frame of reference through which the event could be observed." Laub, "Truth and Testimony," 66. Not wanting to pose the Japanese American internment in pale imitation to the Holocaust event, I have avoided citing Laub's analysis as instructive for the wartime event in the United States. In fact, on the contrary, the U.S. government and the American media constructed the internment spectacle as ostensibly opposed to the fascist spectacle in Europe, as I will discuss below in the introduction. However, I should note that my understanding of the "frame" that surrounded the internment spectacle is informed as much by Laub's work as it is by discussions of the "play frame" within performance studies and anthropology.

21. Caruth, *Trauma*. Ruth Leys published a strong critique of Caruth's claim "that the traumatic experience stands outside or beyond representation as such." Leys finds no psychoanalytic basis for Caruth's discussions of the unrepresentable literalness of traumatic repetitions. However, I think that much of Leys' critique hinges upon her dismissal of Caruth's disciplinary positioning as a "literary critic"; the dismissal is clear when Leys complains of Caruth's "sloppiness in her theoretical arguments . . . in the name of close reading." Ruth Leys, *Trauma: A Genealogy* (Chicago: University of Chicago Press, 2000). In response, Shoshana Felman printed an extensive endorsement of Caruth (and an indictment of Leys' methodology) in the notes to her own recent book. Felman calls Caruth's critics (namely Leys) "parasitic on the topic" of trauma and claims that these critics "reduce the momentous stakes of trauma to the triviality of academic conflict." In the end, Felman unequivocally claims, "Caruth's theorization of trauma is largely recognized and widely cited as canonical, despite the recent academic controversies it has given rise to." Felman, *The Juridical Unconscious*, 175.

22. Caruth, *Trauma*, 7–8.

23. Caruth, *Unclaimed Experience*, 20–21.

24. Twenty-five thousand emigrants had left Japan by 1900, most for Hawaii and California, prompting one American observer to quip, "Whin the gallant Commodore kicked opn th' door, we didn't go in. They came out." George Feifer, *Breaking Open Japan: Commodore Perry, Lord Abe, and American Imperialism in 1853* (New York: Smithsonian Books, 2006), 295–296.

25. Ibid., 111 (emphasis added).

26. Francis L. Hawks, *Commodore Perry and the Opening of Japan: Narrative of the Expedition of an American Squadron to the China Seas and Japan, 1852–1854: The Official*

Report of the Expedition to Japan (Gloucestershire: Nonsuch Books, 2005 [1856]), 232, 235.

27. Ibid., 332.

28. De Certeau writes of sixteenth-century "inaugural scenes" of discovery and conquest, but I see no reason why this would be less applicable to the late blooming of U.S. imperialism in Asia. Michel de Certeau, *The Writing of History,* trans. Tom Conley (New York: Columbia University Press, 1988), xxv.

29. Diana Taylor, *The Archive and the Repertoire: Performing Cultural Memory in the Americas* (Durham, NC: Duke University Press, 2003), 13.

30. George Feifer points out that many Japanese consider the Perry opening to be a traumatic intercultural encounter (Kishida Shu even has a book titled *The Black Ships Trauma*), and he argues that the repetition of this trauma occurs in the minds of Japanese observers to subsequent American naval landings in Tokyo Bay and Uraga Bay. In 1907, President Theodore Roosevelt sent America's Great White Fleet to Japan as a "thinly veiled threat" to ensure the stemming of Japanese immigration to the United States. This fleet's spectacular arrival made "visions of Commodore Perry dance in Japanese heads." Likewise, when the U.S. battleship *Missouri* arrived in Uraga Bay in September 1945 for the surrender ceremony ending the Pacific War, MacArthur "bore a striking resemblance to the Commodore, especially in his proud self-assurance, talent for self-dramatization, and advocacy of a permanent military presence in Asia." Many Japanese referred to this seeming repetition of the Perry voyage as their nation's "second opening" by the United States. However, Feifer contains his interest to how the Perry trauma replayed in the Japanese psyche instead of how the Perry *scenario* was reenacted or reprised by America in a range of historical contexts. As a result of this focus, Feifer does not explore how Perry's use of spectacle in containing Japan became entrenched in U.S. policy thereafter, nor does he even mention the Japanese American internment in his book. Feifer, *Breaking Open Japan,* 296, 315.

31. Henry A. Giroux writes of both shock and awe and of the two-pronged attack of spectacle, existing as "both an act of cultural production and a consuming practice." I thus emphasize both the staging of the event and the arrangement of the audience. Giroux, *Beyond the Spectacle of Terrorism: Global Uncertainty and the Challenge of the New Media* (Boulder, CO: Paradigm Publishers, 2006), 22, 24–25.

32. Debord, *The Society of the Spectacle,* 12.

33. Giroux, *Beyond the Spectacle of Terrorism,* 26, 29, 30.

34. Rey Chow, "The Fascist Longings in Our Midst," in *Ethics after Idealism: Theory—Culture—Ethnicity—Reading* (Bloomington: Indiana University Press, 1998), 15, 20, 24. Chow gestures toward spectacle's potential, as an analytical framework, for exploding the Western conceit of a Cartesian divide separating the internal mind from the external body—a map of subjectivity Westerners rarely extend to non-Western others, particularly Asians, who are (mis)understood as pure surface. However, it is Diana Taylor who realizes the richness of spectacle as a *methodology* for analyzing the national identity construction of an entire political regime, in this case that of Argentina during the Dirty War. Taylor contends that political spectacles "function as a site for the mutual construction of that which has traditionally been labeled 'inner' (from phantoms to fan-

tasy) and that which has usually been thought of as 'outer' (political reality, historical facticity)." *Disappearing Acts,* 29.

35. Rey Chow, "Where Have All the Natives Gone?" in *Writing Diaspora: Tactics of Intervention in Contemporary Cultural Studies* (Bloomington: Indiana University Press, 1993), 33–34, 52.

36. Sociologist Kai Erickson rightfully extends the concept of trauma to include communal injuries, stating that "'trauma' has to be understood as resulting from a *constellation of life experiences* as well as from a discrete happening, from a *persisting condition* as well as from an acute event. . . . The effects are the same, and that, after all, should be our focus." Erickson, "Notes on Trauma and Community," in Caruth, *Trauma,* 185.

37. Caruth, *Trauma,* 4.

38. D. Taylor, *Disappearing Acts,* 19.

39. Anne Anlin Cheng, *The Melancholy of Race: Psychoanalysis, Assimilation, and Hidden Grief* (New York: Oxford University Press, 2001), 12.

40. Felman, *The Juridical Unconscious,* 174. Caroline Chung Simpson explores the internment's traumatic reverberations for all Americans in the postwar era, arguing that "The inexhaustible reenactments and retellings of the internment have prolonged its suspension as an unfinished story; in the postwar era especially it hovers as an event at once safely postponed and dangerously mutable. In some instances, the merest allusion to internment, especially one that purported to deny its significance as a trauma, might be simultaneously threatened by the unanswered question of what it tries to exclude." Caroline Chung Simpson, *An Absent Presence: Japanese Americans in Postwar American Culture, 1945–1960* (Durham, NC: Duke University Press, 2001), 6. Simpson's enlargement of the internment to a national trauma that implicates all Americans—if only in its apparent absence from discourse and representation—should be understood as an important methodological move in Asian American studies and race studies generally.

41. Judith Butler, "Endangered/Endangering: Schematic Racism and White Paranoia," in *Reading Rodney King/Reading Urban Uprising,* ed. Robert Gooding-Williams (New York: Routledge, 1993), 15; Vicki Bell, "On Speech, Race and Melancholia: An Interview with Judith Butler," *Theory, Culture and Society* 16, no. 2 (1999): 169. For more on performative acts, see J. L. Austin, *How to Do Things with Words* (Cambridge, MA: Harvard University Press, 1962); Judith Butler: *Gender Trouble: Feminism and the Subversion of Identity* (New York: Routledge, 1990), and *Bodies That Matter: On the Discursive Limits of Sex* (New York: Routledge, 1993).

42. For a very different interpretation of "performative citizenship," see Jonathan Lepofsky and James C. Fraser, "Building Community Citizens: Claiming the Right to Place-Making in the City," *Urban Studies* 40, no. 1 (2003): 127–142. Urban geographers Lepofsky and Fraser identify "performative acts" as one of the main tactics that impoverished urban communities use to assert flexible citizenship in the face of globalization. They focus on twenty-first-century urban populations in the industrial world.

43. Shimakawa, *National Abjection,* 4–9.

44. Jacques Derrida, *Archive Fever: A Freudian Impression,* trans. Eric Prenowitz (Chicago: University of Chicago Press, 1995).

45. Herman Rappaport, *Later Derrida: Reading the Recent Work* (New York: Routledge, 2002), 76, 89.

46. As Palumbo-Liu puts it in describing U.S. attempts to exclude Asians from citizenship, "'Whiteness' became the signified of the *will* of Congress. That is, whatever Congress had in mind when it decided on whom to accept as naturalizable, a necessary component was 'whiteness.'" *Asian/American*, 39.

47. Nayan Shah, *Contagious Divides: Epidemics and Race in San Francisco's Chinatown* (Berkeley: University of California Press, 2001), 7–8, 15–16.

48. Despite this distinction between our methodologies, I share Shah's intention to explore how such discourses of performative citizenship played out with both exclusionary and inclusive possibilities. Much as Shah demonstrates how Chinese American community leaders seized upon the public health repertoire to resist racist characterizations of Chinatown, I attempt to show how Japanese American internees seized upon the myth of performative citizenship to highlight the contradictions of the internment policy and of U.S. immigration policies generally.

49. Giroux, *Beyond the Spectacle of Terrorism*, 32.

50. Esther Kim Lee, *A History of Asian American Theatre* (New York: Cambridge University Press, 2006), 20.

51. Debord, *The Society of the Spectacle*, 136, 131.

52. Throughout this book, I follow Karen Shimakawa's application of Kristeva's "abjection" to Asian American history and culture. Shimakawa, *National Abjection*, 10–11.

Chapter 1: "A Race of Ingenious Marionettes"

1. William Shakespeare, *Hamlet*.

2. Matthew Calbraith Perry quoted in Rhoda Blumberg, *Commodore Perry in the Land of the Shogun* (New York: Lothrop, Lee, and Shepard Books, 1985), 36.

3. Osman Edwards, *Japanese Plays and Playfellows* (New York: John Lane, 1901), 4.

4. Perry's official title was Commander-in-Chief of the United States Expedition to the China Seas and Japan. In the first phase of the Japan expedition a contingent of the squadron landed in July 1853, at which time Perry delivered a presidential letter demanding the Japanese open their country to foreign contact. Perry then left, instructing the Japanese that he would return the following year with the expectation that they would sign a treaty with the United States. In the interval, Perry spent time in China, devising his strategy for what he called "the sequel," which commenced on Japan's shores in February 1854. The final treaty would be signed a year after the initial landing, in July 1854. Feifer, *Breaking Open Japan*, 260; Matthew Calbraith Perry, *The Japan Expedition, 1853–1854: The Personal Journal of Commodore Matthew C. Perry*, ed. Roger Pineau (Washington, D.C.: Smithsonian Institution Press, 1968), 159.

5. Frank Kermode, *The Age of Shakespeare* (New York: Random House, 2005), 17.

6. Upton Close, *Challenge: Behind the Face of Japan* (New York: Farrar and Rinehart, 1934), 356.

7. D. Taylor, *Disappearing Acts*, 119.

8. Feifer, *Breaking Open Japan*, 260.

9. Hawks, *Commodore Perry*, 43.

10. Blumberg, *Commodore Perry*, 39.

11. Feifer, *Breaking Open Japan*, 231.

12. John Curtis Perry quoted in ibid., 182. After defeating China in the Opium War, the British Empire forced the Chinese to submit to the unequal terms of the 1842 Treaty of Nanking. American trade privileges with China followed from this treaty, which marked the first of a series of unequal agreements between China and dominating foreign powers. The 1844 Treaty of Wanghia, which dictated China's relations with the United States, copied the terms of the 1842 document. Yet while China had submitted to a status akin to one of Britain's colonies, Japan remained obstinate in its superior stance of national isolation and rejection of Western subordination.

13. Anonymous captain quoted in ibid., 189.

14. Hawks, *Commodore Perry*, 27–29.

15. Blumberg, *Commodore Perry in the Land of the Shogun*, 39; Hawks, *Commodore Perry and the Opening of Japan*, 12.

16. D. Taylor, *Disappearing Acts*, 119.

17. Feifer, *Breaking Open Japan*, 119.

18. Ibid., 119–120. Subsequent Perry spectacles on this mission even presented the musicians fully armed. See Hawks, *Commodore Perry*, 332.

19. Kayama quoted in Feifer, *Breaking Open Japan*, 120 (emphasis added).

20. Feifer points out that to this day Americans almost universally praise Perry's expedition and "stress that Perry 'used no force whatsoever.'" *Breaking Open Japan*, 260. De Certeau, *The Writing of History*, xxv.

21. Hawks, *Commodore Perry*, 333.

22. Feifer, *Breaking Open Japan*, 116; Hawks, *Commodore Perry*, 346. While the American presence onshore generally numbered 300–500, at least five thousand Japanese generally lined the shore for these disembarkments.

23. Debord, *Society of the Spectacle*, 14.

24. Perry quoted in Blumberg, *Commodore Perry*, 36.

25. Hawks, *Commodore Perry*, 248.

26. Feifer, *Breaking Open Japan*, 231.

27. John H. Schroeder, *Matthew Calbraith Perry: Antebellum Sailor and Diplomat* (Annapolis, MD: Naval Institute Press, 2001), 68–69.

28. Hawks, *Commodore Perry*, 370.

29. D. Taylor, *The Archive and the Repertoire*, 45.

30. Hawks, *Commodore Perry*, 374.

31. Ralph Ellison, *Shadow and Act*, quoted in Cheng, *The Melancholy of Race*, 41. Cheng draws from Eric Lott and Michael Rogin to argue that racial masking, especially blackface minstrelsy, is a form of what she calls white melancholia, an argument from which I depart somewhat in the following analysis, which emphasizes the "theft" of Lott's *Love and Theft* but not at all the "love."

32. Hawks, *Commodore Perry*, 374.

33. Blumberg, *Commodore Perry,* 90–91, 106. Richard Wiley has written an entire novel based around the baffling phenomenon of Perry's retinue performing blackface minstrelsy for the Japanese. However, only the opening of the novel deals with the actual blackface performances—contending that they frightened at least the Japanese women—and the rest of the book deals with the fictional adventures of two of the American minstrel performers on furlough in the xenophobic Japanese countryside. I found fascinating Wiley's contention that at least one Japanese woman was unsettled by the uncanny "mirror image" of her nineteenth-century aristocratic makeup (whitened face and blackened teeth) and the makeup of the minstrel performers (blackface and whitened lips). Richard Wiley, *Commodore Perry's Minstrel Show* (Austin: University of Texas Press, 2007), 37.

34. Hawks, *Commodore Perry,* 250.

35. Perry quoted in Feifer, *Breaking Open Japan,* 123.

36. Ibid., 298–303.

37. Palumbo-Liu, *Asian/American,* 32.

38. I allude here to my citation above of Perry's blithe reference to the Japanese as "these people of forms and ceremonies." Hawks, *Commodore Perry,* 232.

39. Chow, "Where Have All the Natives Gone?" 52, 60.

40. Palumbo-Liu repeatedly stresses the importance of discerning that the peril's particular meaning varies depending on which ethnic group (e.g., Chinese vs. Japanese immigrants) it targets and in what particular historical moment: "The Yellow Peril has to be read within particular historical specificities which show that the various mutations of the 'peril' stem from particular economic and political phenomena in the United States itself." *Asian/American,* 34.

41. Shah, *Contagious Divides,* 12, 22.

42. Palumbo-Liu, *Asian/American,* 38–40.

43. Edward Said, *Orientalism* (New York: Pantheon Books, 1978), 20–23, 48. Although Said generally understood "the Orient" to mean the Middle East, I think that at the end of World War II, when the United States was confidently anticipating victory over and assumption of a colonial role in postwar Japan, the Orientalist citational network should certainly be extended to include Japan. Moreover, the similarity between the Japanese American internment and the postwar occupation of Japan (the latter, in theory, controlled by the Allied powers as a whole, but in actuality heavily dominated by the United States) is evident in the fact that scholars have likened both situations to colonialism. Japan scholar John Dower has described General Douglas MacArthur's "neocolonial military dictatorship" in his Pulitzer Prize–winning book on the Occupation, *Embracing Defeat: Japan in the Wake of World War II* (New York: W. W. Norton, 1999), 81. Internment scholar Harry Kitano, himself a former internee of the Topaz WRA camp, describes the Japanese American internment as "domestic colonialism" because it meets all four of Robert Blauner's conditions of the colonial model: involuntary entry, forced acculturation, domination by the colonizing group, and pervasive racism. In Roger Daniels, Sandra C. Taylor, and Harry H. L. Kitano, *Japanese Americans: From Relocation to Redress* (Seattle: University of Washington Press, 1991), 154. The U.S. government foretold these structural similarities even before war's end and thus

activated the Japanese American camps as laboratories for policies and personnel to be deployed in postwar occupied Japan.

44. Jonas Barish, *The Antitheatrical Prejudice* (Berkeley: University of California Press, 1981), 191.

45. Ibid., 91, 50, 85.

46. Jean-Christophe Agnew, *Worlds Apart: The Market and the Theater in Anglo-American Thought, 1550–1750* (New York: Cambridge University Press, 1986).

47. See, for instance, the account of Chicago School sociology provided in Henry Yu, *Thinking Orientals: Migration, Contact, and Exoticism in Modern America* (New York: Oxford University Press, 2001).

48. Jennifer Robertson, *Takarazuka: Sexual Politics and Popular Culture in Modern Japan* (Berkeley: University of California Press, 1998), 101–103, 105.

49. Chow, *Ethics After Idealism*, 15.

50. As Mari Yoshihara has argued, Benedict drew from this repetitive network in her study of Japanese culture-at-a-distance but innovated on it by focusing not on Japanese women but instead on rendering the practices of Japanese men as feminized. This feminization went hand-in-hand with the theatricalization I am adding to the equation, in part because theatricality has always been associated in the West with femininity and emasculation. Mari Yoshihara, *Embracing the East: White Women and American Orientalism* (Oxford: Oxford University Press, 2003), 172.

51. Ruth Benedict, *The Chrysanthemum and the Sword: Patterns of Japanese Culture* (Boston: Houghton Mifflin, 1989 [1946]), 7.

52. Benedict's recourse to theatre metaphors stemmed not only from her citations of the Japanese theatricalizing discourse but also from her interests in aesthetics as a whole. As C. Douglas Lummis notes in his critique of *The Chrysanthemum and the Sword*, Benedict came to the field of anthropology not through the social sciences (which was ordinarily the case) but through literature; throughout her anthropological career she considered her studies to be works of aesthetic criticism. C. Douglas Lummis, *A New Look at the Chrysanthemum and the Sword* (Tokyo: Shohakusha, 1982), 29.

53. Benedict, *The Chrysanthemum and the Sword*, 223, 217, 262–263.

54. Ibid., 172, 175, 196–197.

55. Ibid., 2.

56. Edwards, *Japanese Plays and Playfellows*, 2, 7, 17–18, 21.

57. Ibid., 2–4.

58. Ibid., 31.

59. Ibid.

60. Kojin Karatani, "Uses of Aesthetics: after Orientalism," *boundary* 2 25. no. 2 (1998). Like Karatani, I have taken instruction from Said's corporate approach of indicting the body of Orientalist work as a whole rather than vilifying individual authors; Said's approach is not only fair but it also shifts attention to the uncanny coherence and pervasive power of Orientalism. In my cataloging of theatricalizing texts about Japan from the theatre, sociology, and anthropology fields (among others), I have avoided impugning individual writers and artists (many of whom, like Ruth Benedict and Bertolt Brecht, I greatly admire) in favor of demonstrating how this discourse has gained

strength through its circulation and, in fact, through losing a clear connection to its originators.

61. Edwards, *Japanese Plays and Playfellows,* 74–76.

62. Ibid.

63. Ibid., 78.

64. Ibid., 69, 71.

65. Benedict, *The Chrysanthemum and the Sword,* 197.

66. As Samuel L. Leiter and Stanca Scholz-Cionca (along with several of their colleagues) demonstrate, the first wave of Western sources on Japanese theatre appeared decades after Edwards' book. "The first comprehensive studies—introductions, historical surveys, and narrowly focused research (on subjects like religious themes in drama)—appeared during the 1920s. The earliest study of Japanese masks was written in the mid-1920s in Germany and remains to the present day a valuable reference, still used even by Japanese researchers." Stanca Scholz-Cionca and Samuel L. Leiter, "Introduction," in *Japanese Theatre and the International Stage,* ed. Samuel L. Leiter (Leiden: Brill, 2001), 22. This suggests how stagnant the discourse on Japanese theatre remains and how influential early manifestations of it were.

67. In the influential realm of French theory, we can see how the theatricalizing discourse circulated through Edwards remains unquestioned in Roland Barthes' *Empire of Signs.* Written in French in 1970, Barthes enacts Western anxieties about Japan different than the ones that animated Edwards' fin de siècle assessment of Japanese theatre. In his three essays on *bunraku* (puppet theatre) and Kabuki, Barthes offers not a feudal soul for modern Japan, but a lack of soul altogether. Contrasting Japanese theatre to Western theatre, Barthes claims for the former none of the latter's concern with "inwardness." Instead, beneath the surface of Japanese spectacle (including, in other essays, *pachinko* gambling and ritualized bowing) there is merely emptiness, nothingness. For Barthes, Japanese culture and society are pure aesthetic. Roland Barthes, *Empire of Signs,* trans. Richard Howard (New York: Hill and Wang, 1982).

68. Palumbo-Liu, *Asian/American,* 32.

69. Although Noh is known for being a masked theatre, it is worth pointing out that usually only the main character, or *shite,* wears a mask.

70. David Ewick, "Craig, Edward Gordon, and *The Mask,* 1905–29," *Japonisme, Orientalism, Modernism: A Critical Bibliography of Japan in English Language Verse, 1900–1950;* http://www.themargins.net/bib/D/d17.html. Accessed 15 October 2003.

71. Olga Taxidou, *The Mask: A Periodical Performance by Edward Gordon Craig* (Amsterdam: Harwood Academic Publishers, 1998), 98.

72. Ibid., 82, 104, 97.

73. Ezra Pound and Ernest Fenollosa, *The Classic Noh Theatre of Japan* (New York: New Directions, 1959), 3, 6, 58.

74. William Butler Yeats, "Introduction to *Certain Noble Plays of Japan,*" in Pound and Fenollosa, *The Classic Noh Theatre of Japan,* 151, 155–156, 161.

75. Edward Braun, *The Director and the Stage* (New York: Holmes and Meier, 1982), 123; Vsevold Meyerhold, *Meyerhold on Theatre,* trans. Edward Braun (New York: Hill and Wang, 1969), 60, 59, 123.

76. Braun, *The Director and the Stage,* 115.

77. Ibid.

78. Meyerhold wrote in 1907: "The means of expression must now be architectural, rather than pictorial as they were before." *Meyerhold on Theatre,* 98, 58. Genet quoted in Leonard Cabell Pronko, *Theater East and West: Perspectives toward a Total Theater* (Berkeley: University of California Press, 1967), 131.

79. Meyerhold, *Meyerhold on Theatre,* 99.

80. Ibid., 99, 102.

81. Ibid., 51, 57. Reviewer quoted in Braun, *The Director and the Stage,* 119.

82. Nick Worrall, "Meyerhold's Production of the Magnificent Cuckold," *The Drama Review* 17, no. 1 (1973): 23, 27.

83. Sergei Eisenstein, *Film Form: Essays in Film Theory,* trans. Jay Leyda (New York: Harcourt, Brace, 1949), 18.

84. Hugh Wilkinson, *The Asiatic Society of Japan Bulletin No. 7* (1995).

85. Eisenstein, *Film Form,* 44, 24, 26.

86. Said, *Orientalism,* 96.

87. Moreover, both reinforced their limited knowledge with citations from other Western sources, perpetuating a system of assumptions that resembles Said's Orientalism. Perhaps the most disappointing realization is that the Orientalist presumption of mastery was used as a shortcut in the pursuit of knowledge about the traditional Japanese theatre—a theatre whose history and training process these same Western theorists praised for its humility, discipline, and commitment.

88. Eisenstein, *Film Form,* 27, 26, 34. Meyerhold refers to the same anecdote in a 1936 lecture (published in 1962) about Chaplin and Eisenstein titled "Chaplin and Chaplinism." The loose web of associations that make up the context of Meyerhold's reference is a near-perfect demonstration of Orientalist discourse.

89. Ibid., 23.

90. Percival Lowell, *The Soul of the Far East* (New York: Macmillan, 1911), 1; Julian Street, *Mysterious Japan* (Garden City, NJ: Doubleday, Page, 1921), 48. In a description of Japan as the diametric opposite of the West, the Asian other consistently lands on the artificial or "unnatural" side of the binary. Lowell, for instance, describes the Japanese as "preposterously unnatural" by birthright. *The Soul of the Far East,* 3.

91. Close, *Challenge,* 383; Percival Lowell, *Occult Japan or the Way of the Gods: An Esoteric Study of Japanese Personality and Possession* (Boston: Houghton Mifflin, 1894), 283.

92. Lowell, *Occult Japan,* 283.

93. Ibid., 329, 288. Lowell goes on to supply many micro and macro examples of this imitativeness, emphasizing with widely varying degree its sincerity or lack thereof.

94. Lowell, *The Soul of the Far East,* 15, 6–7.

95. Close, *Challenge,* 356.

96. Street, *Mysterious Japan,* 58, 64, 49, 75.

97. Close, *Challenge,* 8–9, 357.

98. Ibid., 278, 290.

99. Ibid., 309, 310.

100. Ibid., 275.

101. David Matsumoto, *Unmasking Japan: Myths and Realities about the Emotions of the Japanese* (Palo Alto: Stanford University Press, 1996); Fumie Kumagai and Donna J. Keyser, *Unmasking Japan Today: The Impact of Traditional Values on Modern Japanese Society* (Westport, CT: Praeger, 1996); Robert Craigie, *Behind the Japanese Mask: A British Ambassador in Japan, 1937–1942* (London: Kegan Paul, 1945); Hal Porter, *The Actors: An Image of the New Japan* (Sydney: Angus and Robertson, 1968; William Bohnaker, *The Hollow Doll (a Little Box of Japanese Shocks)* (New York: Ballantine Books, 1990).

102. Craigie, *Behind the Japanese Mask*, 9.

103. Porter, *The Actors*, 1.

104. Bohnaker, *The Hollow Doll*, xv.

105. Homi K. Bhabha, "The Other Question: Stereotype, Discrimination, and the Discourse of Colonialism," in *The Location of Culture* (London: Routledge, 1994). For two instances of writers who seek to subvert dominant ideas of Japan but end up reinscribing the theatricalizing discourse to do so, see Joy Hendry, *Wrapping Culture: Politeness, Presentation, and Power in Japan and Other Societies* (Oxford: Clarendon Press, 1993), and Matsumoto, *Unmasking Japan*.

106. Ezra F. Vogel, "Foreword," in Benedict, *The Chrysanthemum and the Sword*, x.

107. In his study of Chicago School sociologists and their reliance on Asian American informants as "marginal men," Henry Yu argues that American social science from the 1920s forward relied on the "stage as a metaphor for social life" that both naturalized "the assumption of prescribed roles and proper performance" and "transformed race and exotic identity into an object." *Thinking Orientals*, 113–114, 66. Sociologists like Robert E. Park likened race to a mask or referred to a "racial uniform" in order to celebrate the performativity (constructedness, mobility, mutability) of marginalized identities in modern societies like U.S. cities. Benedict and her colleagues in the Culture and Personality School of liberal anthropology (Franz Boas, Margaret Mead, et al.) certainly drew from sociology's tradition of theatrical metaphors. More important, though, in studies of foreign others like *The Chrysanthemum and the Sword*, the methodology of juxtaposing the foreign object with the American subject inevitably downplayed the extent to which American society at large was depicted as theatrical. Instead, in keeping with the ideological pressures of a nation at war, Benedict emphasized the honest artlessness of America in order to overstate the difference offered by artful Japan as "the most alien enemy the United States had ever fought."

108. Vogel, "Foreword," in Benedict, *The Chrysanthemum and the Sword*, x. One of the topics about which Benedict evidently grilled these Japanese American informants was Japanese propaganda and historical movies, which she needed help deciphering beyond the mere issues of language. Benedict supplemented this information by reading Japanese novels in translation.

109. Christopher Shannon, "A World Made Safe for Differences: Ruth Benedict's *The Chrysanthemum and the Sword*," *American Quarterly* 47, no. 4 (1995): 664.

110. Ibid., 673.

111. Park quoted in Yu, *Thinking Orientals*, 66.

112. Palumbo-Liu, *Asian/American*, 300–301.

113. Benedict, *The Chrysanthemum and the Sword,* 29, 225.

114. Ibid., 196–197, 217.

Chapter 2: Spectacularizing Japanese American Suspects

1. J. Edgar Hoover, *Persons in Hiding* (Boston: Little, Brown, and Company, 1938), viii.

2. Frederick L. Collins, *The FBI in Peace and War* (New York: G. P. Putnam's Sons, 1943), 257. Hoover authorized Collins' text, and he also wrote the book's introduction.

3. Weglyn, *Years of Infamy,* 52–53.

4. Not a single Japanese American was tried, much less convicted, of espionage or sabotage during World War II.

5. Both "happy" and "lark" were terms unabashedly used by William Randolph Hearst's press in its 1942 coverage of the evacuation and internment of local Japanese Americans. See "First Thousand Japs Leave L.A.," *Los Angeles Examiner,* 24 March 1942; "Pasadena and Glendale Japs," *Los Angeles Examiner,* 14 March 1942. The American mass media's contribution to this construction of Japanese American persecution as a harmless farce is treated at length in the following chapter.

6. Robert Gid Powers, *G-Men: Hoover's FBI in American Popular Culture* (Carbondale: Southern Illinois University Press, 1983), 180, xvi.

7. Courtney Ryley Cooper, *Ten Thousand Public Enemies* (Boston: Little, Brown, 1935), 293.

8. D. Taylor, *Disappearing Acts,* 107.

9. John J. Floherty, *Inside the F.B.I.* (Philadelphia: J. B. Lippincott, 1943), 142.

10. For instance, in the FBI-commissioned book *The FBI Story,* Don Whitehead remarks about "the decision to move some 120,000 Japanese-Americans from their homes and farms on the West Coast to relocation centers": "It was a tragic upheaval which Hoover looked upon as a mixture of politics and hysteria and not as an urgent measure of national defense." Don Whitehead, *The FBI Story: A Report to the People* (New York: Random House, 1956), 188–189.

11. U.S. Commission on Wartime Relocation and Internment of Civilians (CWRIC), *Personal Justice Denied* (Seattle: University of Washington Press, 1997).

12. Throughout its history, the FBI's xenophobic excesses often went unchecked because anti-immigrant sentiments ran stronger in the United States than fear of repressive policing. See Athan G. Theoharis, *The Boss: J. Edgar Hoover and the Great American Inquisition* (Philadelphia: Temple University Press, 1988).

13. Robert Gid Powers, *Secrecy and Power: The Life of J. Edgar Hoover* (New York: Free Press, 1987), 212.

14. John Tagg, *The Burden of Representation: Essays on Photographies and Histories* (Minneapolis: University of Minnesota Press, 1988), 72, 13.

15. Shah, *Contagious Divides,* 29.

16. Dirk C. Gibson, "Neither God nor Devil: A Rhetorical Perspective on the Political Myths of J. Edgar Hoover" (Ph.D. diss., Indiana University, 1983), 11.

17. Roberta A. Hill, ed., *The FBI's RACON: Racial Conditions in the United States during World War II* (Boston: Northeastern University Press, 1995), 5.

18. Matthew C. Cecil, "Seductions of Spin: Public Relations and the FBI Myth" (Ph. D. diss., University of Iowa, 2000), 33; William W. Turner, *Hoover's FBI: The Men and the Myth* (Los Angeles: Sherbourne Press, 1970), 126–127.

19. Hoover, *Persons in Hiding,* 311.

20. Hoover was instrumental in shifting the Hollywood hero from the gangster to the detective. In 1935, G-men movies replaced gangster films at the box office pinnacle owing to a 1934 censorship code that banned the latter for their violence and glamorization of crime. Powers, *G-Men,* 65.

21. Cooper, *Ten Thousand Public Enemies,* 48; Hoover, *Persons in Hiding,* xvii–xviii.

22. Cooper, *Ten Thousand Public Enemies,* 17.

23. Hoover, *Persons in Hiding,* 312.

24. Cooper, *Ten Thousand Public Enemies,* 4–5, 7.

25. Powers, *G-Men,* 210–211.

26. Hoover, *Persons in Hiding,* 280–281.

27. Ibid., 17–18, 43, 206, 162.

28. Cooper, *Ten Thousand Public Enemies,* 321.

29. Hoover, *Persons in Hiding,* 162.

30. Ibid., 16.

31. Cooper, *Ten Thousand Public Enemies,* 11.

32. Ibid., 188, 192.

33. D. Taylor, *Disappearing Acts,* 97; Tagg, *The Burden of Representation,* 72.

34. Leon G. Turrou, *How to Be a G-Man* (New York: R. M. McBride, 1939), 10.

35. The FBI endorsed, and Hoover often co-wrote with, various approved authors, including Frederick Collins and Courtney Ryley Cooper. Hereafter I refer to these FBI-sanctioned authors as "FBI writers." Most of Hoover's books and articles were reputedly either co-written with or ghostwritten by Cooper, who, as Athan Theoharis put it, was "the voice of Hoover himself." *The Boss,* 119.

36. Cecil, "Seductions of Spin," 33, 37, 217.

37. Turrou, *How to Be a G-Man,* 178 (emphasis added).

38. Cooper, *Ten Thousand Public Enemies,* 339, 353.

39. Powers, *G-Men,* 200.

40. Theoharis, *The Boss,* 59–60.

41. Jay Robert Nash, *Citizen Hoover: A Critical Study of the Life and Times of J. Edgar Hoover and His FBI* (Chicago: Nelson-Hall, 1972), 215.

42. Cooper, *Ten Thousand Public Enemies,* 173–174, 171.

43. Ibid., 61.

44. Turrou, *How to Be a G-Man,* 131, 133.

45. Foreword to Hoover, *Persons in Hiding,* xviii.

46. Ibid., 8–9, 13, 27.

47. I allude to a chapter of Hoover's *Persons in Hiding* called "The Woman Behind the Crime."

48. Hoover, *Persons in Hiding,* 20, 26, 142–143, 156, 163–164.

49. Homi K. Bhabha, "Of Mimicry and Man: The Ambivalence of Colonial Discourse," in *The Location of Culture*, 86.

50. Collins, *The FBI in Peace and War*, 237–238.

51. Ibid., 238–239.

52. Ibid., 229.

53. J. Edgar Hoover, Memo to Francis Biddle, 2 February 1942.

54. Bob Kumamoto, "The Search for Spies: American Counterintelligence and the Japanese American Community, 1931–1942," *Amerasia Journal* 6, no. 2 (1979): 47.

55. Collins, *The FBI in Peace and War*, 238.

56. Ibid., 227.

57. Federal Bureau of Investigation, internal memo, "Japanese Activities on the West Coast,"13 November 1941.

58. Collins, *The FBI in Peace and War*, 229.

59. Kumamoto, "The Search for Spies," 67.

60. J. Edgar Hoover and Courtney Ryley Cooper, "Stamping Out the Spies," *American Magazine,* January 1940, 83. Powers argues for the representativeness of this article, saying "The argument Hoover presented in 'Stamping Out the Spies' became the FBI's line in all its wartime publicity. . . . Throughout the war Hoover kept telling the public to stay out of the spy hunt." *G-Men,* 220. While the post–Pearl Harbor closure of Japanese-language schools (primarily aimed at Nisei, who attended after regular school hours and/or on Saturdays) has been well documented in internment accounts, the seemingly contradictory criminalization of English-language students of Japanese descent has merited little mention.

61. Collins, *The FBI in Peace and War,* 227.

62. Ibid., 233, 247.

63. Whitehead, *The FBI Story,* 200.

64. Hoover, "Big Scare," *American Magazine,* August 1941, 67.

65. Collins, *The FBI in Peace and War,* 240–243.

66. Ibid.

67. Powers, *G-Men,* 203, 228.

68. Baz Kershaw, "Curiosity or Contempt: On Spectacle, the Human, and Activism," *Theatre Journal* 55, no. 4 (2003): 604–605.

69. Powers, *G-Men,* 228.

70. *New Republic* quoted in Whitehead, *The FBI Story,* 175.

71. Theoharis, *The Boss,* 158–160.

72. Jon McKenzie, *Perform or Else: From Discipline to Performance* (London: Routledge, 2001), 73.

73. Theoharis, *The Boss,* 119; Powers, *Secrecy and Power,* 197.

74. Powers, *G-Men,* 217–218.

75. Hoover and Cooper, "Stamping Out the Spies," 22–23.

76. Collins, *The FBI in Peace and War,* 259.

77. Hoover, "Big Scare," 67.

78. Collins, *The FBI in Peace and War,* 264.

79. Ibid.

80. Hoover and Cooper, "Stamping Out the Spies," 84.

81. Hoover, "Big Scare," 24–25.

82. Dan B. Markel, "Mrs. Roosevelt Urges Women to Set Brave Example in War: U.S. Civilian Morale Has Roots in Home, Mrs. Roosevelt Says at Tacoma Parley," *Seattle Post-Intelligencer,* 14 December 1941, 1.

83. Francis MacDonnell, *Insidious Foes: The Axis Fifth Column and the American Home Front* (New York: Oxford University Press, 1995), 153.

84. Bosworth, *America's Concentration Camps,* 75.

85. "Public Believed First War Reports Only Gag: Reporter Finds It Difficult to Make People Grasp Facts of Japanese Hawaii Attack," *Los Angeles Times,* 8 December 1941; Edward Hunter, "Jap Spies Not So Funny—Joke's on Us," *New York Post,* 10 December 1941.

86. Quoted in MacDonnell, *Insidious Foes,* 82. See also "Peril Real! S. F. Must Blackout Totally," *San Francisco Examiner,* 10 December 1941; "They Wouldn't Believe It: Passersby Think Raid Alarm Is Gag," *New York Post,* 9 December 1941.

87. Collins, *The FBI in Peace and War,* 245–246; D. M. Ladd, Memo to J. Edgar Hoover Re: Conferences between representatives of the FBI, ONI, and G-2 concerning plans for the apprehension of German, Italian and Japanese alien enemies in the territory of Hawaii, 26 November 1941. Plan I related to a state of war between the United States and Japan but no threat of an invasion of the Hawaiian Islands. Plan II envisioned the same conditions of war as Plan I but "with threats of surprise raids against" Hawaii. Plan III prepared for imminent invasion and called for "absolute martial law." Plan I called for 234 Japanese aliens to be temporarily detained, Plan II for these 234 plus 54 U.S. citizens of Japanese descent, and Plan III for permanent detention of all suspect Japanese regardless of citizenship.

88. Collins, *The FBI in Peace and War,* 245–248 (emphasis added).

89. Whitehead, *The FBI Story,* 183 (emphasis added).

90. Collins, *The FBI in Peace and War,* 245–246.

91. "Roundup of Japanese Aliens in Southland Now Totals 500: Officers, Working under FBI, Continue Hunt; Asiatic, Who Had Pledged Loyalty, Found with Guns," *Los Angeles Times,* 9 December 1941; "U.S. Seizes 736 Japs: Those Held Assured Fair Hearing," *New York Post,* 8 December 1941; "Sixty Aliens Held in FBI Roundup," *Los Angeles Times,* 10 December 1941; "Foreign-Born Japanese Here Rounded Up," *Seattle Post-Intelligencer,* 8 December 1941.

92. Makabe quoted in John Tateishi, *And Justice for All: An Oral History of the Japanese American Detention Camps* (Seattle: University of Washington Press, 1984), 251.

93. Hosokawa, *Nisei,* 217.

94. Yamashita quoted in Arthur A. Hansen, ed., *Japanese American World War II Evacuation Oral History Project Part I: Internees* (Westport, CT: Meckler, 1991), 19.

95. MacDonnell, *Insidious Foes,* 181.

96. Ladd, Memo to Hoover. Moreover, in a 26 December 1941 memo to his assistant directors, Hoover approvingly related the opinion of West Coast theatre of war commander John DeWitt that mass raids on all coastal Japanese Americans should be supervised by the FBI "so that it will be done efficiently and without any fan-fare." J. Edgar Hoover, Memo to Tamm Tolson and D. M. Ladd, 26 December 1941.

97. "S.F. Rounds Up Japs, Swings to Defense," *San Francisco Examiner,* 8 December 1941.

98. "Roundup of Japanese Aliens in Southland," *Los Angeles Times,* 9 December 1941.

99. Quoted in Audrie Girdner and Anne Loftis, *The Great Betrayal: The Evacuation of the Japanese-Americans during World War II* (London: Collier-Macmillan, 1969), 5.

100. Carey McWilliams, *Prejudice—Japanese-Americans: Symbol of Racial Intolerance* (Boston: Little, Brown, 1944), 178.

101. "Entire City Is Put on War Footing," *New York Times,* 8 December 1941. Although the FBI initially rebuffed press inquiries, Attorney General Biddle gave a press release about the FBI raids on 9 December 1941. Francis Biddle, Memo to the press, 9 December 1941.

102. "Entire City Is Put on War Footing," *New York Times,* 8 December 1941.

103. Ibid.

104. "All Jap Assets, 736 Nationals Are Seized in U.S.: Forbid Any of Enemies to Leave Country," *Chicago Tribune,* 9 December 1941.

105. "Chicago Japs Gloomy, Hide Behind Doors," *Chicago Tribune,* 9 December 1941.

106. J. D. Swenson, Memo to J. Edgar Hoover Re: Japanese aliens, 18 November 1941; Theoharis, *The Boss,* 23.

107. "Entire City Is Put on War Footing," *New York Times,* 8 December 1941.

108. Hoover, "Big Scare," 66.

109. J. Edgar Hoover, Teletype memo to all Special Agents in Charge, 7 December 1941. I have not reproduced the all-capital letters in which this teletype was originally printed.

110. Whitehead, *The FBI Story,* 182.

111. "S.F. Rounds Up Japs, Swings to Defense," *San Francisco Examiner,* 8 December 1941.

112. Yoneda quoted in Lawson Fusao Inada, ed., *Only What We Could Carry: The Japanese American Internment Experience* (Berkeley: Heyday Books, 2000), 155.

113. Tsukamoto quoted in Tateishi, *And Justice for All,* 6; Ishii quoted in Hansen, *Japanese American World War II Evacuation,* 62; Swanson quoted in Girdner and Loftis, *The Great Betrayal,* 112.

114. David L. Eng, *Racial Castration: Managing Masculinity in Asian America* (Durham, NC: Duke University Press, 2001), 30.

115. Hosokawa, *Nisei,* 239. The leading internment scholar, Roger Daniels, makes a similar point, noting that despite the fruitlessness of FBI raids (none of the prisoners was ever convicted of anything), "the mere fact of these searches, widely reported in the press, added to the suspicion with which Japanese were viewed. These searches, like so much of the anti-Japanese movement, were part of a self-fulfilling prophecy: one is suspicious of the Japanese, so one searches their houses; the mere fact of the search, when noticed ('the FBI went through those Jap houses on the other side of town'), creates more suspicion." *Concentration Camps USA,* 43.

116. Palumbo-Liu, *Asian/American,* 38.

117. Edward H. Spicer, Asael T. Hansen, Katherine Luomala, and Marvin K. Opler,

Impounded People: Japanese-Americans in the Relocation Centers (Tucson: University of Arizona Press, 1969), 50.

118. Michael Taussig, *Mimesis and Alterity: A Particular History of the Senses* (New York: Routledge, 1993), 174.

119. Representatives Wolverton and Woodruff quoted in U.S. Government, *Congressional Record* (Washington, D.C.: U.S. Government Printing Office, 1941), 9521–9522.

120. Funabiki quoted in U.S. Government, "Japanese-American and Aleutian Wartime Relocation," *House of Representatives Committee on the Judiciary,* 98th Congress, Second Session (Washington, D.C.: U.S. Government Printing Office, 1984), 764. For an example of the post–Pearl Harbor narrative that posited that Japan shattered America's idyllic Sunday morning, see "Attack Shatters S.F. Sunday Quiet: Smiles Leave Faces to Be Replaced by Air of Grim Determination," *San Francisco Examiner,* 8 December 1941.

121. Kumamoto, "The Search for Spies," 47.

122. Powers, *G-Men,* 189.

123. Cooper, *Ten Thousand Public Enemies,* 84.

124. J. Edgar Hoover, Memo to Francis M. Shea, 17 December 1941.

125. Cooper, *Ten Thousand Public Enemies,* 132, 136.

126. Turrou, *How to Be a G-Man,* 115.

127. Collins, *The FBI in Peace and War,* ix–x.

128. Cooper, *Ten Thousand Public Enemies,* 99.

129. Ibid., 99, 78.

130. Turrou, *How to Be a G-Man,* 45.

131. Ibid., 87.

132. Gibson, "Neither God Nor Devil," 274–275.

133. Cooper, *Ten Thousand Public Enemies,* 130, 148.

134. Puchner rightly contrasts antitheatrical modernism to "the (pro)theatricalist avant-garde" of Brecht and his ilk, which advocated overt theatricality in order to empower the audience and "lead art back to the public sphere." Martin Puchner, *Stage Fright: Modernism, Anti-Theatricality, and Drama* (Baltimore: Johns Hopkins University Press, 2002), 9–11, 4–6, 125.

135. Hoover, *Persons in Hiding,* xii-xiii.

136. Turrou, *How to Be a G-Man,* 159.

137. Powers, *G-Men,* 214.

138. See Cooper, *Ten Thousand Public Enemies,* 31; W. Turner, *Hoover's FBI,* 253.

139. Quoted in Gibson, "Neither God nor Devil," 42. MacDonnell put it this way: "The Bureau publicity department tried to portray its agents as well-educated, clean-cut professionals; the kind of respectable middle-class figures who would gladly lend a lawnmower to a neighbor or volunteer to coach the local sandlot baseball team." *Insidious Foes,* 177.

140. Theoharis, *The Boss,* 91, 104.

141. Bhabha, "Of Mimicry and Man," 88–90.

142. Hosokawa, *Nisei,* 234, 240.

143. The vast majority of the Japanese Americans immediately seized by the FBI

after Pearl Harbor were indeed men, although, as Michi Nishiura Weglyn has pointed out, fifty women were included in the roundups. Weglyn, *Years of Infamy.*

144. "First S.F. Japanese Prisoner," *San Francisco Examiner,* 8 December 1941.

145. Allan Sekula, "The Body and the Archive," *October* 39, no. 4 (Winter 1986): 14.

146. Ibid., 11, 15.

147. Tagg, *The Burden of Representation,* 12.

148. "The New War in the Pacific: Japanese and Chinese Reactions," *New York Times,* 8 December 1941.

149. "Detained," *San Francisco Examiner,* 10 December 1941; "Suspects in S. F.," *San Francisco Examiner,* 10 December 1941.

150. Miles Orvell, *The Real Thing: Imitation and Authenticity in American Culture, 1880–1940* (Chapel Hill: University of North Carolina Press, 1989), 228.

151. Tagg, *The Burden of Representation,* 12; Powers, *G-Men,* 189.

152. Kumamoto, "The Search for Spies," 71.

153. "Slow Motion," *San Francisco Examiner,* 31 March 1942.

Chapter 3: Performative Citizenship and Anti-Japanese Melodrama

1. D. Taylor, *Disappearing Acts,* 92.

2. Chow, *Writing Diaspora,* 61–62.

3. The Supreme Court's *Korematsu v. United States* (323 U.S. 214) argued that the government's exclusion and internment of Japanese Americans violated the U.S. Constitution and was decided in favor of the government on 18 December 1944. In 1983, Korematsu filed a writ of *coram nobis,* and his original conviction for evading the exclusion orders was overturned. But technically the 1944 Korematsu decision remains one of only two Supreme Court rulings upholding racial discrimination that have not been overturned by "strict scrutiny."

4. Korematsu's statements are from a documentary feature made about his life and his famous case: *Of Civil Wrongs and Rights: The Fred Korematsu Story,* dir. Eric Paul Fournier (National Asian American Telecommunications Association, 2000). Louis Althusser details the "interpellation" process in "Ideology and Ideological State Apparatuses (Notes towards an Investigation)," in *Lenin and Philosophy* (New York: Verso, 1978), 174.

5. D. Taylor, *Disappearing Acts,* 121.

6. Daniels, *Concentration Camps USA,* 32.

7. See Morton Grodzins, *Americans Betrayed: Politics and the Japanese Evacuation* (Chicago: University of Chicago Press, 1949), 19; McWilliams, *Prejudice,* 112; Jacobus tenBroek, Edward N. Barnhart, and Floyd W. Matson, *Prejudice, War, and the Constitution* (Berkeley: University of California Press, 1958), 85.

8. The government would not complete evacuation of all Japanese Americans from the West Coast military zones until 7 August 1942, but major cities like San Francisco and Los Angeles had already been emptied by the beginning of summer.

9. The patriotic pageantry of previous eras in American history had also blatantly

excluded marginalized ethnic groups whose inclusion would not have been politically expedient. See, for instance, David Glassberg, *American Historical Pageantry: The Uses of Tradition in the Early Twentieth Century* (Chapel Hill: University of North Carolina Press, 1990). But World War II's pageants were the first to capitalize on the cosmopolitan cachet of demonstrably including every ethnic group that made up the U.S. "melting pot"—and to use this inclusiveness as ammunition for the ostracism of a singled-out minority.

10. Debord, *The Society of the Spectacle.*

11. Chow, *Writing Diaspora,* 60–61. Melodrama in the theatre was the modern update on classical morality plays, but both share what Peter Brooks calls "Manichaestic terms" insofar as their characters personify the polarization of good and evil through human scenarios that subsume the gray areas of everyday life into a simple but thrilling conflict that "suggests the need to recognize and confront evil, to combat and expel it, to purge the social order." Melodramatic Manichaeism, "arguing its logic of the excluded middle, and imagining a situation—the moment of revolutionary suspension—where the world is called upon to make present and to impose a new society, to legislate the regime of virtue," leaves no room for contemplation of middle-ground solutions or compromise, demanding instead immediate action. Peter Brooks, *The Melodramatic Imagination: Balzac, Henry James, Melodrama, and the Mode of Excess* (New Haven, CT: Yale University Press, 1976), 13, 15. Film scholar Linda Williams demonstrates melodrama's inherent multimedia quality through Henry James' metaphor of a "'leaping fish' alighting first in one medium and then in another." Melodramatic myths of U.S. race relations, such as the *Uncle Tom's Cabin* incarnations that Williams analyzes, leap off the pages and stages of their origin stories to become a "melodramatic mode" that governs everyday interactions and public policy in race-conscious America. The white-Asian melodrama of the "Yellow Peril," originating later in the nineteenth century than the black-white Uncle Tom melodrama (but in no less potent or long-lasting form), can be seen to have similarly "leaping" tendencies, alighting from novels to theatre and from film to newspapers. Linda Williams, *Playing the Race Card: Melodramas of Black and White from Uncle Tom to O. J. Simpson* (Princeton, NJ: Princeton University Press, 2001), 6, 25. For corresponding scholarship on white-Asian melodramas, see Robert G. Lee, *Orientals: Asian Americans in Popular Culture* (Philadelphia: Temple University Press, 1999). For more on the studied disregard of political economy that characterizes melodrama, see Marcia Landy, *Imitations of Life: A Reader on Film and Television Melodrama* (Detroit: Wayne State University Press, 1991).

12. The *Time* article was published on the occasion of William Randolph Hearst's seventieth birthday and is quoted in David Nasaw, *The Chief: The Life of William Randolph Hearst* (Boston: Houghton Mifflin, 2000), 469. *Patria* starred famed ballroom dancer Irene Castle as the title heroine, and the resident Japanese villain, Baron Huroki, was played by Warner Oland, a white actor who would soon gain fame as a popular yellowface movie star by portraying the evil Japanese American in *The Pride of Palomar* (1922) and the sage, feminized Chinese American detective in the Charlie Chan film series (starting in 1925). According to Hearst scholar Louis Pizzitola, "*Patria* was billed as a serial about war preparedness or, rather, the lack of it. It was also a fast-moving tirade against Japan and Mexico, framed within opulent sets and threaded by elegant

fashion shows." Louis Pizzitola, *Hearst over Hollywood: Power, Passion, and Propaganda in the Movies* (New York: Columbia University Press, 2002), 155–156.

13. Joseph Timmons: "Jap Ambassador's Threat Brought Exclusion Law," *Los Angeles Examiner,* 17 April 1942; "Right of Free Immigration One of Japan's Important Goals in War," *Los Angeles Examiner,* 18 April 1942.

14. Joseph Timmons, "Nation Saved from Jap Peril by California Stand: Labor First to See Menace of Immigration Flood, 40 Years Ago; Alien Land Law Passed," *Los Angeles Examiner,* 13 April 1942.

15. Joseph Timmons, "Whites Ousted by Jap Farmers: Alien Land Law Passed to Protect Owners, Labor," *Los Angeles Examiner,* 14 April 1942.

16. Williams, *Playing the Race Card*, 44.

17. Joseph Timmons, "Fight to Halt Jap Influx Told: Growing Body of Unassimilated Aliens Proved Menace to State," *Los Angeles Examiner,* 15 April 1942.

18. Joseph Timmons, "Japs Sought to Kill Land Law by 'Gentlemen's Pact,'" *Los Angeles Examiner,* 16 April 1942.

19. Timmons: "Jap Ambassador's Threat Brought Exclusion Law," *Los Angeles Examiner,* 17 April 1942; "Right of Free Immigration One of Japan's Important Goals in War," *Los Angeles Examiner,* 18 April 1942.

20. Sumiko Higashi has argued that the melodramatic mode was naturally imposed upon Japanese Americans after Pearl Harbor because of their racial difference: "A racialized population with innate characteristics that were considered not only biological but cultural, the Japanese could not be identified as American and so were not morally trustworthy. Unlike other social actors in melodramatic texts, they were racially different and so could not assert claims to a democratic order based on ethical conduct." Sumiko Higashi, "Melodrama, Realism, and Race: World War II Newsreels and Propaganda Film," *Cinema Journal* 37, no. 3 (1998): 49. While Higashi's explanation is sound, I believe it is important to analyze how specific policies and public information officials like Hearst actively constructed Japanese ostracism from the terms of performative citizenship. This melodramatic exclusion was not inevitable.

21. These articles were all published on the same page in the *San Francisco Examiner,* 11 January 1942. This juxtaposition of articles is representative of the coverage of the home front in the Hearst press.

22. "The 'Comedy Is Finished,'" *New York Journal-American,* 13 February 1942.

23. Using the publicity power and editorial influence of his newspaper empire, Hearst transformed the rural community rite of Manitowac, Wisconsin, into a national holiday that theatricalized city streets with spectacular pageantry and patriotic speeches. Gerold Frank, "American Day Rally Draws 1,250,000," *Los Angeles Examiner,* 18 May 1942, 1, 4; "Arnold Tells Citizen Duty," *Los Angeles Examiner,* 18 May 1942, 8; "'I Am American' Fete Here May 17," *Los Angeles Examiner,* 28 April 1942, 9.

24. D. Taylor, *Disappearing Acts*, 93.

25. "Pictorial Review," *San Francisco Examiner,* 11 May 1942, 10.

26. Giroux, *Beyond the Spectacle of Terrorism*, 32.

27. "S. F. Parade to Open Citizenship Week: 15,000 Due to March Today," *San Francisco Examiner,* 10 May 1942 (emphasis added).

28. Writing in 1944 about Japanese Americans' civic demonstrations, McWilliams

marveled, "Today these prewar acts of loyalty are actually referred to, by such persons as Mayor Fletcher Bowron of Los Angeles, as suspicious circumstances." *Prejudice,* 113–114.

29. Lili M. Kim, "The Pursuit of Imperfect Justice: The Predicament of Koreans and Korean Americans on the Homefront during World War II" (Ph.D. diss., University of Rochester, 2001), 161, 167.

30. "Koreans Here in Fete, Ask U.S. Recognition," *Los Angeles Examiner,* 2 March 1942.

31. "Victory House Program Will Honor MacArthur," *Los Angeles Examiner* 28 March 1942.

32. On the American Legion's anti-Japanese agitation, see MacDonnell, *Insidious Foes,* 88; McWilliams, *Prejudice,* 60–61.

33. Magner White, "Southland Acclaims Its New U.S. Citizens: American Day Rites Bring Thunderous Applause, *Los Angeles Examiner,* 18 May 1942; "Big Parade Today Honors New Citizens: Martial Music, Drill Teams to Feature L.A. Spectacle," *Los Angeles Examiner,* 17 May 1942.

34. "Big Parade Today Honors New Citizens," *Los Angeles Examiner,* 17 May 1942.

35. Writing in the postwar period, Huizinga found his concept of play particularly applicable to Japanese culture, an assumption descended from that wartime fountainhead of Ruth Benedict's *The Chrysanthemum and the Sword.* Huizinga remarked that "the extraordinary earnestness and profound gravity of the Japanese ideal of life is masked by the fashionable fiction that everything is only play" and noted that the term for polite, honorific Japanese language, *"asobase kotoba,"* literally translates to "play language." Expanding from this observation, he argues that in Japan, "The convention is that the higher classes are merely playing all they do" and "masking" their elevated status "behind play." Johan Huizinga, *Homo Ludens: A Study of the Play-Element in Culture* (Boston: Beacon Press, 1950), 8, 10, 20, 34–35.

36. Frank Raymond, "Sports Keep Morale of Japs High at Camp: Boy Runner in Heavy Boots Circles Tanforan Track in Six Minutes," *San Francisco Examiner,* 17 May 1942, 10.

37. "Santa Anita Will Hold ONE Race," *Los Angeles Examiner,* 23 March 1942.

38. "3000 Japs Go to Reception Center Today: Santa Anita Park Will House Evacuees from Port Area; Parley Slated for April 7," *Los Angeles Examiner,* 3 April 1942.

39. To take but one example, in the *Los Angeles Examiner* from February to May 1942, Hearst ran at least thirty-five newspages that contained at least three internment-related articles each. These events made it to the newspaper's front page at least sixteen times in February and March. The notion of an honorific photo archive of celebrated personages comes from Sekula, "The Body and the Archive."

40. Simpson, *An Absent Presence,* 21.

41. For more on human-interest journalism, see James Curran et al., "The Political Economy of the Human-Interest Story," in *Newspapers and Democracy: International Essays on a Changing Medium,* ed. Anthony Smith (Cambridge, MA: MIT Press, 1980); Charles Ponce de Leon, *Self-Exposure: Human-Interest Journalism and the Emergence of Celebrity in America, 1890–1940* (Chapel Hill: University of North Carolina Press, 2002).

42. Sekula, "The Body and the Archive," 11.

43. Uno quoted in Inada, *Only What We Could Carry*, 70.

44. Yoshiko Uchida, *Desert Exile: The Uprooting of a Japanese American Family* (Seattle: University of Washington Press, 1982), 70. Ironically, one Hearst article provides an accurate description of this dehumanizing transposition but without apparent consciousness of the demoralizing effect on internees: "Where the tote board once tabulated millions of dollars wagered on equine speed a recreation hall is being built. In the infield, famous in peacetime for its gigantic palette of flowers, a cavernous warehouse stands. Stable space now is occupied by two-room apartments. A pungent odor arises not from expensive horseflesh but from thousands of gallons of disinfectant. And the smell of fresh paint likewise assails the nostrils." "1000 Harbor Japs Moved into Santa Anita Center: Expect 2000 More at Race Track Tomorrow," *Los Angeles Examiner*, 4 April 1942.

45. "1000 Harbor Japs Moved into Santa Anita Center," *Los Angeles Examiner*, 4 April 1942.

46. "Japanese Exodus: Great Credit Due Gen. Dewitt, Clark," *Los Angeles Examiner*, 11 April 1942.

47. "1000 Harbor Japs Moved into Santa Anita Center," *Los Angeles Examiner*, 4 April 1942. (emphasis added).

48. Ibid. One article remarked of the evacuation, "There are 'Sayonaras' or farewells, not tearful, for the Japanese don't cry much." "Little Tokyo Deserted as Exodus Grows," *Los Angeles Examiner*, 9 March 1942.

49. "Jap Evacuation System Speeded; 600 from S. F. Reach Santa Anita: Downey Area Ordered Cleared; 5000 Already at Race Track," *Los Angeles Examiner*, 8 April 1942.

50. Helen MacGill Hughes, *News and the Human Interest Story* (Chicago: University of Chicago Press, 1940), 46, 106.

51. "1000 Harbor Japs Moved into Santa Anita Center," *Los Angeles Examiner*, 4 April 1942. The menu is repeated almost verbatim in the caption to one of the accompanying photographs.

52. "Last of Japs Depart from Harbor Zone," *Los Angeles Examiner*, 6 April 1942.

53. "Jap Jitterbugs Amaze Elders at Santa Anita," *Los Angeles Examiner*, 11 April 1942.

54. "Santa Anita Camp Couple Will Wed," *Los Angeles Examiner*, 12 May 1942.

55. "Japs Wed at Manzanar: No Honeymoon until after the War," *Los Angeles Examiner*, 21 April 1942.

56. "Pasadena and Glendale Japs Go to Tulare," *Los Angeles Examiner*, 14 May 1942.

57. Tateishi and Fujikawa quoted in Inada, *Only What We Could Carry*, 62–63.

58. Uchida, *Desert Exile*, 76.

59. According to the 1942 diary of Manzanar publicity director Robert Brown, Lee accompanied the 23 March 1942 caravan of internees and journalists to the camp. Brown read from his diary in an oral history conducted by Arthur Hansen for the *New York Times* Oral History Program and Cal State University Fullerton (Glen Rock, NJ: Micrfilming Corporation of America, 1977), 26.

60. James Lee, "L. A. Japs Arrive in Owens Valley: Holiday Spirit Marks Start of Historic Movement," *Los Angeles Examiner*, 22 March 1942.

61. James Lee, "De Witt Visits Jap Evacuee Post; 1000 More Leave Today," *Los Angeles Examiner,* 23 March 1942.

62. James Lee, "L. A. Japs Arrive in Owens Valley," *Los Angeles Examiner,* 22 March 1942.

63. Ibid.

64. "Japs' Departure Like Excursion: 500 Off for Manzanar with No Tears, No Apparent Regret," *Los Angeles Examiner,* 2 April 1942 (emphasis added).

Chapter 4: "Manzanar, the Eyes of the World Are upon You"

1. Sue Kunitomi Embrey, foreword to the Toyo Miyatake Manzanar Photographic Archive Project. The title of this chapter comes from "Presses Roll for First Printed Free Press," *Manzanar Free Press,* 22 July 1942, 1.

2. "Interpretation and Education," National Park Service; http://www.nps.gov/learn/. Accessed 1 July 2006.

3. "Remembering Manzanar," National Park Service pamphlet, 2006. At the time, Manzanar's project director, Ralph Merritt, heralded the newly built auditorium as "the family living room for all the members of our Manzanar community." "History of the Auditorium," National Park Service; http://www.nps.gov/manz/auditoriumhistory.htm. Accessed 15 July 2006.

4. According to Manzanar National Historic Site superintendent Frank Hays, despite the NPS's suspicious stance toward reconstruction, "The approved plan for Manzanar calls for reconstruction of the camp's barbed wire fence, camp entrance sign, guard tower, and barracks buildings. . . . One or more of the camp barracks buildings that still exist in the local area will also be relocated and restored" for a demonstration block at the site. Frank Hays, "The National Park Service: Groveling Sycophant or Social Conscience: Telling the Story of Mountains, Valley, and Barbed Wire at Manzanar National Historic Site," *Public Historian* 25, no. 4 (2003): 78. It is also important to note that the site now has two public entrances, so passing the guardhouses en route to the Interpretive Center is optional for tourists. In addition to the three remaining original buildings, Manzanar's internee cemetery still stands with the famed obelisk that serves as a rallying point for those who travel to the camp each year for the annual Manzanar Pilgrimage.

5. The other nine camps were Tule Lake (California), Gila River (Arizona), Poston (Arizona), Minidoka (Idaho), Rohwer (Arkansas), Jerome (Arkansas), Granada/Amache (Colorado), Heart Mountain (Wyoming), and Topaz (Utah). Manzanar's nomination as the most viable campground for commemoration was successful "because of the large number of recognizable artifacts and remains on the site." Manzanar Committee founder Sue Kunitomi Embrey oral history in *Last Witnesses: Reflections on the Wartime Internment of Japanese Americans,* ed. Erica Harth (New York: Palgrave, 2001), 196. This is not to say that other camps did not have well-built auditoriums; rather, after the war many camp structures were sold or donated to the surrounding area. For example, the auditorium from the Topaz camp became part of the campus at Southern Utah State College (now University) until it was dismantled in the 1980s. Sandra C. Taylor, *Jewel*

of the Desert: Japanese American Internment at Topaz (Berkeley: University of California Press, 1993), 220.

6. Robert T. Hayashi, "Transfigured Patterns: Contested Memories at the Manzanar National Historic Site," *Public Historian* 25, no. 4 (2003): 56.

7. National Park Service, "Remembering Manzanar," information pamphlet, 2006.

8. Cynthia Gates Fujikawa, panel discussion at Manzanar Family Day at East West Players, Los Angeles, 14 May 2005.

9. Hays, "The National Park Service," 75.

10. Oral history of Jack B. Hopkins, Owens Valley (Lone Pine) resident, conducted 20 December 1973, in *Camp and Community: Manzanar and the Owens Valley,* ed. Jessie A. Garrett and Ronald C. Larson (Fullerton, CA: California State University Japanese American Oral History Project, 1977), 46.

11. Harry Ferguson, "Manzanar Nice Place—It Better Than Hollywood," *San Francisco News,* 21 April 1942. Available at http://sfmuseum.org/hist8/manzanar1.html. Accessed 20 June 2006.

12. Ishizuka, *Lost and Found,* 125–126.

13. Ferguson, "Manzanar Nice Place," *San Francisco News,* 21 April 1942, 1; Hays, "The National Park Service," 75.

14. Hays, "The National Park Service," 95.

15. Harth, *Last Witnesses,* 196.

16. Although Houston herself eventually settled upon a childhood extracurricular career as a majorette, in *Farewell to Manzanar* she narrates how this decision followed only after a long period of experimentation in the diversity of performance activities offered in the camp, ranging from *odori* (traditional folk dance) and ballet to Catholicism and its "elaborate ceremonies." Moreover, Houston suggests that this search for the perfect performing art was also a search for identity within the political imperatives of the internment and that settling on baton twirling represented a "desperate desire to be acceptable" in mainstream America that would extend into adolescence and beyond. She notes that although "classes of every kind were being offered all over camp: singing, acting, trumpet playing, tap-dancing, plus traditional Japanese arts like needlework, judo, and kendo," it was baton twirling that stuck. "Since then I have often wondered what drew me to it at that age [ten years old]," Houston goes on to write. "I wonder, because of all the activities I tried out in camp, this was the one I stayed with, in fact returned to almost obsessively when I entered high school in southern California a few years later. By that time I was desperate to be 'accepted,' and baton twirling was one trick I could perform that was thoroughly, unmistakably American. . . . Even at ten, the Japanese in me could not compete with that." Jeanne Wakatsuki Houston and James D. Houston, *Farewell to Manzanar* (New York: Bantam, 1973), 113, 159, 108–9.

17. For an apt summation of the debates concerning the lack of resistance offered by internees, see Lon Kurashige, "Resistance, Collaboration, and Manzanar Protest," *Pacific Historical Review* 70, no. 3 (2001): 387–417.

18. Jacques Derrida discusses "logocentrism," or the Western dominance of the spoken and written word, in *Of Grammatology,* trans. Gayatri Chakravorty Spivak (Baltimore: Johns Hopkins University Press, 1974), 3. For more on how literacy and text

have come to epitomize Western modernism—and how orality has been denigrated as a sign of backwardness and primitivism—see Walter J. Ong, *Orality and Literacy: The Technologizing of the Word* (London: Routledge, 1999).

19. "Hull Denounces Tokyo 'Infamy,'" *New York Times*, 8 December 1941; Senator Mead quoted in U.S. Government, *Congressional Record*, 9514–9.

20. U.S. Government, *Congressional Record*, 9524, 9532 (emphasis added). The quotations are from Representatives Capozzoli, Wolverton, and Dirksen.

21. "Tokyo Acts First: Declaration Follows Air and Sea Attacks on U.S. and Britain," *New York Times*, 8 December 1942: 1; U.S. Government, *Congressional Record*, 9519.

22. D. Taylor, *The Archive and the Repertoire*, 24.

23. See "The Shot That Came from Behind a Screen," *Chicago Tribune*, 10 December 1941, 10.

24. WRA deputy director Colonel C. F. Cress quoted in Harlan D. Unrau, *The Evacuation and Relocation of Persons of Japanese Ancestry during World War II: A Historical Study of the Manzanar War Relocation Center* (Washington, D.C.: National Park Service, 1996), 388.

25. Ibid., 390–392.

26. Ibid.

27. *WRA Final Report* quoted in ibid., 577–578. Likewise, Sandra Taylor notes that the administration at the Topaz camp "was in the habit of making a festival out of every possible event, as a morale-building device." *Jewel of the Desert*, 154.

28. See, for instance, Garrett and Larson, *Camp and Community*.

29. "Presses Roll for First Printed Free Press," *Manzanar Free Press*, 22 July 1942, 1.

30. Clem Albers, "WRA no. B-146" (War Relocation Authority Records, vol. 20, sec. C).

31. Bhabha, "Of Mimicry and Man," 86 (emphasis in original).

32. Shimakawa, *National Abjection*, 10–11.

33. D. Taylor, *The Archive and the Repertoire*, 19 (emphasis in original).

34. Taken from the film based on her one-person show, *Old Man River*, "smiling into the camera" expresses Fujikawa's incredulous reaction when she discovered Ansel Adams' photographs of Manzanar internees, which she found when researching a sixth-grade class presentation. *Old Man River*, dir. Allan Holzman, perf. Cynthia Gates Fujikawa (1999).

35. There is evidence to suggest that internees at other camps also kept track of their spectacularization by the outside press and politicians, albeit in an unpublished and more ad hoc fashion. For instance, Harold Stanley Jacoby, who worked on the WRA staff at Tule Lake Relocation Center from its opening in May 1942 to July 1944, remarked that "it was always a matter of fascination to me that the Sunday edition of the *San Francisco Examiner*, a paper that was blatantly anti-Japanese American in its tone and editorial policy, by a margin of three-to-one regularly outsold the rival *San Francisco Chronicle*, which was more understanding to the plight of the evacuees." Such overwhelming preference in their consumption of a Hearst newspaper that regularly

spectacularized the "Japanese problem" on the West Coast demonstrates a vigilant witnessing on the part of Tule Lake internees. Harold Stanley Jacoby, *Tule Lake: From Relocation to Segregation* (Grass Valley, CA: Comstock Bonanza Press, 1996), 59.

36. "Manzanar Lures Newshounds," *Manzanar Free Press*, 27 July 1942, 1. The first of the open houses for outside visitors was held 27 April 1942, and the WRA proposed holding them every Saturday from 1 to 5 p.m. thereafter. "Independence Citizens Pay Visit to Manzanar," *Los Angeles Examiner*, 28 April 1942. These open houses and "Reciprocity Day" events continued throughout the war; see, for instance, "Women's Club Enjoys Center Tour," *Manzanar Free Press*, 28 April 1945, 3.

37. Eighty-eight percent of Manzanar internees had been "evacuated" from Los Angeles County; 72 percent came from the city of Los Angeles. So this population was largely urban. Arthur A. Hansen and David A. Hacker, "The Manzanar Riot: An Ethnic Perspective," *Amerasia Journal* 2, no. 2 (1974): 127.

38. Lon Kurashige, *Japanese American Celebration and Conflict: A History of Ethnic Identity and Festival in Los Angeles, 1934–1990* (Berkeley: University of California Press, 2002).

39. Elena Tajima Creef, *Imaging Japanese America: The Visual Construction of Citizenship, Nation, and the Body* (New York: New York University Press, 2004), 32.

40. Katherine Krater oral history in Garrett and Lawson, *Camp and Community*, 87.

41. According to the Cal State Fullerton Oral History Project, "Manzanar and Tule Lake were the only two camps where the people in the surrounding areas would not allow the internees to come into their towns." Manzanar public information officer Robert Brown has said that "the camp was actually much more cosmopolitan than the surrounding towns." Garrett and Lawson, *Camp and Community*, 38–39.

42. Kurashige, *Japanese American Celebration and Conflict*, 76.

43. Bowron quoted in "Fealty Vowed by Japanese: Speeches and Dances Mark Official Opening of Nisei Festival," *Los Angeles Times*, 26 August 1941, 2.2.

44. Kurashige, *Japanese American Celebration and Conflict*, 76; Hansen and Hacker, "The Manzanar Riot," 128.

45. Kurashige is not the only scholar to find camp performance toothless and reactionary. In his dissertation and subsequent publication, Robert Cooperman concluded that the theatre staged by Nisei internees merely performed assimilation for the appeasement of the white captors. Robert Cooperman: "Nisei Theater: History, Context, and Perspective" (Ph.D. diss., Ohio State University, 1996), and "The Americanization of Americans: The Phenomenon of Nisei Internment Camp Theater," in *Re-Collecting Early Asian America: Essays in Cultural History*, ed. Josephine Lee, Imogene L. Kim, and Yuko Matsukawa (Philadelphia: Temple University Press, 2002), 326–339.

46. "Welcome Visitors," *Manzanar Free Press*, 18 September 1943, 2.

47. "Approximately 291 Outsiders," *Manzanar Free Press*, 22 September 1943, 1. I use "social drama" in the same spirit in which *Free Press* writers used it but also to invoke the meaning used by anthropologist Victor Turner in *Dramas, Fields, and Metaphors: Symbolic Action in Human Society* (Ithaca, NY: Cornell University Press, 1975).

48. Brown in Hansen, *Japanese American World War II Evacuation,* 25–26.

49. "Free Press Staff Acts as 'Guides,'" *Manzanar Free Press,* 22 September 1943, 2.

50. Much of the testimony of Owens Valley residents, as that which follows, is compiled in the oral history *Camp and Community,* which was originally called simply *Jap Camp* to reflect the blunt attitude of the Owens Valley residents who ambivalently watched as a Japanese American internment camp was constructed in—and helped save the economy of—their community. Independence resident Anna Kelley's testimony of 6 December 1973 is consistent with the testimony of those who discuss Manzanar "open house" events. Kelley testifies about "programs that were held out at the camp to which people from the communities were invited," insisting that "there were a great many, and a lot of people did go." Garrett and Lawson, *Camp and Community,* 67, 85.

51. Benzi Zhang, "Mapping Carnivalistic Discourse in Japanese-American Writing." *MELUS* 24, no. 4 (Winter 1999): 19–40.

52. "Free Press Staff Act as 'Guides,'" *Manzanar Free Press,* 22 September 1943; "Approximately 291 Outsiders," *Manzanar Free Press,* 22 September 1943; "Inyo Residents Visit," *Manzanar Free Press,* 22 September 1943, 1; "Scenery Painted," *Manzanar Free Press,* 22 September 1943, 1.

53. Togo Tanaka and Joe Grant Masaoka, Documentary Report 47, 12 August 1942 (Japanese American Evacuation and Resettlement Records, BANC MSS 67/14c/, O 10.06). I am grateful to Lon Kurashige's article, "Resistance, Collaboration, and Manzanar Protest," for bringing this document to my attention.

54. "Hospital Open House Program Slated," *Manzanar Free Press,* 11 September 1942, 3.

55. WRA anthropologists noted the egalitarian impulse behind such intercultural performances. According to Edward Spicer et al., most of the camps' drama groups "set as their aim the production of entertainment which would appeal to the wide variety of tastes among the center people. They secured the elaborate costumes and trained young and old in traditional drama of the feudal period—*kabuki.*" *Impounded People,* 222–223.

56. Weglyn, *Years of Infamy,* 125.

57. "July 4 Carnival Plans Complete," *Manzanar Free Press,* 26 June 1943, 1.

58. "July Carnival," *Manzanar Free Press,* 29 May 1943, 1; "Carnival 'Colossal Success,'" *Manzanar Free Press,* 7 July 1943, 3.

59. "Carnival Committee Formulates Plans for Coming Events," *Manzanar Free Press,* 16 June 1943, 3.

60. "Carnival 'Colossal Success,'" *Manzanar Free Press,* 7 July 1943.

61. Kumamoto, "The Search for Spies," 66–67.

62. Thomas James writes that traditional Japanese cultural practices were generally "beyond the ken of administrators and teachers" in the WRA camps and "invisible from the vantage point of official policy." As a result, James maintains, "the spontaneous mobilization of the cultural resources of [Japanese Americans] was among the most significant educational achievements of the war years." Thomas James, *Exile Within:*

The Schooling of Japanese Americans 1942–1945 (Cambridge, MA: Harvard University Press, 1987), 107.

63. "July Carnival," *Manzanar Free Press,* 29 May 1943. I deduced the origin of these Japanese music recordings because brown wax cylinders were no longer used for recording music by the early twentieth century. Therefore, the recordings of Japanese music played on the carnival's entertainment program had necessarily been imported from Japan decades prior to the evacuation, most likely brought with Japanese immigrants to the United States and smuggled into Manzanar despite evacuation taboos against Japanese Americans' possessing any such markers of transnational identification with the enemy.

64. Takashi Kubota: "Evening for Issei," Japanese Section, *Manzanar Free Press,* 10 May 1944, 3 and "Observing the Consultation Night for Issei," Japanese Section, *Manzanar Free Press,* 17 May 1944, 1. Translations provided by the *Free Press* staff and corroborated by Tomoyuki Sasaki. Such intergenerational cross-casting points to the flawed logic that forms the basis of Robert Cooperman's study of so-called Nisei Theater; in it he focuses only upon English-language drama presentations performed by Nisei internees at six camps (not including Manzanar). Not surprisingly, with this mode of sampling, Cooperman finds mere capitulation to WRA assimilationist cultural policies. Cooperman: "Nisei Theater" and "The Americanization of Americans."

65. The WRA officially reassigned Tule Lake Relocation Center (the other Japanese American internment camp in California) as Tule Lake Segregation Center in July 1943. It would be the last camp to close, remaining open until 1946. On the loyalty questionnaire, Manzanites who refused to renounce allegiance to the Japanese emperor and/or refused to pledge service to the U.S. military—or, at the extreme, asked to be deported to Japan—were considered sociopolitical contaminants by the WRA. Treated as a contagion or a metastasizing cancer, these "disloyals" were, to borrow from Michi Weglyn, "surgically" removed from Manzanar and the other eight camps. *Years of Infamy,* 154. See chapter 5 for more on Tule Lake and the loyalty questionnaire.

66. Internee photographer Toyo Miyatake recorded several instances of intergenerational performance with his illicit camera at Manzanar. In one photograph, an Issei man and his Nisei son recite *gidayu* (theatrical chanting) for an intercultural celebration of the father's sixtieth birthday. In another Miyatake photograph, an Issei man applies makeup to a Nisei boy in preparation for a *buyo* (classical Japanese dance) performance by Issei Tomiko Baba. Both photographs are available through the Toyo Miyatake Manzanar Photographic Archive Project and also in Toyo Miyatake, *Miyatake Tōyō no shashin, 1923–1979* (Tokyo: Bungei Shunjū, 1984).

67. Ralph Merritt, office diary for 16 June 1944, quoted in U.S. Government, "Manzanar National Historic Site, California: The History and Preservation of the Community Auditorium-Gymnasium Historic Structure Report" (Washington, DC: U.S. Government Printing Office, 1999), 16.

68. Ibid.

69. "'Loud and Clear' Received Well," *Manzanar Free Press,* 17 June 1944, 1 (emphasis added). Assessments of the degree of censorship exercised upon the *Free Press* by the

administration vary widely; the WRA insisted at the time and in its Final Report that the internees were free to publish what they wished, except for what appeared in the Japanese language section of the newspaper. Former Nisei staff members have widely divergent recollections of how "free" their press really was. But certainly by this late point in the war, any censorship had dipped to its most lax level. See John D. Stevens, "From behind Barbed Wire: Freedom of the Press in World War II Japanese Centers," *Journalism Quarterly* 48 (1971): 279–287.

70. The two resolutions against the Hood River Post of the American Legion quoted here are from the Legion's Justice Department Post and Los Angeles No. 8 Post.

71. "Justice Department Assails Hood River," *Manzanar Free Press,* 13 January 1945, 1; "Condemn Hood River's American Legion," *Manzanar Free Press,* 13 January 1945, 1.

72. James, *Exile Within,* 55, 132.

73. "Adult Activity Hall Opens for Daily Inspection," *Manzanar Free Press,* 27 January 1945, 1. See also "Adult English Activity Hall Holds Open House," *Manzanar Free Press,* 31 January 1945.

74. James, *Exile Within,* 137.

75. Dorothy Swaine Thomas and Richard Nishimoto, *The Spoilage: Japanese-American Evacuation and Resettlement during World War II* (Berkeley: University of California Press, 1946). I agree with Brian Masaru Hayashi, who pointedly criticizes internment scholars, like Thomas and Nishimoto, who read the political dynamics of the camps through a "domestic-only framework," failing to take into account prewar transnational identities held by Japanese Americans. Brian Masaru Hayashi, *Democratizing the Enemy: The Japanese American Internment* (Princeton, NJ: Princeton University Press, 2004), 3.

76. "Elegance of Manzanar Arts: Gorgeous Entertainment, Gift from CACA," *Manzanar Free Press,* 6 January 1945; "Great New Year's Entertainment Show," *Manzanar Free Press,* 17 January 1945. Translations provided by Tomoyuki Sasaki.

77. Lafcadio Hearn, *Kwaidan: Stories and Studies of Strange Things* (Champaign, IL: Project Gutenberg, 1932), 42–44.

78. Some of the *kanji* in the titles and descriptions of these five pieces in the program are illegible, so I was not able to analyze these parts of the evening in full detail. In particular, I found the title of this *jōruri* performance entirely unreadable in the reproduction available.

79. James R. Brandon and Samuel L. Leiter, eds., *Masterpieces of Kabuki: Eighteen Plays on Stage* (Honolulu: University of Hawai'i Press, 2004), 7–8.

80. Chikamatsu Yanagi, Chikamatsu Kosuiken, and Chikamatsu Chiyōken, *The Picture Book of the Taikō* (Ehon Taikōki), trans. Samuel L. Leiter, in Brandon and Leiter, *Masterpieces of Kabuki,* 170.

81. Brandon and Leiter, *Masterpieces of Kabuki,* 9.

82. Kawatake Mokuami, *The Three Kichisas and the New Year's First Visit to the Pleasure Quarters,* trans. Kei Hibino and Alan Cummings, in Brandon and Leiter, *Masterpieces of Kabuki,* 244–245.

83. Kawatake, *The Three Kichisas,* in Brandon and Leiter, *Masterpieces of Kabuki,* 253–254.

84. "CACA's New Project," *Manzanar Free Press,* 16 December 1944. Translation provided by Tomoyuki Sasaki. The 20–21 January 1945 New Year's program was the outgrowth of this union. See also "Meeting of Various Artists," *Manzanar Free Press,* 1 January 1945. Translation provided by Tomoyuki Sasaki.

85. Two days before the United States dropped the 6 August 1945 atomic bomb on Hiroshima, the *Manzanar Free Press* announced the cessation of organized community activities at the camp, including "Japanese entertainment." The article attributed the stoppage to a diminished WRA staff and the monopolization of internees' energies by impending resettlement. Manzanar Relocation Center closed three and a half months later, on 21 November 1945. "Community Activities to Cut Down Local Functions," *Manzanar Free Press,* 4 August 1945, 2.

Chapter 5: Transnational Theatre at the Tule Lake Segregation Center

1. D. Taylor, *The Archive and the Repertoire,* 210.

2. Debord, *The Society of the Spectacle,* 136.

3. Ibid., 131.

4. Spicer et al., *Impounded People,* 222–224.

5. Noboru Shirai, *Tule Lake: An Issei Memoir,* trans. Ray Hosoda (Sacramento, CA: Tom's Printing, 2001), 72.

6. I borrow here from Shirai's description of the WRA's "divide-and-conquer policy" for administrating Tule Lake. Ibid., 74.

7. Weglyn, *Years of Infamy,* 136. It should be remembered that Issei (along with all Asian immigrants) were ineligible for U.S. naturalization at this time. These polarizing questions are usually referred to by their numbers on the registration form: 27 and 28.

8. Ibid., 135.

9. Takezawa, *Breaking the Silence,* 52.

10. Myer's letter to Stimson quoted in Dillon S. Myer, *Uprooted Americans: The Japanese Americans and the War Relocation Authority during World War II* (Tucson: University of Arizona Press, 1971), 163 (emphasis added).

11. Thomas and Nishimoto, *The Spoilage,* 87 (emphasis added).

12. Richard Drinnon, *Keeper of Concentration Camps: Dillon S. Myer and American Racism* (Berkeley: University of California Press, 1987), 53–54.

13. Myer, *Uprooted Americans,* 238.

14. Ibid., 145–146, 286. The rhetoric describing internee registration and Nisei military service as "dramatic [displays]" and "performances" pervades the wartime accounts of white administrators and researchers working in the camps. Japanese American Evacuation and Resettlement Study (JERS) head researcher Dorothy Swaine Thomas, for instance, contended that "The remarkable *performance* of the Japanese Americans who served in the Army, the unabated favorable publicity they received, and the contacts they established in American communities prior to overseas service were undoubtedly primary factors in promoting community acceptance of resettlers [after they left the camps]." Dorothy Swaine Thomas, *The Salvage* (Berkeley: University of California Press, 1952), 107 (emphasis added). See also Bosworth, *America's Concentra-*

tion Camps, 169; Michael John Wallinger, "Dispersal of the Japanese Americans: Rhetorical Strategies of the War Relocation Authority, 1942–1945" (Ph.D. diss. University of Oregon, 1975), 262–264, 285.

15. Yasuko Takezawa has found that the WRA also "carefully graded" every one of these seventy-five thousand completed questionnaires, adding and deducting points based on characteristics pertaining to the respondent such as the following: religion (Shinto, Buddhist, Christian); travel to Japan; ability to read/write/speak Japanese; and conviction of a crime (one of the *least* damning admissions on the questionnaire). As Takezawa notes, "Subjects were then classified as 'white,' 'brown,' and 'black,' according to their degree of eligibility for leave." *Breaking the Silence,* 99. This color-based classification system clearly tracked along dominant U.S. racial lines, betraying the actual terms of American performative citizenship.

16. Weglyn, *Years of Infamy,* 154.

17. tenBroek et al., *Prejudice, War, and the Constitution,* 163.

18. Shirai, *Tule Lake,* 141.

19. Jacoby, *Tule Lake,* 42.

20. "Issei Staff Reorganized," *Tulean Dispatch,* 15 July 1942, 3.

21. "Recreation Notes," *Tulean Dispatch,* 17 October 1942, 2.

22. "Newell to Have Café Society," *Tulean Dispatch,* 12 October 1942, 1.

23. Shimoda went on to a professional acting career after the war, performing on Broadway and with Asian American theatre companies such as Los Angeles' East West Players. E. Lee, *A History of Asian American Theatre,* 20.

24. "Cabaret International Goes Over Big," *Tulean Dispatch,* 3 November 1942, 5; Francis Stewart, "Entertainers at the Cabaret Internationale Program held at This Relocation Center" (photograph), 1 November 1942 (War Relocation Authority Photographs of Japanese American Evacuation and Resettlement). Note that dates given indicate when the photo was filed, not when it was taken.

25. "Cabaret Comments," *Tulean Dispatch,* 10 November 1942, 3.

26. "Merry-Go-Round by Yuri," *Tulean Dispatch,* 4 November 1942, 3.

27. "Hilarious Antics of 'Nuthouse Gang' Keep Tuleans Screaming for More," *Tulean Dispatch,* 16 September 1942, 2; "Colonists Laugh as 'Gang' Goes on Tour," *Tulean Dispatch,* 19 October 1942, 1.

28. Francis Stewart, "Men and Women in Costumes at the Harvest Festival" (photograph), 31 October 1942 (Special Collections, J. Willard Marriott Library, University of Utah, P0144 #025).

29. Eric Lott, *Love and Theft: Blackface Minstrelsy and the American Working Class* (New York: Oxford University Press, 1993), 29.

30. *Hellzapoppin',* dir. H. C. Potter, perf. Ole Olsen and Chic Johnson (1941).

31. "Hilarious Antics of 'Nuthouse Gang,'" *Tulean Dispatch,* 16 September 1942. The dialogue came from two of the troupe's standard fifteen-minute bits: "Chinese Play Day" and a self-described minstrel show. "Harvest Festival Stage Show to Be Presented," *Tulean Dispatch,* 29 October 1942, 1.

32. "Nuthouse Gang to Tour City Sunday for Preview," *Tulean Dispatch,* 17 October 1942, 3.

33. "From the Recreation Department," *Tulean Dispatch,* 24 September 1942. Translation provided by Tomoyuki Sasaki.

34. "Regulations Concerning Entertainment Events," *Tulean Dispatch,* 3 October 1942. Translation provided by Tomoyuki Sasaki.

35. Shirai, *Tule Lake,* 77.

36. Ibid., 141.

37. Depending on which characters are counted, *Chūshingura* can be referred to as the tale of forty-six or forty-seven *rōnin.* The play was written for puppet performance in 1748 by Takeda Izumo, Miyoshi Shōraku, and Namiki Senryū.

38. "Rain or Shine: Issei Show Tonight Bills 'Chushingura'" *Tulean Dispatch,* 29 August 1942. The dry tone of this announcement—in marked contrast to the effusive editorial details in previews and reviews of the Nuthouse Gang and such Nisei troupes—attested to its police-report attitude.

39. "Council OK's Movie House: Japanese Films to Be Shown," *Tulean Dispatch,* 8 October 1942, 1. Other accounts have listed the Community Council's acceptance of the theatre plan as "voted three to one." "Re: Theatre Building; Arguments for and against Construction Given Preliminary to Referendum Voting," *Tulean Dispatch,* 17 October 1942.

40. "Special Election Will Show Public Opinion on Theatre," *Tulean Dispatch,* 12 October 1942, 1.

41. "Re: Theatre Building," *Tulean Dispatch,* 17 October 1942.

42. "'No' Wins Theater Votes," *Tulean Dispatch,* 20 October 1942, 1.

43. "Theater Ballots: Full Returns Revealed," *Tulean Dispatch,* 21 October 1942, 1. Literally in the place of the aborted internee-funded theatre, the WRA later began construction of a government-funded gym-auditorium in December 1942, next to the camp's fire station. "Tule Lake Will Have Gym Auditorium Seating 1500: Construction Has Started," *Tulean Dispatch,* 21 December 1942, 2.

44. Shirai, *Tule Lake,* 76.

45. Ibid.; Thomas and Nishimoto, *The Spoilage,* 44.

46. Gary Y. Okihiro, "Religion and Resistance in America's Concentration Camps," *Phylon* 45, no. 2 (1984): 231, 233. Okihiro quotes from a postwar article by Tule Lake "community analyst" Marvin K. Opler, who remembered from his time spent in residence at the camp that "Folklore which had been remembered by a handful of Issei, and perpetuated in a small circle, was seized upon by Issei and Nisei alike in a broadening sphere where it was deemed important to strike back at administrative pressures, programs, and politics with the dignified weapons of Japanese culture." Marvin K. Opler, "Japanese Folk Beliefs and Practices, Tule Lake, California," *Journal of American Folklore* 63 (October–December 1950): 385–397.

47. "Harvest Festival," *Tulean Dispatch,* 9 October 1942, 4.

48. "Parade Honors Go to Engei Club Entry," *Tulean Dispatch,* 3 November 1942, 1.

49. "500 Participants in Mardi Gras Parade Saturday," *Tulean Dispatch,* 30 October 1942, 3.

50. Ibid.; Francis Stewart, "The Harvest Day Festival Parade" (photograph), 31

October 1942 (War Relocation Authority Photographs of Japanese-American Evacuation and Resettlement); "Parade Honors Go to Engei Club Entry," *Tulean Dispatch,* 3 November 1942.

51. I am inspired in my use of the term "poach" by Michel de Certeau's argument that reading (interpreted broadly in the sense that the world itself might be understood as a readable text) is a form of poaching in which consumers are far from passive. De Certeau argues that consumers do not "become similar to" the text they read but instead "'make something similar' to what one is, make it one's own, appropriate or reappropriate it." Michel de Certeau, *The Practice of Everyday Life,* trans. Stephen Rendall (Berkeley: University of California Press, 1984), 166.

52. "Filing of Show Asked by 'Rec,'" *Tulean Dispatch,* 30 November 1942, 1.

53. "Blackout Throws Cabaret Show into Confusion," *Tulean Dispatch,* 18 November 1942, 1.

54. "Construction Show on Dec. 5–6," *Tulean Dispatch,* 28 November 1942, 3.

55. "Mammoth Stage Show at Factory Today, Sun.," *Tulean Dispatch,* 5 December 1942, 1, 3 (emphasis added).

56. "Construction Show on Dec. 5–6"; see also "Fabulous Entertainment Sponsored by the Construction Department," *Tulean Dispatch,* 12 December 1942: Japanese section.

57. "Mammoth Stage Show," *Tulean Dispatch,* 5 December 1942; "Great Entertainment at the Construction Show Sponsored by the Construction Department," *Tulean Dispatch,* 4 December 1942, Japanese section. Translation provided by Tomoyuki Sasaki.

58. Takeda Izumo, Shōraku Miyoshi, and Senryū Namiki, *Chūshingura: The Treasury of Loyal Retainers,* trans. Donald Keene (New York: Columbia University Press, 1971), 100. Note that Kampei's suicide is not the glorified sort of *hara-kiri* scene that Western observers of Japanese theatre and society so exoticized in the decades leading up to World War II. Kampei does not ceremoniously prepare for the *seppuku,* and the event is not depicted as the beautifully cruel resolution of his fate. Rather, Kampei sees himself cornered by fate and desperately stabs himself to the shock of all present. It is important that the *Chūshingura* scene that contains an onstage instance of glorified suicide—Lord Hangan's own *seppuku*—is not known to have been performed by the internees at Tule Lake.

59. Ibid., 103.

60. Ibid., 112.

61. Ibid., 16–17.

62. Ibid.

63. "'Hidden Talent' Search On," *Tulean Dispatch,* 6 February 1943, 1.

64. "Entertainment Talent Sign-Up Deadline Is Feb. 28," *Tulean Dispatch,* 17 February 1943, 3.

65. "Eugene Okada's Our Town," *Tulean Dispatch,* 15 March 1943, 3.

66. "Eugene Okada's Our Town," *Tulean Dispatch,* 11 May 1943, 2; "Ozaki, Kumasaka Win First Places in Talent Contest," *Tulean Dispatch,* 11 May 1943, 3.

67. "Daybreak by Yukio Ozaki," *Tulean Dispatch,* 20 April 1943.

68. Paul Green, *White Dresses*, in *Out of the South: The Life of a People in Dramatic Form* (New York: Harper and Brothers, 1939).

69. Tule Lake's town-camp interaction differed from Manzanar's open-house relationship with Owens Valley residents, whom the WRA frequently invited to the camp for "Reciprocity Days" and other performances of hospitality. By contrast, as Jacoby argues, the townspeople of Tulelake (the camp name was spelled as two words for clarity's sake) did not even pretend to tolerate the thousands of Japanese Americans interned in their midst. Jacoby writes, "The population of Tulelake was made up largely of World War I veterans, who were not too happy over the presence of a 'Jap Camp' in their neighborhood. While I know of no overt efforts to annoy the camp, that possibility was very much in the minds of some of the evacuees, who felt that a military police unit between the camp and the town might prove a protection for them." *Tule Lake*, 15.

70. "Program Honors Newspapermen," *Tulean Dispatch*, 22 May 1943, 2. These nineteen journalists and photographers arrived on Monday, 17 May 1943, and stayed through that Wednesday. These members of the press came from several Northern California newspapers, the *New York Times*, wire services, and various OWI departments around the world.

71. "Newspapermen Visit Colony," *Tulean Dispatch*, 19 May 1943, 2.

72. Quoted in Jacoby, *Tule Lake*, 57.

73. "First Outdoor Program on 26," *Tulean Dispatch*, 23 June 1943, 5.

74. "Folk Dancing Will Be Taught for 4th Program," *Tulean Dispatch*, 19 June 1943, 1.

75. "'Ondo' Practices Held Every Night for Fourth of July Celebration Program," *Tulean Dispatch*, 23 June 1943, 5.

76. "Bald Head, Whiskerino Contests Set," *Tulean Dispatch*, 23 June 1943, 5.

77. "Celebrating Independence Day: Planning a Variety of Entertainments," *Tulean Dispatch*, 2 July 1943, Japanese section. Translation provided by Tomoyuki Sasaki.

78. Ibid.

79. Gary Okihiro has described "special cultic occasions" like New Year's Day as opportunities for "Japanese of all ages" to come together in a large gathering and affirm their shared ethnicity and cultural heritage. I agree that such holidays served as opportune stages upon which to communally enact such rituals—if only because the WRA often granted paid time off for internee-workers—but these were by no means *blank* stages. Rather, the "cultic occasions" that brought cross-generational masses of internees together existed as ever-present backgrounds that shaped and determined the contextual meaning of these communal performances. In this case, the diasporic context remained very much present in the performance experience and its social meaning. "Religion and Resistance," 228.

80. Quoted in Jacoby, *Tule Lake*, 81–82.

81. Shirai, *Tule Lake*, 241. Of these renunciants, 4,978 later had their U.S. citizenship restored through postwar litigation.

82. Weglyn, *Years of Infamy*, 242.

83. Shirai, *Tule Lake*, 167.

84. Ibid.
85. Fortas quoted in Wallinger, "Dispersal of the Japanese Americans," 249–250.
86. Roosevelt quoted in tenBroek et al., *Prejudice, War, and the Constitution*, 172.
87. Roosevelt quoted in S. Taylor, *Jewel of the Desert*, 186.
88. Bosworth, *America's Concentration Camps*, 210.
89. T. S. Eliot, "The Hollow Men" (1925).

Bibliography

Agnew, Jean-Christophe. *Worlds Apart: The Market and the Theater in Anglo-American Thought, 1550–1750.* New York: Cambridge University Press, 1986.

Althusser, Louis. *Lenin and Philosophy.* New York: Verso, 1978.

Austin, J. L. *How to Do Things with Words.* Cambridge, MA: Harvard University Press, 1962.

Barish, Jonas. *The Antitheatrical Prejudice.* Berkeley: University of California Press, 1981.

Barthes, Roland. *Empire of Signs.* Trans. Richard Howard. New York: Hill and Wang, 1982.

Bell, Vicki. "On Speech, Race and Melancholia: An Interview with Judith Butler." *Theory, Culture and Society* 16, no. 2 (1999).

Benedict, Ruth. *The Chrysanthemum and the Sword: Patterns of Japanese Culture.* Boston: Houghton Mifflin, 1989 [1946].

Bhabha, Homi K. *The Location of Culture.* London: Routledge, 1994.

———. "Of Mimicry and Man: The Ambivalence of Colonial Discourse." In Bhabha, *The Location of Culture.*

Blumberg, Rhoda. *Commodore Perry in the Land of the Shogun.* New York: Lothrop, Lee, and Shepard Books, 1985.

Bohnaker, William. *The Hollow Doll (a Little Box of Japanese Shocks).* New York: Ballantine Books, 1990.

Bosworth, Allan R. *America's Concentration Camps.* New York: W. W. Norton, 1967.

Brandon, James R., and Samuel L. Leiter, eds. *Masterpieces of Kabuki: Eighteen Plays on Stage.* Honolulu: University of Hawai'i Press, 2004.

Braun, Edward. *The Director and the Stage.* New York: Holmes and Meier, 1982.

Brooks, Peter. *The Melodramatic Imagination: Balzac, Henry James, Melodrama, and the Mode of Excess.* New Haven, CT: Yale University Press, 1976.

Butler, Judith. *Bodies That Matter: On the Discursive Limits of Sex.* New York: Routledge, 1993.

———. "Endangered/Endangering: Schematic Racism and White Paranoia." In *Reading Rodney King/Reading Urban Uprising,* ed. Robert Gooding-Williams. New York: Routledge, 1993.

———. *Gender Trouble: Feminism and the Subversion of Identity.* New York: Routledge, 1990.

Caruth, Cathy, ed. *Trauma: Explorations in Memory.* Baltimore: Johns Hopkins University Press, 1995.

———. *Unclaimed Experience: Trauma, Narrative, and History.* Baltimore: Johns Hopkins University Press, 1996.

Cecil, Matthew C. "Seductions of Spin: Public Relations and the FBI Myth." Ph.D. diss., University of Iowa, 2000.

Certeau, Michel de. *The Practice of Everyday Life.* Trans. Stephen Rendall. Berkeley: University of California Press, 1984.

———. *The Writing of History.* Trans. Tom Conley. New York: Columbia University Press, 1988.

Cheng, Anne Anlin. *The Melancholy of Race: Psychoanalysis, Assimilation, and Hidden Grief.* New York: Oxford University Press, 2001.

Chikamatsu, Yanagi, Kosuiken Chikamatsu, and Chiyōken Chikamatsu. *The Picture Book of the Taikō (Ehon Taikōki).* Trans. Samuel L. Leiter. In Brandon and Leiter, 158–179.

Chow, Rey. *Ethics after Idealism: Theory—Culture—Ethnicity—Reading.* Bloomington: Indiana University Press, 1998.

———."Where Have All the Natives Gone?" In Chow, *Writing Diaspora.*

———. *Writing Diaspora: Tactics of Intervention in Contemporary Cultural Studies.* Bloomington: Indiana University Press, 1993.

Close, Upton. *Challenge: Behind the Face of Japan.* New York: Farrar and Rinehart, 1934.

Colborn-Roxworthy, Emily. "'Manzanar, the eyes of the world are upon you': Internee Performance and Archival Ambivalence at a Japanese American Concentration Camp." *Theatre Journal* 59, no. 2 (May 2007): 189–214.

———. "Role Play Training at a 'Violent Disneyland': The FBI Academy's Performance Paradigms." *TDR: The Journal of Performance Studies* 48, no. 4 (Winter 2004): 81–104.

———. "Trading 'Earnest Drama' for Prophecy: Performing Japanese American Internment after 9/11." *Journal of Dramatic Theory and Criticism* (Spring 2006): 27–49.

Collins, Frederick L. *The FBI in Peace and War.* New York: G. P. Putnam's Sons, 1943.

Conquergood, Dwight. "Performance Studies: Interventions and Radical Research." *Drama Review* 46, no. 2 (Summer 2002): 145–156.

Cooper, Courtney Ryley. *Ten Thousand Public Enemies.* Boston: Little, Brown, 1935.

Cooperman, Robert. "The Americanization of Americans: The Phenomenon of Nisei Internment Camp Theater." In *Re-Collecting Early Asian America: Essays in Cultural History.* Ed. Josephine Lee, Imogene L. Kim, and Yuko Matsukawa, 326–339. Philadelphia: Temple University Press, 2002.

———. "Nisei Theater: History, Context, and Perspective." Ph.D. diss., Ohio State University, 1996.

Craigie, Robert. *Behind the Japanese Mask: A British Ambassador in Japan, 1937–1942.* London: Kegan Paul, 1945.

Creef, Elena Tajima. *Imaging Japanese America: The Visual Construction of Citizenship, Nation, and the Body.* New York: New York University Press, 2004.

Daniels, Roger. *Concentration Camps USA: Japanese Americans and World War II.* New York: Holt, Reinhart, and Winston, 1971.

Daniels, Roger, Sandra C. Taylor, and Harry H. L. Kitano, eds. *Japanese Americans: From Relocation to Redress.* Seattle: University of Washington Press, 1991.

Debord, Guy. *The Society of the Spectacle.* Trans. Donald Nicholson-Smith. New York: Zone Books, 1995 [1967].

Derrida, Jacques. *Archive Fever: A Freudian Impression.* Trans. Eric Prenowitz. Chicago: University of Chicago Press, 1995.

———. *Of Grammatology.* Trans. Gayatri Chakravorty Spivak. Baltimore: Johns Hopkins University Press, 1974.

Dower, John. *Embracing Defeat: Japan in the Wake of World War II.* New York: W. W. Norton, 1999.

Drinnon, Richard. *Keeper of Concentration Camps: Dillon S. Myer and American Racism.* Berkeley: University of California Press, 1987.

Edwards, Osman. *Japanese Plays and Playfellows.* New York: John Lane, 1901.

Eisenstein, Sergei. *Film Form: Essays in Film Theory.* Trans. Jay Leyda. New York: Harcourt, Brace, 1949.

Eng, David L. *Racial Castration: Managing Masculinity in Asian America.* Durham, NC: Duke University Press, 2001.

Ewick, David. "Craig, Edward Gordon, and *The Mask,* 1905–29." In *Japonisme, Orientalism, Modernism: A Critical Bibliography of Japan in English Language Verse, 1900–1950.* http://www.themargins.net/bib/D/d17.html.

Feifer, George. *Breaking Open Japan: Commodore Perry, Lord Abe, and American Imperialism in 1853.* New York: Smithsonian Books, 2006.

Felman, Shoshana. *The Juridical Unconscious: Trials and Traumas in the Twentieth Century.* Cambridge, MA: Harvard University Press, 2002.

Felman, Shoshana, and Dori Laub. *Testimony: Crises of Witnessing in Literature, Psychoanalysis, and History.* New York: Routledge, 1992.

Floherty, John J. *Inside the FBI.* Philadelphia: J. B. Lippincott, 1943.

Fujikawa, Cynthia Gates. Panel discussion at Manzanar Family Day at East West Players. Los Angeles, 14 May 2005.

Garrett, Jessie A., and Ronald C. Larson, eds. *Camp and Community: Manzanar and the Owens Valley.* Fullerton, CA: California State University Japanese American Oral History Project, 1977.

Gibson, Dirk C. "Neither God nor Devil: A Rhetorical Perspective on the Political Myths of J. Edgar Hoover." Ph.D. diss., Indiana University, 1983.

Girdner, Audrie, and Anne Loftis. *The Great Betrayal: The Evacuation of the Japanese-Americans during World War II.* London: Collier-Macmillan, 1969.

Giroux, Henry A. *Beyond the Spectacle of Terrorism: Global Uncertainty and the Challenge of the New Media.* Boulder, CO: Paradigm Publishers, 2006.

Glassberg, David. *American Historical Pageantry: The Uses of Tradition in the Early Twentieth Century.* Chapel Hill: University of North Carolina Press, 1990.

Gotanda, Philip Kan. *Fish Head Soup and Other Plays.* Seattle: University of Washington Press, 1991.

Green, Paul. *White Dresses*. In *Out of the South: The Life of a People in Dramatic Form*. New York: Harper and Brothers, 1939.

Grodzins, Morton. *Americans Betrayed: Politics and the Japanese Evacuation*. Chicago: University of Chicago Press, 1949.

Hansen, Arthur A., ed. *Japanese American World War II Evacuation Oral History Project Part I: Internees*. Westport, CT: Meckler, 1991.

———. "Oral History and the Japanese American Evacuation." *Journal of American History* (September 1995): 625–639.

Hansen, Arthur A., and David A. Hacker. "The Manzanar Riot: An Ethnic Perspective." *Amerasia Journal* 2, no. 2 (1974).

Harth, Erica, ed. *Last Witnesses: Reflections on the Wartime Internment of Japanese Americans*. New York: Palgrave, 2001.

Hawks, Francis L. *Commodore Perry and the Opening of Japan: Narrative of the Expedition of an American Squadron to the China Seas and Japan, 1852–1854: The Official Report of the Expedition to Japan*. Gloucestershire: Nonsuch Books, 2005 [1856].

Hayashi, Brian Masaru. *Democratizing the Enemy: The Japanese American Internment*. Princeton, NJ: Princeton University Press, 2004.

Hayashi, Robert T. "Transfigured Patterns: Contested Memories at the Manzanar National Historic Site." *Public Historian* 25, no. 4 (2003).

Hays, Frank. "The National Park Service: Groveling Sycophant or Social Conscience: Telling the Story of Mountains, Valley, and Barbed Wire at Manzanar National Historic Site." *Public Historian* 25, no. 4 (2003).

Hearn, Lafcadio. *Kwaidan: Stories and Studies of Strange Things*. Champaign, IL: Project Gutenberg, 1932.

Hellzapoppin'. Dir. H. C. Potter. Perf. Ole Olsen and Chic Johnson. 1941.

Hendry, Joy. *Wrapping Culture: Politeness, Presentation, and Power in Japan and Other Societies*. Oxford: Clarendon Press, 1993.

Higashi, Sumiko. "Melodrama, Realism, and Race: World War II Newsreels and Propaganda Film." *Cinema Journal* 37, no. 3 (1998).

Hill, Roberta A., ed. *The FBI's RACON: Racial Conditions in the United States during World War II*. Boston: Northeastern University Press, 1995.

Hoover, J. Edgar. "Big Scare." *American Magazine,* August 1941.

———. "Introduction." In Collins, *The FBI in Peace and War*.

———. *Persons in Hiding*. Boston: Little, Brown, 1938.

Hoover, J. Edgar, and Courtney Ryley Cooper. "Stamping Out the Spies." *American Magazine,* January 1940.

Hosokawa, Bill. *Nisei: The Quiet Americans*. New York: William Morrow, 1969.

Houston, Jeanne Wakatsuki, and James D. Houston. *Farewell to Manzanar*. New York: Bantam, 1973.

Hughes, Helen MacGill. *News and the Human Interest Story*. Chicago: University of Chicago Press, 1940.

Huizinga, Johan. *Homo Ludens: A Study of the Play-Element in Culture*. Boston: Beacon Press, 1950.

Inada, Lawson Fusao, ed. *Only What We Could Carry: The Japanese American Internment Experience*. Berkeley: Heyday Books, 2000.

Ishizuka, Karen L. *Lost and Found: Reclaiming the Japanese American Incarceration*. Urbana: University of Illinois Press, 2006.

Jacoby, Harold Stanley. *Tule Lake: From Relocation to Segregation*. Grass Valley, CA: Comstock Bonanza Press, 1996.

James, Thomas. *Exile Within: The Schooling of Japanese Americans 1942–1945*. Cambridge, MA: Harvard University Press, 1987.

Karatani, Kojin. "Uses of Aesthetics: After Orientalism." *boundary* 2 25, no. 2 (1998).

Kawatake, Mokuami. *The Three Kichisas and the New Year's First Visit to the Pleasure Quarters (Sannin Kichisa Kuruwa no Hatsugai)*. Trans. Kei Hibino and Alan Cummings. In Brandon and Leiter, 242–255.

Kermode, Frank. *The Age of Shakespeare*. New York: Random House, 2005.

Kershaw, Baz. "Curiosity or Contempt: On Spectacle, the Human, and Activism." *Theatre Journal* 55, no. 4 (2003).

Kim, Lili M. "The Pursuit of Imperfect Justice: The Predicament of Koreans and Korean Americans on the Homefront during World War II." Ph. D. diss., University of Rochester, 2001.

Kumagai, Fumie, and Donna J. Keyser. *Unmasking Japan Today: The Impact of Traditional Values on Modern Japanese Society*. Westport, CT: Praeger, 1996.

Kumamoto, Bob. "The Search for Spies: American Counterintelligence and the Japanese American Community, 1931-1942." *Amerasia Journal* 6, no. 2 (1979).

Kurashige, Lon. *Japanese American Celebration and Conflict: A History of Ethnic Identity and Festival in Los Angeles, 1934–1990*. Berkeley: University of California Press, 2002.

———. "Resistance, Collaboration, and Manzanar Protest." *Pacific Historical Review* 70, no. 3 (2001): 387–417.

Landy, Marcia. *Imitations of Life: A Reader on Film and Television Melodrama*. Detroit: Wayne State University Press, 1991.

Laub, Dori. "Truth and Testimony: The Process and the Struggle." In Caruth, *Trauma*.

Lee, Esther Kim. *A History of Asian American Theatre*. New York: Cambridge University Press, 2006.

Lee, Robert G. *Orientals: Asian Americans in Popular Culture*. Philadelphia: Temple University Press, 1999.

Leiter, Samuel L., ed. *Japanese Theatre and the International Stage*. Leiden: Brill, 2001.

Lepofsky, Jonathan, and James C. Fraser. "Building Community Citizens: Claiming the Right to Place-Making in the City." *Urban Studies* 40, no. 1 (2003).

Leys, Ruth. *Trauma: A Genealogy*. Chicago: University of Chicago Press, 2000.

Loo, Chalsa M. "An Integrative-Sequential Treatment Model for Posttraumatic Stress Disorder: A Case Study of the Japanese American Internment and Redress." *Clinical Psychological Review* 13 (1993): 89–117.

Lott, Eric. *Love and Theft: Blackface Minstrelsy and the American Working Class*. New York: Oxford University Press, 1993.

Lowell, Percival. *Occult Japan or the Way of the Gods: An Esoteric Study of Japanese Personality and Possession.* Boston: Houghton Mifflin, 1894.

———. *The Soul of the Far East.* New York: Macmillan, 1911.

Lummis, C. Douglas. *A New Look at the Chrysanthemum and the Sword.* Tokyo: Shohakusha, 1982.

MacDonnell, Francis. *Insidious Foes: The Axis Fifth Column and the American Home Front.* New York: Oxford University Press, 1995.

Malkin, Michelle. *In Defense of Internment: The Case for Racial Profiling in World War II and the War on Terror.* Washington, D.C.: Regnery Publishing, 2004.

Matsumoto, David. *Unmasking Japan: Myths and Realities about the Emotions of the Japanese.* Palo Alto, CA: Stanford University Press, 1996.

McKenzie, Jon. *Perform or Else: From Discipline to Performance.* London: Routledge, 2001.

McWilliams, Carey. *Prejudice—Japanese-Americans: Symbol of Racial Intolerance.* Boston: Little, Brown, 1944.

Meyerhold, Vsevold. *Meyerhold on Theatre.* Trans. Edward Braun. New York: Hill and Wang, 1969.

Miyatake, Toyo. *Miyatake Tōyō no shashin, 1923–1979* (Toyo Miyatake behind the Camera, 1923–1979). Tokyo: Bungei Shunjū, 1984.

Myer, Dillon S. *Uprooted Americans: The Japanese Americans and the War Relocation Authority during World War II.* Tucson: University of Arizona Press, 1971.

Nasaw, David. *The Chief: The Life of William Randolph Hearst.* Boston: Houghton Mifflin, 2000.

Nash, Jay Robert. *Citizen Hoover: A Critical Study of the Life and Times of J. Edgar Hoover and His FBI.* Chicago: Nelson-Hall, 1972.

Of Civil Wrongs and Rights: The Fred Korematsu Story. Dir. Eric Paul Fournier. National Asian American Telecommunications Association, 2000.

Okamura, Raymond Y. "The American Concentration Camps: A Cover-Up through Euphemistic Terminology." *Journal of Ethnic Studies* 10, no. 3 (Fall 1982): 95–108.

Okihiro, Gary Y. "Religion and Resistance in America's Concentration Camps." *Phylon* 45, no. 2 (1984).

Old Man River. Dir. Allan Holzman. Perf. Cynthia Gates Fujikawa. 1999.

Ong, Walter J. *Orality and Literacy: The Technologizing of the Word.* London: Routledge, 1999.

Opler, Marvin K. "Japanese Folk Beliefs and Practices, Tule Lake, California." *Journal of American Folklore* 63 (October–December 1950): 385–397.

Orvell, Miles. *The Real Thing: Imitation and Authenticity in American Culture, 1880–1940.* Chapel Hill: University of North Carolina Press, 1989.

Palumbo-Liu, David. *Asian/American: Historical Crossings of a Racial Frontier.* Palo Alto, CA: Stanford University Press, 1999.

Perry, Matthew Calbraith. *The Japan Expedition, 1853–1854: The Personal Journal of Commodore Matthew C. Perry.* Ed. Roger Pineau. Washington, D.C.: Smithsonian Institution Press, 1968.

Pizzitola, Louis. *Hearst over Hollywood: Power, Passion, and Propaganda in the Movies.* New York: Columbia University Press, 2002.

Ponce de Leon, Charles. *Self-Exposure: Human-Interest Journalism and the Emergence of Celebrity in America, 1890–1940.* Chapel Hill: University of North Carolina Press, 2002.

Porter, Hal. *The Actors: An Image of the New Japan.* Sydney: Angus and Robertson, 1968.

Pound, Ezra, and Ernest Fenollosa. *The Classic Noh Theatre of Japan.* New York: New Directions, 1959.

Powers, Robert Gid. *G-Men: Hoover's FBI in American Popular Culture.* Carbondale: Southern Illinois University Press, 1983.

———. *Secrecy and Power: The Life of J. Edgar Hoover.* New York: Free Press, 1987.

Pronko, Leonard Cabell. *Theater East and West: Perspectives toward a Total Theater.* Berkeley: University of California Press, 1967.

Puchner, Martin. *Stage Fright: Modernism, Anti-Theatricality, and Drama.* Baltimore: Johns Hopkins University Press, 2002.

Rappaport, Herman. *Later Derrida: Reading the Recent Work.* New York: Routledge, 2002.

Robertson, Jennifer. *Takarazuka: Sexual Politics and Popular Culture in Modern Japan.* Berkeley, CA: University of California Press, 1998.

Said, Edward. *Orientalism.* New York: Pantheon Books, 1978.

Schroeder, John H. *Matthew Calbraith Perry: Antebellum Sailor and Diplomat.* Annapolis, MD: Naval Institute Press, 2001.

Sekula, Allan. "The Body and the Archive." *October* 39, no. 4 (Winter 1986).

Shah, Nayan. *Contagious Divides: Epidemics and Race in San Francisco's Chinatown.* Berkeley: University of California Press, 2001.

Shannon, Christopher. "A World Made Safe for Differences: Ruth Benedict's *The Chrysanthemum and the Sword.*" *American Quarterly* 47, no. 4 (1995).

Shimakawa, Karen. *National Abjection: The Asian American Body Onstage.* Durham, NC: Duke University Press, 2002.

Shirai, Noboru. *Tule Lake: An Issei Memoir.* Trans. Ray Hosoda. Sacramento, CA: Tom's Printing, 2001.

Simpson, Caroline Chung. *An Absent Presence: Japanese Americans in Postwar American Culture, 1945–1960.* Durham, NC: Duke University Press, 2001.

Smith, Anthony. *Newspapers and Democracy: International Essays on a Changing Medium.* Cambridge, MA: MIT Press, 1980.

Spicer, Edward H., Asael T. Hansen, Katherine Luomala, and Marvin K. Opler. *Impounded People: Japanese-Americans in the Relocation Centers.* Tucson: University of Arizona Press, 1969.

Stevens, John D. "From behind Barbed Wire: Freedom of the Press in World War II Japanese Centers." *Journalism Quarterly* 48 (1971): 279–287.

Street, Julian. *Mysterious Japan.* Garden City, NJ: Doubleday, Page, 1921.

Tagg, John. *The Burden of Representation: Essays on Photographies and Histories.* Minneapolis: University of Minnesota Press, 1988.

Takeda, Izumo, Shōraku Miyoshi, and Senryū Namiki. *Chūshingura: The Treasury of Loyal Retainers*. Trans. Donald Keene. New York: Columbia University Press, 1971.

Takezawa, Yasuko. *Breaking the Silence: Redress and Japanese American Ethnicity*. Ithaca, NY: Cornell University Press, 1995.

Tateishi, John. *And Justice for All: An Oral History of the Japanese American Detention Camps*. Seattle: University of Washington Press, 1984.

Taussig, Michael. *Mimesis and Alterity: A Particular History of the Senses*. New York: Routledge, 1993.

Taxidou, Olga. *The Mask: A Periodical Performance by Edward Gordon Craig*. Amsterdam: Harwood Academic Publishers, 1998.

Taylor, Diana. *The Archive and the Repertoire: Performing Cultural Memory in the Americas*. Durham, NC: Duke University Press, 2003.

———. *Disappearing Acts: Spectacles of Gender and Nationalism in Argentina's "Dirty War."* Durham, NC: Duke University Press, 1997.

Taylor, Sandra C. *Jewel of the Desert: Japanese American Internment at Topaz*. Berkeley: University of California Press, 1993.

tenBroek, Jacobus, Edward N. Barnhart, and Floyd W. Matson. *Prejudice, War, and the Constitution*. Berkeley: University of California Press, 1958.

Theoharis, Athan G. *The Boss: J. Edgar Hoover and the Great American Inquisition*. Philadelphia: Temple University Press, 1988.

Thomas, Dorothy Swaine. *The Salvage*. Berkeley: University of California Press, 1952.

Thomas, Dorothy Swaine, and Richard Nishimoto. *The Spoilage: Japanese-American Evacuation and Resettlement during World War II*. Berkeley: University of California Press, 1946.

Turner, Victor. *Dramas, Fields, and Metaphors: Symbolic Action in Human Society*. Ithaca, NY: Cornell University Press, 1975.

Turner, William W. *Hoover's FBI: The Men and the Myth*. Los Angeles: Sherbourne Press, 1970.

Turrou, Leon G. *How to Be a G-Man*. New York: R. M. McBride, 1939.

Uchida, Yoshiko. *Desert Exile: The Uprooting of a Japanese American Family*. Seattle: University of Washington Press, 1982.

U.S. Commission on Wartime Relocation and Internment of Civilians (CWRIC). *Personal Justice Denied*. Seattle: University of Washington Press, 1997.

U.S. Government. *Congressional Record*. Washington, D.C.: U. S. Government Printing Office, 1941.

———. "Japanese-American and Aleutian Wartime Relocation." House of Representatives Committee on the Judiciary, 98th Congress, Second Session. Washington, D.C.: U.S. Government Printing Office, 1984.

———. "Manzanar National Historic Site, California: The History and Preservation of the Community Auditorium-Gymnasium Historic Structure Report." Washington, D.C.: U. S. Government Printing Office, 1999.

———. "National Park Service." http://www.nps.gov/.

Unrau, Harlan D. *The Evacuation and Relocation of Persons of Japanese Ancestry during*

World War II: A Historical Study of the Manzanar War Relocation Center. Washington, D.C.: National Park Service, 1996.

Wallinger, Michael John. "Dispersal of the Japanese Americans: Rhetorical Strategies of the War Relocation Authority, 1942–1945." Ph.D. diss., University of Oregon, 1975.

Weglyn, Michi Nishiura. *Years of Infamy: The Untold Story of America's Concentration Camps.* Seattle: University of Washington Press, 1976.

Whitehead, Don. *The FBI Story: A Report to the People.* New York: Random House, 1956.

Wiley, Richard. *Commodore Perry's Minstrel Show.* Austin: University of Texas Press, 2007.

Wilkinson, Hugh. *The Asiatic Society of Japan Bulletin No. 7* (1995).

Williams, Linda. *Playing the Race Card: Melodramas of Black and White from Uncle Tom to O. J. Simpson.* Princeton, NJ: Princeton University Press, 2001.

Worrall, Nick. "Meyerhold's Production of the Magnificent Cuckold." *The Drama Review* 17, no. 1 (1973).

Yoshihara, Mari. *Embracing the East: White Women and American Orientalism.* Oxford: Oxford University Press, 2003.

Yu, Henry. *Thinking Orientals: Migration, Contact, and Exoticism in Modern America.* New York: Oxford University Press, 2001.

Zhang, Benzi. "Mapping Carnivalistic Discourse in Japanese-American Writing." *MELUS* 24, no. 4 (Winter 1999): 19–40.

Index

Page numbers in **boldface** refer to illustrations.

actor-criminals, 58, 62–63, 67, 72–73, 75, 98
Adams, Ansel, 122, 204n.34
African Americans, 12, 28, 157, 162, 170–171
Ahn, Phillip, 109
Althusser, Louis, 9, 197n.4
ambivalence, 123, 128–130, 161, 175
American Dream, 52, 68–69
American Legion, 74, 109, 142
American Magazine, 71–72, 75
Americanization. *See* assimilation
antitheatrical prejudice, 30–31, 62–63, 66–67, 91–92
archiving, 13–15, 65, 93–94, 124–125, 130. *See also* spectacle-archive
assembly centers, 110, 112–117
assimilation, 15, 17, 27, 54–55, 68, 71, 87, 93, 97, 135–136, 139–140, 142–143, 147, 152–153, 157, 160, 164, 169–172, 203n.16
atomic bombing of Hiroshima and Nagasaki, 7
Austin, J. L., 12, 183n.41
Automatons. *See* dehumanization
avant-garde, 38, 41–42

Barish, Jonas, 30–31
Barker, Ma, 66–67
Barthes, Roland, 188n.67
baseball, 123, 174

baton twirling, 17, 122, 125, 170, 171, 203n.16
beauty pageants, 125, 131, 134
Benedict, Ruth, 16, 31–34, 45, 51–55, 145, 158, 167–168, 190n.107
Bhabha, Homi, 51, 68, 92, 128–130
Biddle, Francis, 84, 99
blackface minstrelsy, 7, 27–28, 156–157, 161–162, 170, 185n.31, 186n.33
Bohnaker, William, 51
Bosworth, Allan, 177
Bowron, Fletcher, 86, 131, 137, 200n.28
Boy Scouts, 174
Brandon, James, 144–146
Brecht, Bertolt, 8, 39
Broadway, 112, 156, 170
Brooks, Peter, 198n.11
Brown, Robert, 126
bunraku, 38–39, 144, 188n.67
Butler, Judith, 11–12, 14
Buy a Bomber, 101, 105, 109
buyo, 136, 144, **165**, 174, 207n.66

Cabaret International, 153–156, 164, 170
camp plays, postwar, 18
Capra, Frank, 88
cartoons, **98**, 98–99, 106, **127**, 138
Caruth, Cathy, 1–2, 5–6, 10, 181n.21
celebrity, 111, **113**, 115. *See also* human-interest journalism
Chekhov, Anton, 174
Chicago, 83–84, 151
Chinatown, 60, 68

Chinese, versus Japanese, 50–51, 54, 107, 185n.12
Chinese Americans, 13–14, 30, 54, 60, 90, 107–108
Chinese culture, 157, 162
Chow, Rey, 9–10, 29–30, 32, 100, 103
Chrysanthemum and the Sword, The, 16, 31–33, 51–52, 54
Chūshingura, 55, 145, 158, 166–168
Civil Liberties Act, 18, 121
Close, Upton, 45, 47–50
Collins, Frederick, 57, 64, 70, 76
Commission on Wartime Relocation and Internment of Civilians (CWRIC), 18, 59, 180n.8
Community Activities Cooperative Association (CACA), 147
Community Activities Department, 137
Community Council, 159–161
Congress, U.S., 87–88, 104, 106, 125–126, 175
Conquergood, Dwight, vii
Constitution, U.S., 13, 142, 197n.3
Construction Department, 159, 164–168, 173
Cooper, Courtney Ryley, 64, 75, 90–91
Cooperman, Robert, 205n.45, 207n.64
Craig, Edward Gordon, 38–40, 91
Craigie, Robert, 51
Cress, C. F., 204n.24
criminology, 95
cultural nationalism, 71, 135–140, 147

dance, 17, 28, 50, 108–109, 116–117, 128, 136, 139, 144, 152–158, 170, 171
Daniels, Roger, 101, 195n.115
de Certeau, Michel, 7, 182n.28, 212n.51
Debord, Guy, 4, 8, 15, 25, 102, 148
dehumanization, 3, 43, 47–48, 63, 74, 89, 91, 103–104, 113–115, 201n.44
depersonalization. *See* dehumanization
Depression, the, 58, 87, 89, 103, 117
Derrida, Jacques, 13, 203n.17
Deshima, 22
DeWitt, John, 108, 150, 194n.96
Dies, Martin, 74
Draft. *See* Selective Service
Drinnon, Richard, 151

East West Players, 122
Edwards, Osman, 34–38, 46, 48
Eisenstein, Sergei, 39, 43–45
Eliot, T. S., 177
Embrey, Sue Kunitomi, 120
Endo, Mitsuye, 142, 176
Enemy Alien Registration Section, 60
Eng, David, 86
Engei Club, 162
Erickson, Kai, 183n.36
espionage, 58, 65, 67–78, 97, 108, 191n.4
evacuation notices, 6, 126
Ex parte Mitsuye Endo, 142, 176–177

farce, 58, 110, 119
Farewell to Manzanar, 125, 203n.16
fascism, 8–9, 40, 102, 107
Feifer, George, 182n.30, 185n.20
Felman, Shoshana, 1, 4–5, 11, 181n.21
Fenollosa, Ernest, 38, 40
Ferguson, Harry, 123
festivals, 131–139, 143–144, 156, 161–163, **163**
feudalism, 35–37, 40, 44–45, 48, 55, 144–146, 158
fifth column, 77–78, 97
Filipino Americans, 30, 107–109
fingerprinting, 90
Fortas, Abe, 176
Forty-Seven Ronin. See Chūshingura
442nd Regimental Combat Team, 55, 151, 209n.14
Fourth of July observance, 137–140, 173–175
Frizzell, Louis, 134, 141
Fujikawa, Cynthia Gates, 122, 130, 204n.34
Fujikawa, Fred, 117
Funabiki, Kiku Hori, 88

gangsters, 58, 61–63, 66–67
gender, 66–69, 76, 117
Genet, Jean, 42
German Americans, 72, 74, 96–97, 110, 194n.87
German espionage, 70, 72, 74, 77
Gestapo. *See* Nazism
Giroux, Henry, 8–9, 14, 107, 182n.31
G-men (Federal Bureau of Investigation

agents), 58, 63, 64, 66, 77, 91, 99, 192n.20
Gōdō troupe, 167–168
Gotanda, Philip Kan, 1
Gramsci, Antonio, 74
Green, Paul, 170–171

haiku, 44
Hammerstein, Oscar, 170–171
hara-kiri, 37–38, 50, 212n.58. See also *seppuku*
Harlem Congaroo Dancers, 157
Harth, Erica, 124
Hawaiian culture, 109, 134, 161–162, 165
Hayashi, Brian Masaru, 208n.75
Hayashi, Robert, 121
Hays, Frank, 122, 202n.4
Hearst, William Randolph, 16–17, 82, 99, 101, 103–108, 112, 191n.5
Hellzapoppin', 156, 158, 170
heteronormativity, 66–68, 72, 76, 92–93
Higashi, Sumiko, 199n.20
Hitler, Adolf. *See* Nazism
Hollywood, 110, 116, 118, 123, 154, 156, 158, 159, 198n.12
Holocaust, comparison to internment, 3, 129, 179n.6, 180n.18, 181n.20. *See also* Nazism
Honolulu, 79, 81
Hood River (Oregon), 142
Hoover, J. Edgar, 57–81, 83, 87, 89, 91–92, 99
Hōrai, 144
horse stalls, 114–116, 201n.44
Hosokawa, Bill, 80, 86, 93
Houston, Jeanne Wakatsuki, 125, 203n.16
Huizinga, Johan, 110, 112, 200n.35
Hull, Cordell, 125
human-interest journalism, 111, 113, 115–116, 119
hysteria, 50, 76–77, 79, 81, 97, 107, 191n.10

I Am an American Day, 106–110, 112
Ichikawa Sadanji, 41, 43
identification tags, 133
immigration law, 84, 90, 104, 107

Independence Day, U.S. *See* Fourth of July
intercultural dynamics, 124–125, 134–135, 137, 139, 162–164, 173–175
intergenerational dynamics, 55, 135, 139–141, 153, 162–164, 174, 207n.66, 213n.79
Inyo County. *See* Owens Valley
Ishii, Amy Uno, 3, 86
Ishizuka, Karen, 123, 179n.6
Italian Americans, 72, 110, 194n.87
Ito, Michio, 40
Iwata, Jack, **138, 165**

Jacoby, Harold Stanley, 204n.35, 213n.69
James, Thomas, 206n.62
Japanese American Citizens League (JACL), 70–71, 132, 136
Japanese American National Museum (JANM), 123, 180n.6
Japanese child rearing, 33–34
Japanese Empire, 32, 34, 41, 45
Japanese Evacuation and Resettlement Study (JERS), 209n.14
Japanese immigration, 6, 181n.24, 182n.30
Japanese isolation, 23–24, 35, 185n.12
Japanese language schooling, 71, 193n.60
"Japanese problem," 59, 81, 97, **98**, 99, 103–104
Japanese traditional performing arts, 36, 38, 40–42, 55, 124–125, 138, 143, 147, 153, 158, 160, 174, 189n.87, 207n.66. *See also* Kabuki; Noh
Japonisme, 22, 91, 134
Jerome Relocation Center, 85
jōruri. See bunraku
jujitsu, 91

Kabuki, 29, 37, 39, 41–45, 55, 134, 136, 144–146, 152, 158, 162, 166–168, 180n.13, 188n.67, 206n.55
Kanagawa, Treaty of, 26
Karatani, Kojin, 36
Kataoka, Ichiro, 93–94, **94**
Kawakami Otojiro, 37–39, 41
Keene, Donald, 168

Kelley, Anna, 206n.50
Kelly, George "Machine Gun," 63, 67
Kelly, Kathryn Thorne, 67, 69
Kershaw, Baz, 73
Kim, Lili M., 200n.29
King, Rodney, police beating of, 12
Kitano, Harry, 186n.43
Know Your Enemy—Japan, 88
Korean Americans, 108–109
Korematsu, Fred, 100–101
Korematsu v. United States, 100, 197n.4
Krater, Katherine, 133
Kumamoto, Bob, 138
Kurashige, Lon, 131–132, 203n.17

Laub, Dori, 180n.18, 181n.20
Lee, Esther Kim, 15
Lee, Frank, 109
Lee, James, 118–119
Leiter, Samuel, 144–146, 188n.66
Leys, Ruth, 181n.21
Lippman, Walter, 99
Little Theatre, 170–172, **172, 173,** 174
Little Tokyo, 109–110, 131
Los Angeles, 68, 80, 82, 86, 103–105,
    108–110, 114, 123, 131–132, 142
Lott, Eric, 156
Loud and Clear, 134, 141
Lowell, Percival, 45–47
loyalty questionnaire, 149–152, 169–170

MacArthur, Douglas, 109, 182n.30,
    186n.43
Makabe, Wilson, 80
makoto, 33–34, 55
Manzanar community auditorium,
    120–121, 124, 141–142
Manzanar Free Press, 17, 54, 125–130,
    132–134, 137–138, 141–143, 147
Manzanar High School, 141
Manzanar Interpretive Center. *See* Man-
    zanar National Park
Manzanar National Park, 17, 120–122,
    129
Manzanar "riot," 135–137, 140
Mardi Gras, 161–162
Mask. *See* theatricalizing discourse
mass media, 3, 16, 65, 76, 80, 82–83, 86,
    88, 93, 96–97, 100–119, 123, 128,

129, 133, 138, 141, 171, **172, 173,**
    204n.35, 213n.70
McKenzie, Jon, 74
McWilliams, Carey, 82
Meiji era. *See* Westernization of Japan
melodrama, 62, 65–66, 69, 89, 103–106,
    108, 142, 145, 166–167, 198n.11,
    199n.20
Merritt, Ralph, 139–141, 202n.3
Mexican culture, 136, 165
Mexico, 103, 198n.12
Meyerhold, Vsevold, 39, 41–45
"military necessity," 1, 4, 129
mimicry, 2, 44–46, 49, 55, 68, 71, 87,
    92–95, 129
Minidoka Relocation Center, 170
Miranda, Carmen, 154, **155,** 156
Miyatake, Toyo, 120, 207n.66
model minority myth, 1, 69, 125, 179n.3
modernism, 38–39, 41, 58, 74, 79, 87,
    91–92
Mori, Chiye, 126
motion picture industry, 77–78, 103,
    192n.20
Murayama, Sada, 174
music performance, 136, 139, 141, 144,
    147, 158, 165, 171, 174
Myer, Dillon, 150–151

National Archives, U.S., 125, 130
National Park Service, U.S., 17, 120–122,
    124
national security, 9, 57, 84, 133. *See also*
    "military necessity"
naturalism. *See* realism
Nazism, 2–3, 11, 58, 72, 74, 113,
    114–115, 118, 123, 129
New Deal, 58, 95, 103, 124
New Year's celebration, 143–146, 148
New York City, 82–84
Nihon buyo. See buyo
Nippon Kaigun Kyokai, 71
Nisei Week, 131, 134, 139
Nishimoto, Richard, 143
Noh, 29, 38–43, 48, 134, 136, 144
Nomura, Kichisaburo, 69
no-no boys, 151
Nuthouse Gang, 156–157, 162, 170

occupation of Japan, 33, 186n.43
odori, 134, 136, 137, 139, 158, 162
Office of War Information (OWI), 32–33, 53, 160–161, **172**
Okamura, Raymond, 2–3
Okihiro, Gary, 161, 213n.79
"Ol' Man River" *(Show Boat),* 170–171
ondo, 139, 173–174
Ong, Walter, 204n.18
open houses, 130–134, 171–172, 205n.36, 206n.50
Opler, Marvin K., 211n.46
Orientalism, 30–31, 35–36, 44, 187n.60
Owens Valley, 118, 120, 122–123, 128, 131–134, 141, 206n.50
Ozaki, Yukio, 170–171

Palumbo-Liu, David, 30, 53, 86, 179n.3
Park, Robert E., 53, 190n.107
Patria, 103, 198n.12
Patriotism. *See* performative citizenship
Pearl Harbor, 1, 32, 49, 57, 59, 71, 78–80, 85, 86–88, 102, 105, 125–126, **127**, 138, 164, 176
performative citizenship, 13–14, 16, 68, 102, 106–109, 113, 119, 135, 142–143, 149–152, 161, 169–170, 175–176, 183n.42, 210n.15
performativity, 11–14, 84, 125, 135, 150–151, 175
Perry, Commodore Matthew C., 6–8, 11, 15, 19–29, 182n.30, 184n.4
photography, 93–97
Picture Book of the Taikō, The, 144
play, 110, 112, 118–119
police. *See* surveillance
Porter, Hal, 51
post-traumatic stress disorder (PTSD), 3
postwar relocation. *See* resettlement
Pound, Ezra, 38–40
Powers, Robert Gid, 58, 62, 73, 75, 89, 91
Progressive Era, 74
Propaganda. *See* public relations
public opinion, 57, 61, 64–65, 89, 99, 101, 125, 150, 176
public relations, 58, 61–66, 73–74, 89, 123, 126–137, 141, 143, 151, 160–161, 172

public sphere, 100, 102, 106–107
Puchner, Martin, 91, 196n.134
puppet theatre. *See bunraku*

questions 27 and 28. *See* loyalty questionnaire

racial performativity. *See* performativity
raids, Federal Bureau of Investigation (FBI), 74, 78–83, 85–88, 92–93, 96, 99, 138, 194nn.87, 96, 195n.115
rape, comparison of internment to, 3–4
Rape of Nanking, 32
Reagan, Ronald, 121
realism, 18, 20, 34, 39, 41, 45, 47, 54, 56, 65–66, 91, 96, 103, 174
Recreation Department, 153, 157–158
redress, 121
reenactment, 132–133, 183n.40
registration. *See* loyalty questionnaire
renunciation of citizenship, 175, 213n.81
repertoire, 130–131, 136, 158
resettlement, 142–143, 151, 175–176
resistance, 125, 130, 135, 141, 147, 159–161
Robertson, Jennifer, 32, 187n.48
Roosevelt, Eleanor, 77
Roosevelt, Franklin, 58, 84, 106, **127**, 151, 154–155, 176–177, 179n.6
Roosevelt, Theodore, 182n.30
Runyon, Damon, 112
Russo-Japanese War, 29, 38, 73

Said, Edward, 30–31, 35, 44, 186n.43
samurai, 37, 145, 158, 161, **163**, 166–168
San Francisco, 13, 82, 85, 88, 93–94, **94**, 105, 115
San Jose, 84–85
Santa Anita Race Track, 112–117
segregation, 140, 148–149, 151, 175, 207n.65
Sekula, Allan, 93–94, 114
Selective Service, 150–151
seppuku, 166–167, 212n.58. See also *hara-kiri*
Shah, Nayan, 13–14, 30, 60, 68
Shakespeare, William, 19–20, 46
shikata ga nai, 1, 123

Shimakawa, Karen, 13, 180n.11, 184n.52
Shimoda, Yukio, 155, 210n.23
shimpa, 37–40
Shinto religion, 162
Shirai, Noboru, 152, 158, 176
Shirrell, Elmer L., 149, 158, 160–161
Shivers, R. L., 81
"shock and awe" military strategy, 7–8,
     25–26
Siamese culture, 154
Sierra Nevadas, 122
silence, 1–2, 177
Simpson, Caroline Chung, 113, 183n.40
sincerity. See *makoto*
Smith, Frank, 155
South Asian immigrants, 30
spectacle-archive, 17, 113–114, 128,
     130–131, 134, 136, 140. *See also*
     archiving
spectacularity, 4, 7–10, 20–21, 25–26, 49,
     59, 79, 84
spectacularization, 5, 12–13, 52, 54–55,
     59, 93, 97, 102, 103, 114, 125, 128,
     130, 151, 161, 176–177; of Asian
     difference, 9–10, 11, 30, 60
spectatorship, 4–5, 8, 62, 73, 75–82, 141
Spoilage, The, 143
Stewart, Francis, 154, 155, 163, 172,
     173, 210n.28, 211n.50
Stone, Harlan, 92
Street, Julian, 45, 47–48
suicide, 146. See also *hara-kiri; seppuku*
sumo wrestling, 26, 174
Supreme Court, United States, 100–101,
     142, 176–177, 197n.3
surrogation, 52–53, 55
surveillance, 60, 64, 71, 75, 84–86, 93,
     137–138, 151

Tagg, John, 60, 64, 95–96
Takeno, Roy, 126
Takezawa, Yasuko, 210n.15
talent search, 169–171
Tanforan Race Track, 112, 114
Tateishi, Yuri, 117
Tatsui, Emon, 123
Taussig, Michael, 87
Taylor, Diana, 4–5, 7, 10, 21, 24, 27, 58,
     64, 100, 101, 107, 126, 128, 130,
     148
Taylorism, 74, 89, 92, 103
Terminal Island, 86, 117
Thai culture, 154
theatricalizing discourse, 8, 15–16,
     21–22, 29, 35–36, 40–42, 46–53,
     55, 59, 70, 86, 88, 91, 148
Thomas, Dorothy Swaine, 143, 209n.14
Three Kichisas, The, 145–146, 148
Timmons, Joseph, 103–105
Topaz Relocation Center, 186n.43,
     202n.5, 204n.27
tours. *See* open houses
transnationalism, 145, 148–149,
     164–165, 167, 172, 175
trauma, 1–6, 10–11, 13, 180n.18,
     181n.21, 183nn.36, 40
Tri-City High School, 170
Tsukamoto, Mary, 85
Tulean Dispatch, 153–158, 160, 163–164,
     169–171
Tulelake, 213n.69
Turner, Victor, 205n.47
Turrou, Leon, 64, 90–91

Uchida, Yoshiko, 114, 118
undercover disguises, 63, 65–66, 69, 73,
     76–78
Uno, Ernest, 114
U.S. citizenship. *See* performative citizen-
     ship
U.S. East Asia Squadron's "opening" of
     Japan, 6–8, 19–29
Utai. See Noh

vaudeville, 153, 156–158
Vietnam War, 1–2, 180n.11
von Kleist, Heinrich, 44

War Relocation Authority (WRA), 2, 124,
     128, 136, 141–143, 148–155, 157,
     159–161, 163, 170, 175–176
Wartime Civil Control Agency (WCCA),
     2
weddings, 117
Weglyn, Michi Nishiura, 57, 150, 175,
     197n.143

Welles, Orson, 78
Westernization of Japan, 15, 29, 35, 36, 49, 52
White Dresses, 170–171
Whitehead, Don, 79, 191n.10
whiteness, 11–14, 27, 58, 87, 92–93, 102, 107–108, 184n.46, 185n.31
Whitey's Lindy Hoppers, 157
Wiley, Richard, 186n.33
Williams, Linda, 104, 198n.11
Wong, Anna May, 109
World War I, 60, 77, 79, 213n.69

Yakko, Sada, 37–39, 41
Yamashita, Kenko, 80–81
Yeats, William Butler, 38–41, 91
Yellow Peril, 30, 86, 95, 108, 112, 198n.11
yellowface, 198n.12
Yoneda, Elaine Black, 85
Yoneda, Karl, 85
Yoshihara, Mari, 187n.50
Yu, Henry, 187n.47, 190n.107

Ziegfeld, Florenz, 154, 158

About the Author

Emily Roxworthy teaches theatre and dance at the University of California, San Diego, where she is also affiliate faculty for the California Cultures in Comparative Perspective initiative and the Department of Ethnic Studies. She received her doctorate in theatre and drama from Northwestern University in 2004. Roxworthy has published articles about Asian American performance, the Japanese American internment, and the political spectacles of the U.S. nation-state. These articles have appeared in *Theatre Journal, TDR: The Journal of Performance Studies,* the *Journal of Dramatic Theory and Criticism,* and *Theatre Research International.* She has also written on the theatricality of the Holocaust and Nazi death camps.

Production Notes for
Roxworthy / The Spectacle of Japanese American Trauma

Designed by University of Hawai'i Press production staff
with Berkeley text and display in Clearface

Composition by Josie Herr

Printed on 55# Glat Offset B18, 360 ppi